Nostradamus Speaks

Nostradamus Speaks

The Classic Guide to His Most Shocking
Prophecies and Predictions

Rolfe Boswell

ST. MARTIN'S
ESSENTIALS
NEW YORK

Published in the United States by St. Martin's Essentials,
an imprint of St. Martin's Publishing Group

All rights reserved. Printed in the United States of America.
For information, address St. Martin's Publishing Group,
120 Broadway, New York, NY 10271.

www.stmartins.com

Designed by Steven Seighman

The Library of Congress Cataloging-in-Publication Data
is available upon request.

ISBN 978-1-250-32528-0 (trade paperback)
ISBN 978-1-250-32575-4 (ebook)

Our books may be purchased in bulk for promotional, educational, or
business use. Please contact your local bookseller or the Macmillan
Corporate and Premium Sales Department at 1-800-221-7945, extension
5442, or by email at MacmillanSpecialMarkets@macmillan.com.

First published in 1941

First St. Martin's Essentials Edition: 2024

10   9   8   7   6   5   4   3   2   1

Helen
"Light" *(Greek)*

Note

The peculiarities of time and place herein expressed as to past, present, and future are an attempt at faithful identification. It is well to remark that no characters in this book are fictitious and that only actual persons have been alluded to or mentioned. The French verses reproduced in most cases are as cited in *Les Vrayes Centuries de Me. Michel Nostradamus,* edited and published at Rouen in 1649 by Cailloue, Viret & Bensongne.

Note

Contents

"Two Witnesses Shall Prophesy a Thousand Two Hundred and Threescore Days"

During his lifetime, Nostradamus enjoyed a well-earned renown as a physician of great wisdom and a prophet of astounding skill and accuracy. While he is now a legendary figure, we have actual early editions of his prophecies which these hurrying years have shown to be accurate time and time again. The most celebrated of his predictions are contained in his so-called *Centuries,* in which he forecasts cardinal events from the sixteenth to at least the end of the twentieth centuries.

The quotation from Revelation xi, 3, heading this first chapter, supports the belief of Nostradamians that their prophet was divinely inspired. He wrote twelve *Centuries* of four-lined prophecies, or a total of 1200, of which 966 have survived. His six-lined predictions are numbered to LVIII (58), of which 54 have survived. This makes a total of 1258 for "two witnesses" of the Apocalyptic "thousand two hundred and threescore."

Everyone would like to know what is going to happen to the world. A true prophet might make his fortune out of accurate knowledge; or, horrified by his vision of the misery in store for humanity, he might give up the ghost. The only human who ever predicted our future with deadly accuracy died in sorrow. There is no doubt that this thaumaturge once lived; we know far more about him than we do about his dramatic contemporary, William Shakespeare.

His right name was Michel de Notredame, commonly Michael

Nostradamus. He was born at Saint-Rémy, in Provence, France, in 1503, of Jewish ancestry, but Catholic parentage. After studying philosophy and the classical and literary humanities at Avignon, he took the degree of doctor of medicine at the medical school of Montpellier in 1529. For some time thereafter he acted as a professor, but later settled at Agen as a medical practitioner.

During the pestilence of 1524–1529, he went from city to city in the south of France, aiding the suffering. Space is lacking to describe here the work of Nostradamus as a medical professor, his struggle against the plague, his treatises on simples, "fardemens," and preserves. He traveled several years in France and Italy but established himself eventually at Salon, near Aix, in Provence. Before this final settlement, however, when another epidemic of the plague began to ravage Europe, Nostradamus was called to Aix and Lyons, where he acquired great distinction through his labors. He treated the stricken with a secret powder which was credited with miraculous cures, winning him a phenomenal reputation.

About 1547, Nostradamus began to believe in his own prophetic powers and soon his claim that he could read the future attracted widespread attention. In 1550 he began writing his famous *Centuries,* mystic prophecies in rhymed quatrains. That same year he began publishing an almanac, containing weather predictions, which enjoyed a wide circulation until his death. He is said to have been the first to publish almanacs forecasting the weather.

Nostradamus lives through the *Centuries.* The first of these rhymed prophecies, a series of seven hundred, was published at Lyons in 1555. Later, he issued an augmented edition, dedicated to King Henry II of France, whose death had been foretold with explicit detail previously. Queen Catherine de' Medici invited him to court to cast the horoscopes of her sons, and the apparent fulfillment of his predictions led, on the accession of Charles IX, to his appointment as physician-in-ordinary to the crown. At the height of his fame, Nostradamus was consulted by all classes for the cure of disease and for divination, too, as his influence increased. Yet, soon afterward, he returned to Salon, where he died on July 2, 1566, exactly as he had foretold.

In times of war, famine, pestilence, and revolution, the great mass of the people becomes curious about the future. Signs and wonders take on added meaning amid national peril. Every world crisis evokes new interpretations of the many prophetic lines of the Old and New Testaments. However, until after the outbreak of World War II, few people in this country even had heard of Nostradamus, and, to those who had, he was little more than a name. In general reference works he usually is dismissed as an impostor and charlatan, though sometimes it is admitted grudgingly that he did foresee some remarkable things about the French Revolution—no mean feat, when we remember that he died 223 years before the first Bastille day.

Nostradamus and his auguries were known to historians and devotees of the occult, but few others had heard of their existence. The *Centuries* probably have suffered some from the pontifical condemnation of Pope Pius VI in 1781, and they still occasion ecclesiastical controversy from time to time. The Vatican is said to have forbidden the book because it was found to contain a prophecy of the abolition of the papal authority. Recently, however, Nostradamus and his writings began again to attract the widespread attention of the French and other Europeans, his abstruse oracles being read by French-speaking people with increasing curiosity. Nostradamus has been denounced as a fraud by many captious critics but followed and proclaimed as one of the world's wise ones by an equal number of eager adherents.

Today the interest in him is almost world wide. He is discussed everywhere and is the star of a series of motion-picture short subjects. Books and articles strive to explain his achievements, and it is somewhat refreshing to find that he was not a semimythical character such as Mother Shipton or Thomas the Rhymer, but a man of position and reputation, neither a fanatic nor a dreamer.

There is a popular Nostradamian cult in Washington. Wherever one goes in the nation's capital, someone is garbling the prognostications of the "learned physician . . . and one of the best astronomers that ever were"—as he is described on the title page of the only English edition of his works in the rare-book collection of the Library of Congress. This volume once belonged to the late Harry Houdini and is filled with checkmarks, presumably made by the magician himself, under predictions which might, by stretching the imagination, be supposed to have come true within the past four centuries.

Sometimes there is a waiting line in the Congressional Library of those hoping to take a peek at the battered old book, printed in 1672 at the "sign of the Bell in London, translated and commented upon by Theophilus de Garencières, doctor in physick," a French physician practicing in London. The Library of Congress has been obliged to put a new, strong binding around it. This cult, apparently inspired by the recent movie shorts, pervades governmental offices, homes, cocktail lounges, and hotel lobbies. A reporter examining the Congressional Library's volume was forced to hurry to pass it along to an Air Corps captain who had taken a few hours' leave to find out whether Nostradamus actually had made the predictions regarding airplanes with which he is credited.

Pascal had an edition of Nostradamus in his library. Aubrey wrote that in his time the work was common. Faust, in his gloomy cell, translating Nostradamus, is said by Goethe to have exclaimed:

"Was it then a god who penned these signs?"

There is, in the New York Public Library, a copy of a book printed in 1606 containing the prophecies of Nostradamus. Verse No. 834 not only gives an account of the activities of two men born in 1758, two centuries after the stanza was written, but also names the men. Several other verses cite men born many years after Nostradamus died. He wrote of the Tuileries, the French royal palace completed in Paris after his death, and mentions Napoleon and several other

French rulers who made history centuries after he wrote his *Centuries*.

Between 1550 and 1566, Nostradamus wrote more than a thousand quatrains and six-lined verses dealing with the immediate future of his times and extending into the succeeding centuries. Like most prophecies, those of Nostradamus were written in a style to conceal their true meaning until after the events foretold had happened. Most quatrains are in crabbed French, but a few are in the Provençal dialect, all reading as if they had been translated from earlier Latin versions. So ambiguous is his style that the adage has it: "As good a prophet as Nostradamus"—that is, so obscure that no one can make out the meaning. In any case, his style is extremely, perhaps wilfully, enigmatic. The quatrains, moreover, are not in any chronological sequence.

Just a century after the death of Nostradamus, his first English translator, Dr. de Garencières, admitted that some of the author's words, though in his own native tongue, were meaningless to him. He translated the recondite French into clumsy English, apologizing that he never had mastered the language of his adopted country.

Each *Centurie* is a hundred quatrains only, not years, and no one ever has succeeded in wholly interpreting the future by their aid, though many attempts have been made, generally with little success. The verses are full of anagrams, puns, plays on words, and cryptic forms, difficult to interpret until the events described have taken place, when their Delphic meaning becomes perfectly clear. However, it is impossible to study Nostradamus without becoming convinced that he was not writing entirely at random.

The *Centuries* include prophecies for all history; but a prophecy concerned more with the religious, political, and geological crises, beginning with the execution of Louis XVI in 1793 and ending A.D. 2000, is the one entitled "Letter to Henry II," treated in an ensuing chapter.

The two-way character of his oracles—Nostradamus was something of a genius in double-talk—makes it almost impossible to identify correctly each country and person described. On a few occasions, Nostradamus has given a definite date and has named a nation accurately. These few citations only have served to enhance the prophet's reputation and discomfit those who mock and traduce him.

The prophecies of Nostradamus, though frequently puzzling, have been confirmed in many amazing instances. Delvers into his prophetic writings concede freely that for long-range forecasting he stands alone. Through the centuries which have elapsed since he made his predictions, Nostradamus' insight into the future has been exceptionally accurate. Along with others who have foretold the course of inventive science, Nostradamus is not to be dismissed too lightly. He is on the record as having, many a time, in his own mystical fashion, delivered the goods.

To bring things down from the sixteenth century to the present era, apparently so filled with strange fulfillments, how many of us know anything of the predictions of Nostradamus beyond certain quotations garbled in the newspapers?

His writings foretold aerial warfare, the use of bombs and poison gas, an "iron cage," which well may be the modern army tank, and even defined almost precisely the construction of the Maginot Line. His quatrain on the masterpiece of André Maginot, the most circumvented man in modern history, said that near a great river would be a vast series of fortifications hollowed into the ground and divided by streams into fifteen segments. The river is interpreted as the Rhine, and the Maginot Line was divided into fifteen main sectors, any one of which could be shut off from the rest by flooding.

Some of the most lucid of other Nostradamian stanzas referred to the beheading of Britain's King Charles I by the Rump Parliament of 1641, Oliver Cromwell, London's fire and plague, the revolt of the American Colonies with their subsequent independence from London's rule, the St. Bartholomew eve massacre in France, Louis XVI, the French Revolution, and many other events which have shaped human history. Quite a large number of prophetic quatrains refer to the rise and fall of Napoleon Bonaparte. Others mention the Franco-Prussian War of 1871 and the loss of Alsace-Lorraine.

Many attempts were made in nineteenth-century France, a most turbulent period, to relate the Nostradamic quatrains to current events. Unfortunately, the task of interpretation fell almost entirely into the hands of fanatical royalists, and Father Torné-Chavigny, one of the most untiring of these commentators, brought ridicule upon France's greatest prophet by being so very certain that the fall of Napoleon III (which he foretold correctly) would be followed by the restoration of the Bourbon monarchy in the person of that Henry V which the Count of Chambord so nearly succeeded in becoming. Subsequent commentators have seen references to Waldeck-Rousseau, Félix Faure, the Dreyfus case, and even to Léon Blum, which neutral readers have found absurdly unconvincing.

What of World Wars I and II? Singularly little, apparently. It is as if the four-dimensional vision of Nostradamus, reaching into the future to observe the French revolutions and the gyrations of two Napoleons, began to weaken as he plunged into the twentieth century. The interpreters lose themselves in a thick, apocalyptic fog through which moves the dim figure of "Le Grand Celtique" and the formidable shade of Antichrist himself. Modern warfare was revealed to the seer as he watched "the armies fight in the air a long time and the iron cage . . . rage in a cyclone of fire."

In general, Nostradamus' predictions for our era bear a somewhat catastrophic character. He sees a king or dictator set up over Europe with his capital at ancient papal Avignon, in France, but this will take place in the year when Saturn will be in conjunction with the sun in water. Now, according to astrological calculations, the sun and Saturn enter the House of Cancer in 1944 and the House of Pisces in 1967—these two dates, therefore, are the ones to be watched for world-shaking changes.

Other Nostradamian writings brought out again in recent months by interpreters foreshadow horrible aerial warfare in Italy, followed by a Red revolution there, an invasion by the Germans, a great slaughter of priests, and the translation of the Papacy, by no means so improbable an event as it would have seemed a few years ago. Some commentators believe that Nostradamus has predicted the loss of British colonies and dominions across the seas, reducing the empire upon which the sun never sets to just the British Isles. Hitler, however, will fare quite as poorly, being beaten, so Nostradamus is believed to have predicted, between two rivers by a brilliant young general who will save the world.

Meanwhile, interpretations of two quatrains are said to have Hitler worried. One of these is a prediction that a certain leader is to die by a throat injury. German astrologers have reported that Hitler's horoscope shows a sudden death from a throat injury. Could not "a throat injury" also be induced by a hempen collar attached to a sour-apple tree? The other quatrain is supposed to indicate that Hitler will be put into an iron cage in 1944 and his empire dismembered.

The exact detail with which Nostradamus described future events is to be seen in his psychic vision of the evacuation of British children from danger points in England's great cities. In his description of this heart-rending scene, he wrote: "From within the Isles the children will be transported, two out of seven will be in despair." Since history shows no other record of children having been transported to places of safety, and since "the Isles" very obviously means England, this passage is easily interpreted.

The French soothsayer also forecast that the blockade of the British Isles, if this is Hitler's "secret weapon," would boomerang, with Europeans, not the British, being on the receiving end of the starving. He also foretold that the British Navy would be victorious in a great naval battle, with England at her peak thereafter. However, he seems to have indicated that, win, lose, or draw, England must go through a social revolution after the war with Hitler. Also, he foresaw Russia headed for bloody wars, with the downfall of Communism.

At least thirty-five predictions relating to the destruction of Paris have been annotated. All these describe the devastation of the French capital by fire during a terrible war. The difficulties of correlating these prophecies with the calendar must be apparent when it is observed that this destruction has been interpreted variously as due in 1937, 1940, 2040, and 3420!

Yet some prophecies appear to apply directly to the tumultuous era through which the world is passing. It would appear that there is to be a quick end to the current oppression of dictators and an uprising of Europe's modern serfs against their totalitarian masters, led by a certain great Celtic or French leader. Of particular interest today are the Nostradamian prophecies anent the future of France, the seer's own country. He foresees the coming of this great prince, named Henry, who will reestablish the Bourbon monarchy and free France from Nazi dominion.

There were plenty of signs in the last decade or so that France and the smaller democracies of western Europe were on the toboggan slide to national disaster. French morale and stamina seemed to be on the skids. Most alarming, France appeared to have ceased caring what political clique led her and to what Red hell she headed.

Nostradamus was right about France before and he may be again. Yet, the nature of these signs of French decline is such that they are easier to see only when put into rhymed quatrains in crabbed French.

Unfortunately, a prophet is without honor in his own country—until too late.

Apropos of this, Nostradamus was the raging fad in a Paris hovering between the two surrenders—Munich and Bordeaux—in the summer of 1939. A cult of the sixteenth-century mystagogue, whose supposedly uncanny prophecies of a catastrophic war with aircraft and submarines seemed to be coming true, was the leitmotiv among the bearded sidewalk-café philosophers of the Left Bank.

In predicting the beginning of World War II, Nostradamus said that Germany first would pretend friendship for France, then invade her. It happened that way, and the soothsayer's prestige soared. Too late, the French realized that Nostradamus never has misled them.

However, Nostradamus enables Frenchmen furiously to hope for a savior—Prince Henry, the heir of a long line of great Capetian monarchs. He is destined to lead the people to victory, crushing both internal and external enemies, restoring law, order, and religion. Except for this triumph, which some interpreters believe may be as soon as May or June, 1944, Nostradamus appears to mention no really great decisive battles for the French. Rather, he sees a vast surge of invasions, bloodshed, and inhumanity accompanying general revolution and calamitous suffering of all varieties, but he offers almost no encouragement to mankind.

Nostradamus apparently had a particularly clear idea of dictatorships, calling them the cause of war, but he also viewed the democracies as being responsible for the dictatorships in the first instance. Democracy—the French mode in particular—he indicated, offers nothing but materialism, while dictatorship merely stretches and exaggerates this same materialism to the breaking point. Nostradamus expatiates at great length on the (to him) far-distant French republics, their mental and spiritual bankruptcy, corruption, and weakness, plunging the nation into disaster after disaster.

The League of Nations, to whose innocuous ineptitudes he has devoted several quatrains, Nostradamus apparently regards as the last word in senile and sterile democracy. He appears to have depicted Geneva's fate in terms not lacking in humor:

"From Lake Geneva sermons will bore, first by days, then brought to weeks, then months, then years; then they all will fail."

One commentator on Nostradamus believes that between 1940 and 1946 there will be five Popes, three of whom will be antipopes;

that the current phase of World War II will end in 1941; that the Third French Republic will meet its final doom in April, 1944; that Germany again will be broken up into small states; and that by 1949 a Bourbon king on the French throne will rule Spain and Italy as well.

Much depends upon the spirit in which one reads prophecies such as these; one can read into them whatever one wishes. The Nostradamic *Centuries* are rather difficult to fathom except in their original French and their translation presents many difficulties. It is impossible to pretend that Nostradamus offers any clear guidance to our perplexities, yet, there remain enough quatrains to convince any unprejudiced reader that the sixteenth-century prophet had some ability to see the future. To those who adhere to the pseudo-scientific explanation of history, Nostradamus must be an enigma as insoluble as he is disquieting. Some day, perhaps, the riddle of the Sphinx of Issachar may be read, and we may be able to travel with Dr. Nostradamus in spiritual, though oft-bewildered, communication down the avalanche of these *Centuries*.

2

"Of the Tribe of Issachar"

Michel de Notredame was born at Saint-Rémy, Provence, on Thursday, December 14, 1503, at high noon. His father was Jacques de Notredame, a notary, while his mother was Renée de Saint-Rémy. They were of Jewish descent but of families that had been converted to Christianity. Nostradamus himself claimed to be descended from the tribe of Issachar, deriving thence his gift of prophecy.

Just how he could have been descended from one of the so-called Lost Tribes remains imponderable. The tribe of Issachar is represented particularly as one which consisted mostly of scholars. Nostradamus and his progenitors were scholarly and cultured. The people of the tribe occupied themselves in Biblical times with the study of the Law. The wise men consulted by Ahasuerus were of Issachar. Its tribesmen often figure as persons who united wealth and learning. The ancestors of Nostradamus did just that. Since Nostradamus made this claim of Issachar descent himself, that must be taken at face value, at least.

The Nostradamian saga may begin on September 7, A.D. 70, when Titus took Jerusalem by assault, burned the Temple, demolished the city, and sold into slavery or drove into exile all inhabitants who had escaped death. Approximately 110,000 Jews perished during the siege and at the destruction of Jerusalem. Those Jews who had taken refuge in the mountains or the ruins were compelled, after many unsuccessful efforts, to abandon their country, now a barren desert.

Going forth as refugees, they went into virtually every part of the known world. They found proselytes and believers in all countries of the Roman Empire and in the East as far as the Ganges, where those who had settled during the Babylonish captivity had increased and multiplied. One colony even migrated to China.

It is certain that more than four centuries before the Christian era a fully organized community of Jews existed in Egypt. When Alexandria was founded in 332 B.C., Jews were included in the new settlement, just as they figured in the Hellenistic cities. Some of these may have been of Issachar.

With the final fall of Jerusalem, however, Egypt and all North Africa were filled with many more Jewish colonies, and in the cities of Asia Minor, Greece, and Italy were thousands enjoying the rights of citizens. Hundreds took refuge in the south of France, where they were received hospitably. They made themselves masters of commerce and, as money lenders and brokers, they often were of importance to princes and noblemen. They became physicians, artists, and lawyers. They enjoyed religious and cultural freedom and they were not shut into ghettos as were their kindred in other European lands.

René, titular King of Naples, Sicily, and Jerusalem, and Count of Provence, had two Jewish court physicians. These were Jean de Saint-Rémy and Pierre de Notredame, who not only were skilled in medicine, but were profound and learned, often being consulted by King René on matters of high policy and great estate. Thus was Michel de Notredame born into a world where two wise grandsires could supervise his educational progress.

It was his mother's father, Jean de Saint-Rémy, who undertook the child's education in the humanities and the classics—Latin, Greek and Hebrew—and also inculcated in him a taste for the celestial sciences, as higher mathematics, astronomy, and geometry were then known. Nostradamus himself said that his knowledge of mathematics had come to him hand to hand from his remote ancestors.

Nostradamus was born a Catholic because his parents had embraced Christianity under a compulsory edict of Louis XII, King of France, who had fallen heir to the County of Provence after the death of the more tolerant René. After the death of Jean de Saint-Rémy, Pierre de Notredame, his paternal grandfather, took over the boy's education with firm and skillful guidance. Michel was sent to the University of Avignon to study his humanities courses, which naturally led to the arts of healing. There was no more famous medical faculty in those times than that of the University of Montpellier, where philosophy joined hands with medicine. They even dissected corpses there and demonstrated real knowledge of the fevers and fluxes which so distressed humanity in those days.

Advanced as it was in medical lore while Nostradamus was a student there, Montpellier could not avoid infection by Europe's perennial pest of the Middle Ages, the black plague. In 1525 an epidemic made its filthy and fearful appearance and turned the university town into a pesthole. Grisly as was the pestilence, the greater enemy was fear, terror slaying more humans than did sickness. Even the clouds in the skies assumed frightful forms. Thunderheads and cloudlets seemed to embody the monsters and demons of the Apocalypse, menacing all humanity.

Nor was there any of the suave bedside manner of modern medicos to be found in the physicians who attended the plague-ridden. Their appearance alone was sufficient to jolt the healthy into illness. They resembled the Wellsian (both H. G. and Orson) men from Mars with their leathern jerkins and trunks to fend off the ubiquitous pestilence. Under the hidebound jacket the doctor wore a shirt saturated with evil-smelling oils and essences. Plugs stopped his nostrils and crude goggles masked his eyes. Many patients fainted at the sight of the doctor; and, when they came to, the tinkling bell preceding the tumbrel down the street would throw them into another fit, perhaps the dispatching one.

Nostradamus watched his Montpellier professors scornfully

as they pranced about in their weird attire, fumigating the pest-stricken with incense and aloes and adding amber and musk thereto for the treatment of the wealthier townsfolk. In the very midst of the epidemic, the young medical student realized that research was the answer to mastering a disease not understood fully. His method was close observation, with careful analysis of the excrement.

His stubborn old professors, with their ancient shibboleths, weren't interested in the suggestions of a twenty-two-year-old whippersnapper. However, the deserted villages and towns of the countryside were infested with the epidemic, too. There Nostradamus went, where he could pursue his own methods independently. He roamed the plague-ravaged south of France four years, practicing in Narbonne, Toulouse, Bordeaux, Avignon, and Carcassonne. Oddly enough, whenever this youngster without his medical degree treated a plague patient with the secret powder that he had developed, the victim generally got well.

As his renown spread, he was called to the sickbed of Cardinal da Chiaramonte, the Papal Nuncio who ruled Avignon, and to the Grand Master of the Knights of Rhodes, who also dwelt there. Many physicians, despite their outlandish uniforms, were smitten by the pestilence themselves; but Nostradamus, though constantly at work in the pesthouses, retained his bountiful health, his ruddy-cheeked attendance being a self-advertisement to cure.

After the epidemics ceased, at the end of four years, Nostradamus thought it time to return to Montpellier to finish his medical studies and to take his doctorate. At twenty-six, he upheld his beliefs in several difficult verbal examinations before the entire faculty and many townsfolk with an aplomb winning him the applause and admiration of all. Finally, he received his four-horned doctoral biretta, velvet robe trimmed with fur, golden ring and the golden zone of the Hippocratic fraternity.

His travels through southern France treating the plague sufferers had given the new M.D. a bit of the wanderlust, so he began his practice in the great open. As he followed the winding roads, many patients he had cured of the pestilence and many parents of stricken children he had saved hailed and blessed him. Often the cry was raised: "The good doctor is here."

Young women gave him flowers and gratefully kissed the hands that had healed them. Presents were his and the homes of the high and mighty, as well as of the humble, were opened to him as he passed by. He traveled through Languedoc and Provence two years.

In returning to Toulouse, he passed through Agen, a cathedral town on the Garonne eighty-five miles southeast of Bordeaux, where he met Jules César Scaliger, poet-philosopher and literary critic. These two were on such familiar terms of intimacy that Nostradamus calls his mentor "a Virgil in poetry, a Cicero in eloquence, a Galen in medicine." Scaliger urged Nostradamus to establish his practice at Agen. Here he married Adriète de Loubéjac, a Gascon lady of good family, who bore him a son and daughter.

Settled at last, well-educated and ripe in experience, though still a young man, Nostradamus was dealt a cruel blow by fate. Within a few months, his two children and then their mother died swiftly and suddenly, all of the father's medical arts being of no avail.

Bereft of his all, Nostradamus again let wanderlust have its way. As he rode along on his mule, perhaps he pondered bitterly upon the futility of the physician who could not heal his dearest ones. It may have been then that he began thinking over the unbearable darkness which masks mankind's future. It is possible that he determined to examine the occult and cabalistic lore which enable the versatile to explore that fourth dimension—time. It may be that sorrow itself had brought clairvoyance in its trail.

Few positive facts are known of the donkey-back years. He roamed more widely, went farther afield into Italy—Milan, Genoa and Venice, cities where the new learning of the Renaissance was flowering. He conferred and studied with the alchemists and astrologers of Italy and France.

An anecdote which has been handed down from Nostradamus' travels apparently embodies the first visible manifestation of his budding prophetic gifts. While in Italy he met up with a young Franciscan, Felice Peretti, a poor village boy from the Mark of Ancona. Nostradamus, on being introduced, got down before the young friar on bended knee. His fellow Franciscans asked the reason for this homage.

"I must bow and kneel before His Holiness," Nostradamus replied. The brothers, however, took little stock in this mumbo-jumbo. Fra Felice appeared no different from themselves. However, Brother Peretti went on to teaching canon law at Rimini and Siena and was created a cardinal in 1570. His ambition seemed to go no further. He lived quietly and gave the impression of being a man easy to lead.

The cardinals, thinking he would be mild and indulgent, elected him Pope in 1585, but he threw off all concealment of the natural energy of character which Nostradamus had seen and, now Sixtus V, began vigorous reforms. His aim was to raise the papal see to its former splendor, and his political negotiations show his capacity for statesmanship. He exterminated brigandage in the Papal States, encouraged trade, enforced the law in his domain, and accumulated vast wealth for the papal exchequer. His only expenditure was on many public buildings in Rome, the great dome of St. Peter's being among the works which he executed. Nostradamus died nineteen years before one of the ablest of the Popes had come into his own, just as he had foreseen.

Grieving, lonely, Nostradamus repaired to the Abbey of Orval, in Belgian Luxembourg, whose Benedictine monks were famous locksmiths and ironmasters. He followed the strict regimen of that cloistered order, including the singing of matins at 2 A.M. It was while he was at Orval that another incident transpired to show how he acted his seer's role in the midst of the ordinary affairs of life.

Nostradamus had been called from Orval Abbey to a near-by

castle to attend the ailing mother of its proprietor, the Lord of Florenville. He and the lord of the manor chanced to stroll through the yard, where two young shoats, one white and the other black, were rooting. Lord Florenville, half in jest, asked Nostradamus what would be the fate of the two shoats.

"We shall eat the black one and the wolf shall eat the white one," Nostradamus replied, after a pause. Lord Florenville, intending to catch up Nostradamus, secretly ordered his cook to dress the white shoat for supper. The cook then killed the white pig, dressed it, and spitted it, ready to be roasted when it should be time. Meanwhile, the cook having some business out of the kitchen, a young tame wolf came in and ate up the buttocks of the white shoat, so that it could not be sent to the table.

The cook, coming in and fearing lest his master should be angry, took the black shoat, killed and dressed it, and served it for supper. The lord, not knowing what had befallen and thinking he had made easy japes of the prophet, taunted Nostradamus:

"Well, sir, we are now eating the white pig and the wolf shall not touch it."

"I do not believe it," replied Nostradamus, "it is the black one that is on the table."

The cook was sent for and he confessed the mishap, much to the surprise of everyone, except possibly to Dr. Nostradamus.

Soon thereafter, Nostradamus left Luxembourg to return to his native Provence, but he is believed to have left behind the so-called prophecy of the Abbey of Orval, known much before 1789 and foretelling the French Revolution and its Napoleonic aftermath.

"In those times a young man will come from across the sea and will manifest himself by a counsel of force," the prophecy goes. "But the leaders, alarmed, will send him to flight in the land of the captivity."

In other words, Napoleon will prove to be an able general and the French Directory, jealous of his growing fame, will furnish him with an army and fleet to strike at England in Egypt. The prophecy continues:

"He will return; he will take the title of Emperor; many puissant Kings will tremble, for the eagle will ravish many scepters and crowns. All Europe will be terrified and bleeding, for he will be so powerful, they will believe God fights upon his side."

That prophecy is so explicit that it needs no superfluous commentary.

When Nostradamus reached Marseilles, he began fighting another visitation of the plague. Scarcely had he settled there when he was invited by the Parliament of Provence to go to Aix to save the provincial capital from the epidemic, which had been raging there two hundred days. The town was one vast pesthouse, with homes emptied, devastated by the pestilence, and filthy hovels serving as hospitals, with six victims to each pallet.

Nostradamus remained at Aix for some little time, receiving a salary from the provincial government after the plague broke out in 1546. That he earned it is obvious because he won out against his old enemy; the Parliament voted him a life pension; and wealthy townsfolk gave him fat purses. These he handed out at once to those widowed and orphaned by the epidemic. His success at Aix brought him a call to Lyons, where Dr. Nostradamus conducted yet another campaign against the black plague, with his usual success.

Eventually, this wandering, prophetic, and solitary physician settled down at forty-four in Salon de Craux, in Provence, halfway between Avignon and Marseilles. Here he took his second wife, Anne Ponsard Gemelle. To them were born three sons and three daughters.

Wealthy patients from all over the south of France and north of Italy brought their ailments, real and imaginary, to the skilled Dr. Nostradamus. The drowsy little Provençal town soon owed its more prosperous times to its most notable resident. However, the green tentacles of professional jealousy intruded when rival medicos fathered a whispering campaign that the great Nostradamus was a witch doctor, in league with the Evil One.

Color was lent to their dark hints of sorcery by the good doctor's habit of retiring nights to his attic den, there to pore over dog-eared volumes in many forgotten languages replete with abracadabra and to experiment with his armillary spheres, magical mirrors, brazen tripod, diviner's rod, and retorts full of vitriol, verdigris, aqua fortis and other strange alchemical compounds. There, too, he practiced his own variation of the art of judicial astrology, adding to the usual computations what he told Jean Aymes de Chavigny, his biographer and only pupil, was the true spirit of prophecy, "the gift of Providence." One who has examined Nostradamic methods calls the seer's gift a sixth sense, both inborn and hereditary from his tribe.

The Nostradamic system of astrological supputation differed from those methods used nowadays. Nostradamus called his chart the *Grand Romain* ("Great Roman"). An oblong figure resembling a coffin and representing the "Sepulcher of the Great Roman" is formed by drawing lines from the vowels of the Latin words *Floram Patere*. These two six-letter words are placed around the twelve lines of the zodiac. By using this formula to support his knowledge of judicial astrology, Nostradamus is supposed to have worked out his calculations and prophecies.

In a letter to his eldest son by his second marriage, Caesar Nostradamus, the learned doctor writes that he burned some ancient manuscripts after digesting their contents thoroughly. These works, possibly taken from Egypt and Babylonia after the captivities, may have been handed down to Nostradamus from his remote ancestors through either of his cultured grandsires.

Jean Moura and Paul Louvet, who wrote a thoroughgoing biography of Nostradamus a decade ago, propound the theory that these documents were brought from Egypt by the Hebrews at the Exodus: "They could not have failed to help themselves to all possible data from the initiatory chambers of Egypt's temples, all the geometric, cosmographic and mathematical formulas used for the Torah and in building Solomon's Temple. Then, when the Romans destroyed the Temple at Jerusalem, the Jews were dispersed. Before the Temple was destroyed, however, the documents had vanished. When the Holy of Holies was penetrated, it was vacant."

Of course these secret works never were found. MM. Moura and Louvet suggest that they were handed down from father to son within the tribe of Issachar, some of whose members lived near the Temple and the royal palace at Jerusalem. They also assert that some of the Temple's builders had fled to Provence.

It has been surmised that Nostradamus had turned to his secret studies because of the petty treatment accorded to him by the townsfolk of Salon, egged on by the jealousy of other physicians who feared his growing popularity and widening practice. It well may be that after this withdrawal from the society of others Nostradamus began to delve into the occult and to practice divination. Apparently he began to believe himself directly inspired as to the future.

Perhaps he foresaw the vast changes which were to sweep Europe within the next two centuries, particularly the civil-religious wars which were to devastate the kingdom wherein he lived. He seemed to feel a strange enthusiasm for his new hobby which soon approached fever pitch. As the night lamps burned later and later, the light of the future gleamed more clearly and he began committing his visions to writing, probably in some sort of cabalistic shorthand known only to himself, and more prose than poetic in form.

At last he began writing his *Centuries*, probably in Latin quatrains. His first publications, however, were almanacs forecasting the weather both for fun and for profit. These were successful and popular; moreover, it is reported that they embodied a fair degree of accuracy. The first almanac was issued in 1550.

Nostradamus kept his *Centuries*, in manuscript form, under lock and key in his den, for perhaps five years, fearing the danger of ecclesiastical disapproval and public ridicule. After all his hesitancy, however, he surmounted his qualms by voicing the hope that he might be helpful to posterity and had his work published.

The first edition of the *Centuries* was published at Lyons in March, 1555, by Macé Bonhomme. When the book came off the press, it met a divided public. The more genteel dubbed the Seer of Salon a mere visionary; the vulgar regarded him as a fool. Some accused him of delving into the Black Arts; others thought that he, like Dr. Faustus, had signed on the Devil's dotted line. Apparently the seekers after culture of those days had more time to study and deeper insight into the crabbed Nostradamic style than we have today. To the average well-educated American, the quatrains are likely to be regarded as sheer gibberish until interpreted.

However, Nostradamus became the fad about court and in the *haute monde* which emulated those who hovered in the light about the throne. The Seer of Salon was the topic of polite conversation. Many peers and literati regarded Nostradamus as a prodigy, believing that he was endowed with supernatural insight. It was the uneducated public, knowing only his name, which termed him a faker.

The titled and wealthy traveled from abroad to consult Sir Oracle of Provence. Salon became celebrated. The fours-in-hand of noblemen and wealthy merchants swung up to the doors of the Sphinx of Issachar. Often callers obtained little or nothing for their pains, his answers being cryptic and Delphic. Those who came to mock and taunt were sent kiting, their ears burning with sarcastic remarks.

Rival doctors particularly were stung by their fellow-practitioner's renown and success, renewing more vehemently and positively their charges that Nostradamus was in league with the Old Boy. One sorehead, Laurent Vidal, had a work published at Avignon to report "the abuses, ignorances and seditions of Nostradamus."

Soon all these caustic critics were to have something really to be put out about. As the fame of Nostradamus increased in important circles, it came to the attention of Queen Catherine de' Medici and King Henry II. The Queen hailed from Florence, birthplace of the revival of that learning which was spreading throughout Europe. However, it must be remembered that she also was a Tuscan, in whose veins flowed the blood of those ancient Etruscans who had believed so implicitly in auguries and omens.

Henry II of France, her husband, was more of a skeptic, but he, too, was impressed with the fame of the Seer of Salon. The King had read the thirty-fifth stanza of the first *Centurie*, dedicated to himself, in which Nostradamus predicted that His Majesty would be blinded in an eye in a duel and soon thereafter would die a painful death. Furthermore, he remembered that Lucas Gauric, the royal soothsayer, had cautioned him to eschew the mock combats of chivalry, particularly in his forty-first year, because he was likely to receive a wound in an eye or in the head which would blind or kill him. There is the stage, set for a personal royal interview with the Sphinx of Issachar.

Three months after the publication of Nostradamus' first *Centuries*, Claude de Savoie, Royal Governor of Provence, received a command to arrange for Nostradamus to visit Paris. The seer left Salon on July 14, 1555, the anniversary of the future Bastille Day, taking the swift horses of the royal post, since he was traveling at the King's behest, and he reached Paris on August 15, after a month's tough journey.

Nostradamus entered an inn named for his patron saint, Saint Michel, on the Île de la Cité, near the Cathedral of Notre Dame de Paris, to confront Anne, first Duke of Montmorency and Grand Constable of France, who told the shy little doctor that Their Majesties were awaiting his arrival impatiently. The entire court, with its lords and ladies in waiting and page boys in scents and satins, pressed forward for just one look at the mysterious prophet. His royal hosts, the kingly skeptic and queenly believer, refused to permit Nostradamus to be delayed an instant and he was conducted to the royal apartments immediately.

There Nostradamus learned what was to be his principal task.

The royal couple had three sons. The Queen was the niece of Pope Clement VII, most ill-fated of all the pontiffs, while her father was the nephew of Pope Leo X. She was ambitious, crafty, perfidious, and full of intrigue; her policy was to promote the welfare of her family and to preserve the unity of France.

Like many Florentine women, she was a devotee of soothsayers, diviners, and augurs, always ready to hear more auspices and omens as to her future and that of her family. Nostradamus was sent to the royal château at Blois, where the three young princes were taking the country air. He was to study the boys and return with his astrological report.

Nostradamus succeeded in winning the royal favor, perhaps by promising the ambitious Queen that her three sons should all be kings, which they were, though only because the first two died young soon after their father had been killed, just as Nostradamus had predicted, in a tournament. Luckily, Queen Catherine, believing only what she wanted to believe, failed to grasp that both elder sons were fated to die young, to be succeeded by the youngest. These kings were Francis II, Charles IX, and Henry III.

Henry and Catherine showed Nostradamus great courtesy, lodging him in the palace of the Cardinal Louis de Bourbon-Vendôme, Archbishop of Sens, while he stayed at Paris. While resting there Nostradamus was afflicted with a severe seizure of gout, lasting several weeks. The King sent him a velvet purse with two hundred golden écus, and the Queen sent a hundred more.

Nostradamus also was laden with presents and flattered by noblemen and notables who besought him to unveil their future destinies. Pierre de Ronsard, prince of poets in that poetic age, acclaimed the Sphinx of Issachar in a quatrain which taunted the skeptics for "mocking the prophets of God, chosen from among thy children, and making them appear among you so to tell your troubles to come, but you only laugh at this."

There were scoffers, too, with this sarcastic, punning couplet from the pen of Étienne Jodelle, the dramatic poet, most typical of the biting Renaissance wit:

Nostradamus cum falsa damus, nam fallere nostrum est,
Et cum falsa damns, nil nisi nostra damns.

Which is rudely Englished: "We give our own things when we give false things, for it is our own peculiarity to deceive, and when we give false things, we are only giving our own things."

Despite such slings and arrows, the Nostradamian cult grew apace, and anecdotes as to his prophetic acumen became almost commonplace. There is, for instance, the story of a cadet of the noble family of Beauvau who was serving at court as a page boy. The arrogant young puppy had a cherished dog which failed to return from a nocturnal prowl. The brash youngster hammered on the door of the archiepiscopal palace, demanding Nostradamus. The Seer of Salon, without waiting to hear what the insolent cadet wanted and without bothering to open the door, sang out:

"What is it you wish, oh page of the King? You make much ado for a lost hound! Take the Orléans road and you will find him led back on a leash."

The lad, abashed, but pleased withal, hastened to follow the seer's directions and soon ran across his own bully boy leading in the dog. Adventures such as this one only served to spread the Nostradamian renown.

A life at court, patronized by the high and mighty as a gifted soothsayer and astrologer, was not to the liking of the unworldly country doctor, who returned to home and family at Salon. His reception at Paris, however, had encouraged him and probably had larded his exchequer. He set to work to complete his *Centuries*, writing at least three hundred more quatrains. These further *Centuries* appeared several years later. The date generally given for printed publication is 1558. One commentator asserts that Henry II saw them in manuscript form in 1557, but Anatole le Pelletier, the acknowledged nineteenth-century authority on Nostradamus, declares that they were not published until 1566, the year Nostradamus died. The only thing which is certain is that the dedicatory epistle to Henry II, which is translated in Chapter 4 of this book, is dated June 27, 1558.

There have been many succeeding reprints of the complete *Centuries,* as well as some spurious editions. One of these, in particular, published in 1658 at Lyons, is notable because it contained two interpolations of libeling quatrains vilifying Cardinal Mazarin. Le Pelletier, who detected these frauds, with persevering and resolute research succeeded in identifying 213 authentic quatrains and linking them with happenings in European history which had occurred up to 1866.

Nostradamus now was living much in solitude, spending entire nights in his study, withdrawn into intensive meditation. Thus he considered himself as attaining a participation in the supernatural knowledge which flowed directly from God. He undoubtedly was sincere in believing that coming events were casting their shadows on his telepathic mind.

Furthermore, he certainly lived up to the adage of a prophet being without honor in his own country. As the mystic who traded with powers unknown, he was looked at askance as being in league with the spirits of evil. The superstitious peasantry and citizenry of southern France feared that he had the Evil Eye, though the shopkeepers delighted in the trade he brought to town. Were it not for the fact that he was quite a court favorite, life for the lonely Sphinx of Issachar would have been empty indeed. It was hard enough, with the burghers of Salon keeping him in Coventry unless royalty or nobility was visiting their seer.

Late in 1559, Emmanuel, Duke of Savoy, and his bride, Princess Marguerite, sister of the late King Henry II, patron of Nostradamus, journeyed southward to their duchy, stopping at Salon to visit their prophetic friend at his home. Naturally, Salon gave visiting royalty a hearty welcome and the burgomaster asked Nostradamus to compose and deliver the necessary address in Latin before the ducal newlyweds. When he was thus engaged, there could be no black looks for the good doctor of the town. As soon as the cavalcade had turned the bend in the road to the west, however, the towns-folk made up for the enforced pleasantries with glances more jaundiced than ever for the sorcerer who was far more feared than honored at Salon.

Then, too, the heresies and free thought of Luther, Zwingli, and Calvin were making inroads into the Catholic southland of France, giving the ruder peasantry an excuse for assaulting their betters, burning manor houses, and looting the land. The recognized devotion of Nostradamus to the Holy Roman Church, his constant attendance at Mass on Sundays and holy days, his devoted piety, and the friendship of royalty could not spare him from the threats and insults of the cloddish yokelry. Because he was not of their lowness and dim wit, he was in league with evil. The streets were in clamor, volleys of rocks smashed the windows of the better-class merchants and professional men and the house of the physician who had treated them suffered along with the others of Salon.

The state of his health, too, worried Nostradamus, with gout torturing his legs and rheumatics his bones. Professional jealousy was another sore point; one enemy, Charles Langlois, issued in 1560 *The Contradictions of Nostradamus*, charging the Sphinx of Issachar with predicting falsely. A more unfortunate time to bait Nostradamus scarcely could have been chosen. One after another prophecy was coming true with bewildering swiftness, and the cabinet rooms and counting houses of Europe were agog with anticipation as to what next.

Henry II was killed in a tournament at Saint-Quentin in July, 1559, as Nostradamus had set forth fully in *Centurie* I, Quatrain 35. His eldest son, Francis II, first husband of Mary, Queen of Scots, reigned only a year and a half, succumbing to a fatal illness. Emissaries from the Italian city-states began whispering against Nostradamus the Necromancer. Another royal child died, bringing the Spanish ambassador to warn his own king that, rather than being encouraged by the French royal family, Nostradamus the Sorcerer should be burnt for practicing the Black Art. Yet, the superstitious French nobility doted on the Seer of Salon, with his reputation at its very peak.

Charles IX and his domineering mother, Queen Catherine de' Medici, visited southern France in 1564, trying to calm rebellious cities and towns. During their progress through Provence, they arrived at Salon on November 17, in the midst of another visitation of the recurrent pest, the plague. The burghers sent couriers into the countryside to call home the townsfolk so that Salon at least would appear inhabited and could receive royalty properly. When the burgomaster began welcoming King and royal Dowager with an effusive speech, the young monarch's only reply was:

"I have come to see Nostradamus."

The seer was among the local dignitaries near by, so he was presented immediately, whereupon Charles IX created Nostradamus his physician-in-ordinary and conferred upon him the additional title of royal councilor. Nostradamus then complained sardonically of the scornful treatment his townsfolk accorded to him. However, the people began to show pride in the old man, now past sixty.

His health was poor, with frequent severe attacks of the gout, and the water of dropsy was gaining fast. Nostradamus died twenty months after the first visit of Charles IX to Salon. The salary and position of physician-in-ordinary to the King, however, was a comfort to his weary old age. He also seemed to enjoy the calls of scholars and noblemen, who flocked from near and far to hear him expound his forebodings as to the future, but the close was drawing near. On his return journey through Provence, Charles IX inquired after

Nostradamus, now more and more confined to his home, and left a purse of two hundred écus for his sickly personal physician.

Nostradamus was receiving only his protégé, Chavigny, and a few very close friends who called occasionally. He passed his time poring over his *Centuries* and preparing his will. His grave in the church of the Franciscans was ready in the thick wall between the main entry and St. Martha's chapel. He insisted upon being buried upright so no one might tread over his bones.

Late in the night of July 1, 1566, Chavigny, wishing his patron a good night's rest, murmured the usual parting words: "Till tomorrow, master." Nostradamus, replying, shook his head, sighing: "You will not see me alive at sunrise."

Le Pelletier cites the last of the Nostradamian presages, No. 141, which follows all the *Centuries,* as the stanza which the Sphinx of Issachar wrote bearing upon his own death. Though these lines assign no definite date, they do give complete enough details to appear remarkable:

> *De retour d'Ambassade, don du Roy mis au lieu,*
> *Plus n'en fera. Sera allé à Dieu,*
> *Parens plus proches, amis, frères du sang,*
> *Trouvé tout mort prez du lict et du banc.*

> *Upon the return of the Embassy, the King's gift put in place,*
> *Nothing more will be done. He will have gone to God:*
> *Nearest relations, friends, blood brothers,*
> *Found quite dead near bed and bench.*

So he was found, on his bench, early in the morning of July 2, 1566. The interpretation of this presage and its fulfillment are this: Charles IX, when he returned from his mission of pacification to the far corners of southern France, inquired for the ailing Nostradamus and left the gift of money, which the seer put away safely. Nostradamus did no more work and commended his soul to his Maker. His kinsmen, friends, and brothers found him dead near his bed, seated in his customary place on the bench at its foot.

Nostradamus left behind his second wife, six children, and two brothers—Bertrand, the elder, and Jean, his junior, who was proctor of the Parliament at Aix and a historian and biographer.

Since his fellow townsmen had shunned him in life like the very plague, except when the pestilence was among them all, so Nostradamus hoped they would avoid him in death. The superstitious peasantry dared not go too near the left side of the door of the Franciscan Church at Salon, where Nostradamus was entombed. Like Shakespeare, he warned those who would disturb his bones: "Quietem posteri ne invidete" (Let not posterity disturb his rest).

His widow, however, had a more complete marble tablet erected, with his simple warning Latin phrase expanded and built up in imitation of the elaborate epitaph of Livy, the Roman historian:

D. M.
Clarissimi Ossa
MICHAELIS NOSTRADAMI,
Unius omnium mortalium judicio digni,
Cuius pene divini calamo totius orbis,
Ex astrorum influxu, futuri eventus
Conscriberentur.
Vixit annos LXII. Menses VI. Dies XVII.
Obiit Sallone An. MDLXVI.
Quietem posteri ne invidete. Anna Pontia Gemella
Coniugi opt. v. felicit.

Or, "Here rest the bones of the most illustrious Michael Nostradamus; alone, in the judgment of all mortals, worthy of recording with almost divine pen, under the influence of the stars, the future events of the entire world. He lived sixty-two years, six months, and seventeen days. He died at Salon in the year 1566. Let not posterity disturb his rest. Anne Ponsard Gemelle wishes her husband true happiness."

All his life, Nostradamus was a humble worshiper of God, holding fixedly to the Roman Catholic faith, believing that outside the Church there was no salvation for him. Though he appears to have followed his own train of thought along independently scientific lines, he was completely at odds with Huguenots and Lutherans. He conformed to the rules and forms of the Gallican rite and practiced the tenets of prayer, charity, and fasting. In those troubled times, the Catholic Church was to be obeyed and Nostradamus kept in close touch with the ecclesiastical authorities.

Nostradamus was of small stature, but sturdy in body and healthy and athletic until arthritic gout made its inroads. His forehead was broad, his countenance open, his nose straight and even, and his deep-set gray eyes were kindly, though quite capable of showing burning anger. His general mien was stern, yet an abiding love for his fellow men was manifest despite his grave demeanor. Though his cheeks became wrinkled in his old age, they still were ruddy. He wore a long, thick, forked beard. Even up to the close of his life, he was keenly alert to everything; his wit was penetrating; he was very quick in the uptake in grasping new facts and theories; and his memory was remarkable in its scope and retentiveness. Though, like the wise old owl, he thought more than he spoke, he was perfectly capable of carrying on extensive conversations when they were necessary. He slept only four or five hours a day.

His eldest son by his second marriage was Caesar, born only a few weeks before Nostradamus, on March 1, 1555, dedicated the first seven *Centuries* to the baby. Caesar, who died in 1629, was a historian, like his uncle Jean, delving into the chronicles of old Provence and writing the biographies of the Troubadour poets. Charles, the second son, wrote considerable Provençal poetry, while the third son became a Capuchin monk.

Le Pelletier has described the Nostradamic quatrains as "a sort of game of Taroc cards in rhyme, a cabalistic kaleidoscope. His manner brings him closer to the pagan oracles of Egypt, Greece and Italy than to the grave inspiration of the canonical prophets."

Pierre V. Piobb, a current interpreter in French, believes that no prophet has set down details so precisely as has the Sphinx of Issachar in relation to both time and place. Some years ago, the inevitable German professor made a calculation as to the possibilities of any single Nostradamic prediction being fulfilled haphazardly. According to this supposition there was a chance of approximately one in thirty million. Only Nostradamus himself seems to have been a more able calculator than the adding-machine–minded German.

From the very day of his death, the reputation of Nostradamus has increased. As the years go by, more and more of his predictions come true with specifically accurate detail. Thus, it appears that what he says may be relied upon, when it can be interpreted in advance.

There are two difficulties confronting the would-be interpreter. First, though Nostradamus asserts, by his own statement in his own preface, that he could have dated every prediction from 1555 to the year 3797, yet the Sphinx of Issachar dated very few of them. Only from its context can it be determined if a given prediction has yet come to pass. Secondly, almost no prophecies are expressed clearly. Actually, they are doggerel in the evasive phraseology of parables. Since each group of four lines seldom has any relation to the preceding and succeeding quatrain, it sometimes is virtually impossible to make much sense of any single stanza.

When meanings are entirely obscure, the only method likely to succeed is to let the quatrain stand by itself with the hope that time will make clear all things. In cases in which some lines are clearly applicable to current events and others are not, translations and partial interpretations may be given in the belief that the other details will be made understandable in the not-too-distant future.

Between the Sixth and Seventh of the Nostradamic *Centuries* are these lines in Latin:

Legis Cautio Contra Ineptos Criticos

Qui legent hosce versus, maturé censunte:
Prophanum vulgus & inscium ne attrectato:
Omnesque Astrologi, Blenni, Barbari procul sunto,
Qui aliter faxit, is rité sacer esto.

Words of Warning to Inept Critics

Let those who read these verses ponder them maturely:
Let the profane, vulgar, and ignorant keep their hands off:
Let all astrologers, fools, and barbarians stand aside,
He who acts otherwise be accursed by magic rites.

3

"What Thou Seest, Write in a Book"

The preface to Mr. Michael Nostradamus, his prophecies:

To the son, Caesar Nostradamus, life and felicity. Your late coming, Caesar Nostradamus, my son, has caused me to devote a great deal of time in continuous nightly watches that I might leave a memorial of myself after my death, to the common benefit of mankind, concerning the things which the Divine Spirit has revealed to me by astronomical revolutions. Since it has pleased the immortal God that you came into this world lately and it can be said that your years are yet very few, and your months are incapable of receiving in your weak understanding what I am forced to record of the future, and since it is impossible to leave you in writing what may be obliterated by the perils of the times, for the hereditary word of occult predictions will remain locked up in my breast, considering also that the course of events definitely is uncertain, and that all is governed by the omnipotent rule of God, who inspired us not by a bacchant fury or lymphatic motion, but by astronomical influences. Only those who are inspired by divine power can presage particular things in a prophetic spirit.

Though I often have foretold long before what has come to pass afterwards, and in particular regions, acknowledging all to have been done by divine virtue and inspiration, being willing to hold my peace by reason of the injury, not only of the present, but also of the future, and to put them in writing, because the realms, sects, and religions will be changed so contrarily, to seem in respect to the present diametrically, that if I came to refer to that which will be in the future, those of the realm, sect, religion, and faith would find it so poorly in accord with their petty fancies that they would come to condemn that which future ages shall know and understand to be true. Consider also the sentence of the true Saviour: "Give not that which is holy unto the dogs, neither cast your pearls before the swine, lest haply they trample them under their feet, and turn and rend you." [Matthew vii, 6.]

Which has been the cause of making me hold my tongue in public and keeping my pen from paper; thereafter I was willing for the common advancement to amplify, declaring myself in dark and cryptic sentences, foretelling future events, chiefly the most urgent, and those which I foresaw, whatever human mutation happened, would not offend the hearers, all under dark clouds more than prophetic, for although Thou didst hide these things from the wise and prudent, that is, from the powerful and from kings, Thou didst reveal them to the small and feeble, and the prophets, by means only of the immortal God and good angels, have received the spirit of prophecy, whereby they foresee things and foretell future events.

For there is nothing perfect without Him, whose power and goodness is so great to His creatures; that though they are but men, nevertheless, by the likeness of our good genius to the angels, this heat and prophetic power draw near unto us, as it happens do the rays of the sun, which cast their influence both on elementary and nonelementary bodies. As for ourselves, who are but men, we cannot attain anything by our natural knowledge of the secrets of God our Creator. "It is not for you to know times or seasons, which the Father hath set within his own authority." [Acts i, 7.]

Also, though there is, or may come, some person to whom Almighty God will reveal by impressions made upon his understanding some secrets of the future, according to judicial astrology, as has happened in former times, that a certain power and voluntary faculty possessed them as a flame of fire, so that by his inspiration they were able to judge of divine and human things; for the divine works that are absolutely necessary, God will end.

But, my son, I speak to you too obscurely. But as for the secrets that are received by the subtle spirit of fire, by which the understanding being moved, contemplates the highest celestial bodies, as being active and vigilant to the very pronunciation without fear, or any shameful loquacity. All of which proceeded from the divine power of the eternal God, from Whom all goodness flows.

Now, my son, though I have inserted the name of prophet here, I will not arrogate to myself so sublime a title. For "he who now is called a prophet formerly was called a seer." Prophets are those properly, my son, who see things remote from the natural knowledge of men.

Furthermore, to elucidate, prophets, by means of the perfect light of prophecy, may see divine, as well as human, things; which cannot come to pass, seeing that the effects of future predictions extend a great way. The secrets of God are incomprehensible and the efficient power moves into fields far removed from natural knowledge.

Taking their beginning from the free will, causing those things to appear which otherwise could not be known, either by human auguries or any hidden knowledge or secret virtue under heaven, but only by some indivisible eternal being, or comitial and Herculean agitation, the causes coming to be known by celestial motion.

Therefore, I do not say, my son, since you may not understand me well, because the knowledge of this matter cannot be imprinted in your feeble brain as yet, but that events in the faraway future are comprehendible in the knowledge of human beings. If they are, notwithstanding, merely the creatures of the intellect behind current events, the future can be neither hidden nor obscured from the intelligent soul. But the perfect knowledge of the cause of things cannot be acquired without divine guidance, seeing that all prophetic inspiration receives its original principle from God the Creator; next, from good luck, and afterward from nature.

Therefore, causes independently produced or not produced, the prophecy partly happens where it had been foretold. For the understanding being, intellectually created, cannot see occult things, unless it be by the voice coming from limbo, through the thin flame, to which the knowledge of future events is entrusted.

And, also, my son, I beg you never to employ your understanding on such dreams and vanities which dry up the body and send the soul to perdition, giving trouble to the feeble sense. Similarly shun the vanity of the more execrable magic, already reproved by the Holy Scriptures and divine canons; however, judicial astrology is excepted from this judgment, by means of which inspiration and divine revelation we have drafted our prophecies into writing.

Although this occult philosophy was not forbidden, I never could be persuaded to meddle with it, though many volumes concerning that art, which had been hidden during long centuries, were presented to me. But fearing what might happen, after I had read them, I presented them to Vulcan. That flame was more brilliant than ordinary fire, as if a preternatural flash of lightning suddenly had illumined the house and had thrown it into an unexpected conflagration.

Therefore, that henceforth you might not be troubled in searching for the perfect transformation, as much lunar as solar, and to hunt incorruptible metals in the waters, I have burnt them all to ashes. As to the judgment which comes to be perfected by the help of the celestial judgment, I will manifest to you that you may have knowledge of future things, rejecting the fanatical imaginations that should happen by limiting the particular places, by divine inspiration, supernatural, according to celestial figures, the events, and part of the time, by an occult property, and by a divine virtue, power, and faculty, in the presence of which the three times are comprehended by eternity, revolution being tied to the cause which is past, present, and future, for all things are bared and opened.

Therefore, my son, you may, despite your tender brain, comprehend things which will happen hereafter, and may be foretold by the celestial lights of night, and by the spirit of prophecy; not that I would arrogate to myself the name of a prophet, but as a mortal man, being no farther from heaven by my own sense than I am from the earth by my feet, I cannot err, fail, or be deceived.

I am the greatest sinner in the world, subject to all human afflictions, but being surprised sometimes in the week by a prophetic disposition and by a long computation, pleasing myself in my study, I have made books of prophecies, each one containing a hundred astronomical stanzas, which I have joined obscurely, and are perpetual predictions from this year to the year 3797.

At which figure some, perhaps, will frown, seeing such a vast expanse of time and that I treat of everything under the moon. If you live the natural age of man, you shall see in your climate, and under the heaven of your nativity, the future things which have been foretold. Although God alone knows the eternity of the light proceeding from Him, I say freely to those to whom His incomprehensible greatness has by a long and melancholy inspiration been revealed, that by this occult reason, divinely manifested, chiefly by two principal causes, which are comprehended in the understanding of him who is inspired and prophesies. One is that he clears the supernatural light in the period foretold by the doctrine of the planets, and prophesies by inspired revelation, which is a kind of participation of the divine eternity, whereby the prophet judges what the divine spirit has given him, through God the Creator, and by a natural intuition. So it is that what is predicted is true and has its origin from above. Such light and thin flame is completely efficacious and subliminous, no less than the natural light which makes philosophers so secure. By the principles of the first cause, they have attained the greatest depth of the most profound knowledge.

But that I may not stray too far, my son, from the capacity of your senses, and, also, because I find that learning would be a great loss, and that before the universal conflagration shall happen there are to be so many great inundations that there shall scarcely be any land which is not covered with water. This shall last so long that except for ethnographies and topographies all shall perish. Also, before and after these inundations in many countries, there shall be such scarcity of rain, and such a spate of fire and burning stones shall fall from heaven, that nothing unconsumed will be left and this will happen a little while before the great conflagration.

Although the planet Mars makes an end of its course and is come to the end of its last period, nevertheless it will begin it again. But some shall be gathered in Aquarius for many years; others in Cancer, also for many years. Now we are governed by the moon, under the power of Almighty God; before the moon has finished its circuit, the sun will come, then Saturn. According to the celestial signs, the reign of Saturn will come again, so that, all being calculated, the world draws near to an anaragonic revolution.

From this present time that I write this, before 177 years, 3 months, 11 days, through pestilence, famine, war, and even more by floods, the world between this and that prefixed time, before and after for several times will be so diminished, and the people will be so few, that they will not find enough to till the soil, so that it will remain fallow as long as it has been tilled.

And this, so far as celestial judgment is visible, that we still are in the seventh number of one thousand, which brings all to perfection, we are approaching the eighth, where is the firmament of the eighth sphere, which is in a latitudinarian dimension, where the great eternal God will come to terminate the revolution: where the celestial images will return to their movement, by the superior motion which makes the earth firm and stable, from which it will not deviate from age to age, unless His will be accomplished, and not otherwise.

God the Creator, by the ministrations of His messengers of fire and flame, shows to our external senses, and chiefly to our eyes, the causes of future predictions, signifying the future event, that He will manifest to him who prophesies. The prophecy which is made by the internal light comes to judge of the thing partly with and by the external light.

Though the party seems to have by the eye of understanding, what it has not by the lesion of its imaginative sense, there is no reason why what he foretells should not come by divine inspiration, or by an angelic spirit inspired into the poetic person, anointing him with prophecy, moving the forepart of his fancy, by various nightly apparitions, so that by astronomical ministration he prophesies with a divine certitude, joined to the holy prediction of the future, having no other regard than to the freedom of his mind.

Come, now, my son, and understand what I find by my revolutions, which are agreeing with the divine inspiration: That the sword draws near to us now and the plague and the war more horrid than has been seen in the life of three men before, as also by famine, which will return often. For the stars agree with the revolution, as also He said: "I will visit their iniquities with a rod of iron, and with blows will I smite them."

For the mercies of God shall not be spread for a while, my son, before most of my prophecies shall come to pass. Then often shall occur sinister storms. "I will trample them and break them," said the Lord, "and not show pity." A thousand other accidents which shall happen by the waters and continued rains, as I have more fully declared at large in my other prophecies, written in hortatory style, delimiting the places, times, and prefixed terms, that men coming after may see and know that those accidents are certainly come to pass, as we have marked in other places, speaking more clearly, though the explanation be involved in obscurity, when the time comes for removing ignorance, the case shall be made more clear.

Making an end here, my son, accept this gift from your father, Michael Nostradamus, hoping to expound to you every prophecy of these stanzas and praying to the immortal God that He will grant you a long life in felicity.

From Salon this first of March, 1555.

4

"Things Which Must Shortly Come to Pass"

This chapter is devoted to the so-called Luminary Epistle to King Henry, which many Nostradamians regard as the key to all the prophetic *Centuries*. Whether it be that or merely the Seer of Salon's grateful tribute to the gracious sovereign who became his royal patron, the letter to Henry II is a remarkably astute glimpse of history as it has transpired since March 14, 1547. In this dedication, Nostradamus asserts that he could specify all the dates and name every person and place in his prophecies. Remembering the letter to Caesar, his son, cited in the preceding chapter, we assume that the prophet meant to cover the period from 1547 to 3797.

The prophetic portions of the letter to Henry II comprise, in the original, three long paragraphs. The first of these extends to the coming millennium; the second covers that millenary age itself, while the third goes on from there to the end of time. That is the standard interpretation of Nostradamic scholars.

The original French of the letter which follows is set forth in the Appendix (page 379).

To the most unconquerable, most powerful, and most Christian Henry the Second, King of France, Michael Nostradamus, his most humble and most obedient servant and subject: Victory and felicity.

For that sovereign observation which I have had, O most Christian and most victorious King, since my face, long beclouded, presented itself before the glory of your immeasurable Majesty, since then I have been perpetually fascinated, never ceasing to honor and justly to venerate that day when first I presented myself before a singular majesty so humane. I searched for some occasion by which to vouchsafe high heart and stout courage whereby I could grow into greater knowledge of your most serene Majesty.

In effect, it soon was found that it was impossible for me to declare this, in view of the contrast of the loneliness of my long eclipse and obscurity with my sudden thrusting into the limelight and transport into the presence of the sovereign eye of the first king of the universe. In like manner, I long have been in doubt as to whom I ought to dedicate these three centuries, the others of my prophecies terminating now at one thousand. After long having weighed such a daring act, I have taken my address toward your Majesty, nor being prevented from that, as the very serious author Plutarch relates in his life of Lycurgus, that seeing the offerings and presents made as sacrifices at the temples of the immortal gods of those times, many were astounded at the extent thereof and dared not approach the temples to offer anything at all.

Despite this, I saw your royal splendor accompanied with an incomparable humanity and paid my address thereto. Not as it were to those kings of Persia whom it was not permissible to approach, but to a most prudent and a very wise prince, I have dedicated my nocturnal and prophetic reckonings, composed from a natural instinct accompanied by poetic frenzy which oversteps the rules of verse and for the most part is composed in harmony with astronomical calculation, corresponding to the years, months, and weeks of the regions and countries and for the most part of the towns and cities of all Europe, comprising

Africa and part of Asia by the changing of the regions which approach the nearest to all these climates and composed in a natural manner responsive to those who well will have need of these things, the rhythm being understood as easily as the sense of meaning is difficult.

So, O most humane King, most of the prophetic quatrains are so difficult that there is no seeing the way through them, nor is there any interpreter for them, nevertheless, always hoping to put into writing the years, towns, cities, and regions where most things will occur even from 1585, and 1606, beginning from the present, which is March 14, 1547, and passing much beyond to the Advent, which will be after the beginning of the seventh millennium, profoundly reckoned, so far as my astronomical calculus and other knowledge has been able to enlarge upon, to the time that the adversaries of Jesus Christ and of His Church shall begin to increase greatly.

A significant event in English history occurred in 1585 when it was proclaimed treason for a Catholic priest even to be in England. One result of this act was the attempted invasion by the Spanish Armada in 1588. On April 10, 1606, the first charter for the settlement of Virginia by the London and Plymouth companies was issued. The first permanent settlement of North America by Englishmen resulted from this act.

All this has been composed and calculated as to the days and hours of election and of disposition with all possible certainty. At a period when Minerva was free and favorable, my reckoning looking ahead to events of the times to come, as nearly as the ages past comprise the present, and by this they will know in the course of time and for all the regions what is to happen, all being named as it is written, nothing therein being superfluous, though some might say: There can be nothing true entirely determined which is in the future.

It is equally true, Sire, that my natural instinct, given me by my ancestors, has been adjusted and regulated by long reckoning and the endeavor to free the soul, spirit, and courage from all care, solicitude, and vexation by the repose and tranquility of the spirit. All this finally has to be reconciled and conjectured to an entity by the bronze tripod.

With all this there will be many to attribute to me as my work that which is no more mine than nothing itself. God alone who knows thoroughly human courage, piety, justice, and mercy is the true judge and to Him I pray that He will defend me against the slander of the wicked.

Such folk with equal calumny will bring under inquiry how all your most ancient progenitor kings of France have cured scrofula and other nations have a certain sting of serpents. Others have had a certain flair for the divinatory arts and still others talents which would be too numerous to recount here.

Notwithstanding those who could not be prevented from exercising the malignant spirit of evil, by the passing of time and after my earthly passing, my writing will do more than during my life; however, if I err in reckoning the ages, or could not conform to the wishful thinking of everyone, may it please your Imperial Majesty to excuse me. I protest before God and His saints that I intend to put herein no writings which will be contrary to the true Catholic faith, consulting astronomical calculations to the limit of my knowledge.

Because the space of time of our sires which has preceded us is such, putting myself under the correction of the most sacred judgment, that the first man, Adam, was approximately 1242 years before Noah, not computing the time by the reckonings of the Gentiles, as written by Varro, but merely taking the Holy Scriptures as a guide in my astronomical calculations, to the best of my poor spirit. After Noah, from him and the universal flood, about 1080 years, came Abraham, who was a master astrologer, according to some; he invented first the Chaldean alphabet. After him came Moses about 515 or 516 years later and between the time of David and Moses were about 570 years. Then between the time of David and the time of Our Saviour and Redeemer, Jesus Christ, born of the only Virgin, have been, according to some chronographs, 1350 years. Some there may be who object to this reckoning as not being true, because it differs from that of Eusebius. Since the time of the human redemption up to the execrable allurement of the Saracens there have been approximately 621 years.

Now from this it is easily reckoned what time has elapsed if my computation is not good and valuable for all nations, because it has been calculated by the celestial courses, by the association of intuitive emotion with certain inherited traits from the feeling of my ancient progenitors. But the danger of our times [the Inquisition], O most serene King, requires that such hidden events be not manifested except by enigmatic sentences, having but one sense and only one meaning and without having anything to do with ambiguity and equivocal calculation.

Rather, under a beclouded obscurity from some natural inspiration, resembling the words of the thousand and two prophets who have been from the creation of the world, according to the reckonings and Punic Chronicle of Joel. This proceeds not from fate, but from God and nature. But this prophecy, proceeding from the mouth of the Holy Spirit, which was the sovereign power eternal, in conjunction with the celestial bodies, has caused some of this number to predict great and marvelous events.

As to myself, in this place, I make no claim to such a title—never, it please God. I confess wholly that all comes from God and for that I give Him thanks, honor, and immortal praise and have mixed nothing with it of the divination which proceeds from fate, but from God and nature, and for the most part accompanied with the movement of the celestial courses. Much as if looking into a glowing mirror, as with darker vision is seen the great events, sad and prodigious, and the calamitous happenings which are about to fall on the principal cultures.

First, upon the temples of God; second, upon those who have their support from the earth, this decadence draws nigh, with a thousand other calamitous events which in the course of time will be known to have happened.

Nostradamus here warns the reader that his first long prophetic summary falls in two distinct portions: Spiritual changes, to be followed by temporal revolutions.

Because God will take regard of the long sterility of the great dame, who thereafter will conceive two principal children, but she being in great danger, she to whom she will give birth, risking death with the rashness of the era, in the eighteenth year, and not possible to pass the thirty-sixth, will leave three males and one female, and two of these will not have had the same father. The three brothers will be so different, though united and agreed, that the three and four parts of Europe will tremble. By the least in age will the Christian monarchy be sustained and augmented, sects sprung up and suddenly abased, the Arabs repelled, kingdoms united and new laws promulgated.

Of the other children, the first will inhabit the furious crowned lions, holding their paws upon the intrepid coat of arms. The second, accompanied by the Latins, shall penetrate so far that a second trembling and furious way shall be made to Mount Jove [Rome] and descending to scale the Pyrenees, but he will not be replaced by the antique monarchy.

The French Revolution of 1792 is the origin of this important passage: "Because God will take regard of the long sterility of the great dame." In other words, the prolific Capetian race of French

kings will become a withered stock during the score of years between the execution of Louis XVI at the beginning of the Revolutionary Reign of Terror and the royalist restoration after the defeat
of Napoleon I by the Allies.

The return of the Bourbons gave the throne to "two principal
children," Louis XVIII and Charles X, both of whom were "in great
danger" most of the time because of the rising tide of liberalism
and ideals of liberty which the French Revolution had brought to
the fore. In July, 1830, this flood tide swept in Louis Philippe, Duke
of Orléans, a cousin of the abdicated Charles X, as "Citizen King."
This "July Monarchy" died, as Nostradamus points out, "in the
eighteenth year," since it went down in Europe's spasm of revolutions in 1848.

After the brief interim of the Second Republic came the gaudy
empire of Napoleon III, proclaimed in 1852 and lasting another
eighteen-year period to its crushing defeat by the Germans at Sedan
in 1870, "not possible to pass the thirty-sixth." The flotsam and jet-
sam of all this were: the Count of Chambord, legitimist Bourbon
pretender, grandson of Charles X; the Count of Paris, grandson of
Louis Philippe; Louis Napoleon, the Prince Imperial, only son of
Napoleon III and Empress Eugénie, these constituting the "three
males"; and "one female," Madame la République. Up to this time,
there had been two short-lived republics, those of 1792 and 1848, or
"two of them will not have had the same father."

"The three brothers" were Louis XVIII, Charles X, and Louis
Philippe, "so different" in their policies and outlook, "though
united" in their Capetian ancestry "and agreed" in their desires to
see monarchy hold sway over France. It was the last of these, or, as
Nostradamus puts it, "the least in age," who came from the younger
branch of the royal Bourbons, who did his utmost to "sustain and
augment" the Christian monarchy. However, "sects sprung up and
suddenly abased" Louis Philippe. The upper classes sneeringly called
him "the king of the barricades"; the monarchists were dissatisfied

with him; the republicans had opposed his Orléanist monarchy from the start; the bourgeoisie withdrew their valuable support; and the workingmen had disapproved his rule all along.

In 1827 the Dey of Algiers struck a French consul in the face with a fan. Until Louis Philippe ascended the throne, the insult went unavenged; then French troops were transferred to Algeria and a long, slow process of subjugation was begun. Louis Philippe saw to it that the task was completed in a thorough manner; and, long before there was law or order in any other part of Barbary Africa, Algeria had become peaceful and prosperous. Thus were "the Arabs repelled."

The year Louis Philippe came to the throne, Belgium became independent of Holland in a revolution, and Walloons and Flemings were united in a kingdom under Leopold I. Russia and Prussia wanted to intervene against the Belgians, but Louis Philippe stood firm and his daughter married the new Belgian king. Thus was a "kingdom united."

Louis Philippe's government started as a constitutional monarchy patterned on England's. At first the Orléanist policy was liberal; but, as time passed, it grew more despotic, although the people steadily were becoming more liberal. In that way were "new laws promulgated" to stifle the new democracy.

The first of the other children appears to have been Charles X, who fled France in 1789 and became a recognized leader of the royalist opposition to the Revolution. Until the restoration in 1814, he "inhabited" Edinburgh's royal palace, Holyrood, over which flew "the furious crowned lions, holding their paws upon the intrepid coat of arms" of France's ancient enemy—Britain.

The armies of "the second" Napoleon, benighted nephew of the great emperor-general, "accompanied by the Latins" in revolt against their Austrian rulers, penetrated "so far that a second trembling and furious way" resulted in the eventual liberation of all Italy, when the Franco-Prussian War forced Napoleon III to withdraw from the city of Rome ("Mount Jove") the troops which he had garrisoned there to protect the Pope.

It was Napoleon III's effort "to scale the Pyrenees" by meddling in the matter of the vacant Spanish throne which caused his downfall through the war with Germany in 1870. However, he was not "replaced by the antique monarchy." By the end of 1873 it seemed that the existence of the newly fledged Third Republic would be terminated with Henry V reigning in France. But the French monarchists had reckoned without their host. The republic was saved by the devotion of the Count of Chambord to a symbol. Though he believed that he already was the French king, he refused to accept the crown unless he was permitted to use the ancient Bourbon banner as France's legal flag.

"Henry V could never abandon the white flag of Henry IV," he declared. The tricolor represented the Revolution. Even his own supporters knew that the French people never would give up their red, white, and blue of Liberty, Equality, and Fraternity. The Count of Chambord, last of the old Bourbons, proved that even in the late nineteenth century the Bourbons never learned anything or forgot anything.

A third inundation of human blood will come, but for a long time wars will not be found in Lent. The daughter will be given for the preservation of the Christian Church, the dominator falling into the pagan sect of new infidels. She will have two children, the one faithful and the other unfaithful by the confirmation of the Catholic Church.

"A third inundation of human blood" is the Nostradamian prediction of the First World War of 1914–1918. The first blood tide was the series of revolutionary-Napoleonic wars waged by France; the second slaughter was Napoleon III's Crimean, Italian, Mexican, and Franco-Prussian wars. However, after 1871 France was at peace and "wars will not be found" until the Germans marched in 1914.

France apparently is "the daughter given for the preservation of the Christian Church"; and "the dominator falling into the pa-

gan sect of new infidels" is Germany, where "blood and iron" was
the root policy. Madame la République "will have two children, the
one faithful and the other unfaithful by the confirmation of the
Catholic Church." These are France's Catholic clericals and radical
republicans, at loggerheads half a century over the Church-versus-
State issue.

> The other who, to his great confusion and tardy repentance
> wished to ruin her, will have three regions over an extreme di-
> versity of leagues, that is to say, Rome, Germany, and Spain,
> which will call for diversified sects by military might, forsaking
> the fiftieth to the fifty-second degree of latitude. They will have
> to pay homage to the more distant religions in the regions of
> Europe and in the north above the forty-eighth degree of lati-
> tude, which in a vain timidity will tremble, then the most west-
> ern, southern, and eastern will quaver. Their power will become
> so great that what was brought about by concord and union will
> prove unsupportable by warlike conquests. By nature they will
> be equal, but greatly different in faith.

In other words, Nazi Germany, a nation mentally confused,
sought to ruin France in the 1940 *blitzkrieg*, but Hitler thereafter
hoped by devious means to drive France into the Axis camp through
the machinations of the depraved men of Vichy. The "three regions"
with "an extreme diversity of leagues," as Nostradamus writes, are
"Rome, Germany, and Spain," with their "diversified sects," Fascists, Nazis, and Falangists, ruled "by military might." However,
"the fiftieth to the fifty-second degree of latitude," or England and
Wales from Land's End to St. David's Head, and from Beachy Head
to Orford Ness (the so-called invasion coast), which rectangular
region includes London, heart of the British Empire, will not fall
under the totalitarian yoke.

"The more distant religions in the regions of Europe and in the north above the forty-eighth degree of latitude," apparently indicates the Union of Soviet Socialist Republics, with its many creeds and tongues, "which in a vain timidity [at first] will tremble," signing on Hitler's dotted line on August 24, 1939. The forty-eighth parallel passes through the southerly part of the Ukraine. "Then the most western [Britain and France], southern [the Balkans], and eastern [Russia] will quaver."

The Axis finds its power "become so great that what was brought about by concord and union [the democratic way] will prove unsupportable by warlike conquests [the militaristic way]." The implication is that the entire Jerry-built system will collapse sooner than we think. "By nature they will be equal, but greatly different in faith," may point to the hidden weakness of the Axists.

> After this, the sterile dame of greater power than the second will be received by two peoples. By the first made obstinate by him who had power over all, by the second, and by the third, who shall extend his forces toward the circuit of the east of Europe ["*Drang nach Osten*"], in traps there it is overwhelmed and fallen, but by sea he will extend into Sicily and the Adriatic with his Myrmidons. The Germans will succumb wholly. The barbarian sect will be defeated soundly and driven out by all nations.

"The sterile dame of greater power than the second" daughter is the totalitarian Fascist State, "received by two peoples"—Italy and Germany. The first daughter of the French Republic was the Reign of Terror; the second was the Paris Commune following the Franco-Prussian War, communism being its present-day equivalent.

The first is the "obstinate" Stalin who usurped Lenin's communistic state, substituting his Sovietized imperialism, a totalitarian leviathan with "power over all." Benito Mussolini, the tintype Caesar with his castor-oil brand of fascism, is "the second"; while "the third, who shall extend his forces toward the circuit of the east of Europe," is Hitler with his Nazism. Hitler's Russian campaign, like Napoleon's, may fall "in traps there" and be "overwhelmed."

Then for Hitler, as for Napoleon, there will be a retreat from Moscow, with the last battles coming in the Mediterranean theater, where "by sea he will extend into Sicily and the Adriatic with his Myrmidons." This last bit would indicate that the Nazis are to overrun Italy, if they haven't done so already, as some observers report.

"The Germans will succumb wholly" gives hope for an Allied victory such as overthrew Napoleon. "The barbarian sect [Nazis] will be defeated soundly and driven out by all nations." This prediction made three thousand copies of a thirty-franc French translation of the *Centuries* sell in one New York bookshop during October, 1939:

> Then the great empire of Antichrist will begin in the Arda and Zerfas, to descend in great and innumerable numbers, so that with the coming of the Holy Spirit, proceeding from the twenty-fourth degree, shall make the transmigration, chasing out the abomination of the Antichrist who made war against the royal one, who will be the great Vicar of Jesus Christ, and against His Church and reign for a time and to the end of time. This will be followed by a solar eclipse, more obscure and more gloomy than ever has been seen since the creation of the world up to the death and passion of Jesus Christ and from that time until today.

The above paragraph would seem to bear out the fears of those who warn that the Axis intrigue and British counterplot in the Near East will serve only to provoke Islam into proclaiming a jihad, or holy war, against Christendom. Zerfas, where "the great empire of the Antichrist will begin," is a Nostradamic anagram for Ras Fez, the proper Arabic name for Fez, one of the three sacred capitals of

Morocco and a sacred city in the Middle East. Furthermore, Fez is in the province of Draa, for which Arda is another cryptogram.

"The twenty-fourth degree," from which the Holy Spirit will proceed, passes through Medina, the second holy city of Islam, which contains the tomb of Mohammed and often is called the Prophet's City. The inference here is that "the transmigration, chasing out the abomination of the Antichrist," will begin at El-Medina. If Nostradamus has been interpreted correctly, "the royal one, who will be the great Vicar of Jesus Christ," will be a descendant of the Bourbon family.

Our forefathers paid scholarly attention to Mohammed as the prototype of Antichrist. That is the burden of *A Discourse on Antichrist* by Richard Franklin, published in London in 1675. The New York Public Library's copy of this monograph bears the signature of Increase Mather.

"A solar eclipse, more obscure and more gloomy than ever has been seen since the creation of the world up to the death and passion of Jesus Christ," according to French commentators on the *Centuries*, is the total eclipse of the sun which will be visible from Paris on August 11, 1999, beginning at 10: 28 A.M.:

> There will be in the month of October such a great removal
> made that one would think that the gravity of the earth had lost
> its natural movement and plunged into the abyss of perpetual
> gloom.

"The month of October" when "a great removal" will take place also would be in 1999. This is considered generally to be a forecast of one of the periodic shiftings of continental masses which, some geologists say, have not yet ceased to remake the earth's map. Nostradamus has implied as much in his letter to his son, Caesar.

Several scientists have borne out this geophysical interpretation of the Nostradamic warning. William Boeksche, a German geologist, has forecast radical changes in the earth's surface and climatic alterations affecting the entire world. His phraseology in a talk at Halle was almost Nostradamian when he predicted gigantic terrestrial inundations to which recent strange weather variations, floods, storms, earthquakes, and seismological disturbances are a prelude. He warned that these transformations may come with remarkable rapidity and that the world is on the brink of vast convolutions. He added that new continents and mountain ranges may rise from the depths of the Pacific Ocean.

Dr. Milton A. Nobles, geologist and seismologist, has gone so far as to forecast another deluge wherein entire continents will be destroyed and new ones substituted. He foresees new land rising to double the area of the Western Hemisphere, with New Zealand and Australia being linked in a continent treble their current size. Dr. Nobles also predicts that the earth's axis will be shortened, with the new North Pole in Siberia and the new South Pole in the south Pacific.

All this, he indicates, will mean that the United States will be much nearer the next equator, with Florida's all-year mildness the climate of the entire nation. He predicts new coastlines in the Atlantic and Pacific, turning Los Angeles and San Francisco into cities of the hinterland. He foresees the transformation of the Gulf of Mexico into an inland sea, with Central America and the West Indies joined to the new continent, which will be approximately five thousand miles across.

Though many scientists have jeered at the Nobles theories, there have been earthquakes, volcanic disturbances, and tidal waves in the regions he has indicated. Nostradamus carries on this thought, then harks back to make the most remarkable of his predictions in the letter to Henry II:

> There will be warnings in the springtime and after extreme
> changes ensuing, exchanges of regime and great earthquakes,

with the teeming of the new Babylon [Paris], miserable daughter, swollen with the abomination of the first holocaust and it
will last only seventy-three years and seven months.

"The abomination of the first holocaust" occurred on January
21, 1793, when Louis XVI was guillotined by the extreme radicals
of the French National Convention. "It will last only seventy-three
years and seven months" refers to the duration of the French republics. Here Nostradamus has demonstrated his prophetic insight
with uncanny prescience, since the three French republics did last
an exact seventy-three years and seven months.

From "the abomination" of January 21, 1793, to Napoleon Bonaparte's *coup d'état* of the Eighteenth Brumaire (November 9, 1799),
whereby the conquering general created the Consulate, with himself
as First Consul, is six years and nine months for the duration of "the
first holocaust," or First Republic, which had been organized on
September 25, 1792, by the National Convention, though Louis XVI
languished on for a while in his cell as Louis Capet.

The Second Republic was proclaimed on February 24, 1848, upon
Louis Philippe's abdication. Louis Napoleon Bonaparte, elected
president in the autumnal elections, took office in December, 1848.
On December 2, 1851, the anniversary of his celebrated uncle's re-
sounding military victory of Austerlitz, Napoleon the Little, by a
coup d'état, established a dictatorship, all prominent republicans
being arrested and imprisoned. That was the end of the Second Republic, in three years and nine months, though it was not until the
anniversary of his *coup* a year later that the dictator actually conferred the title of Napoleon III upon himself.

After the fall of the Second Empire, it was expected that the
Bourbon monarchy would be restored; and the first two presidents,
Adolphe Thiers and Marshal MacMahon were, in effect, regents.
However, in May, 1877, the republicans finally gained control of the
French Senate, as well as of the Chamber of Deputies, and though

the monarchistic Marshal clung to the presidency two more years, historians date the Third Republic's legislative competence from May, 1877. It is sixty-three years and one month from that date to the debacle of the Third French Republic on June 22, 1940, when an armistice, signed in the Forest of Compiègne with the conquering Nazis, ushered in another ex-hero marshal, Pétain the defeatist, who may be hoping to hold the historic throne in trust for the Bourbons.

First Republic, six years and nine months; Second Republic, three years and nine months; Third Republic, sixty-three years and one month: total, seventy-three years and seven months.

> Thereafter will issue from the stem which so long had remained fruitless, proceeding from the fiftieth degree, one who will renew the whole Christian Church. There will be made great peace, union, and concord at the same time among the misled and divided children. By various realms will be set up such a peace, which shall dwell attached to the most profound depths, that the resuscitator and promoter of martial faction by the diversity of religions will be united to the kingdom of the furious, who shall counterfeit the wise. The countries, towns, cities, realms, and provinces which had left their original ways to deliver themselves, yet captivating themselves all the more deeply, will become secretly wearied of their liberty and the perfect religion lost will begin to offset the left party only to turn back to the right.

"The fiftieth degree" of latitude passes very close to Givet, in the Belgian province of Namur, where is the Château of Agimont, a conspicuous modern manor with a sixteenth century tower. It is the property of the Count of Paris, now the pretender to the throne of France. He it may be who "will issue from the stem which so long had remained fruitless" to bring "peace, union, and concord ... among the misled and divided children" of France.

The Associated Press has reported from Rome that "French monarchists are working for the restoration of the monarchy in France and seeking Adolf Hitler's consent therefor." John T. Whitaker of the Chicago *Daily News* amplified this report, saying that Marshal Pétain had told Hitler: "I am an old man and I cannot carry on forever." Mr. Whitaker explained that the aged Marshal, a faithful Catholic and monarchist, was a personal friend of the Count of Paris, the Bourbon-Orléanist faction's candidate. The Marshal was said to have felt that if the Count took the throne, Frenchmen of all parties could rally round the king as a symbol midway between democracy and fascism.

The Third French Republic actually was proclaimed at the Hôtel de Ville, in Paris, on September 4, 1870. Seventy-three years and seven months from that date would take us to March, 1944, when it may be that Henry, Count of Paris, will accede to the throne of his forefathers as Henry V, King of the French.

Replacing holiness, so long overcome by their early writ, afterward the great cur will come forth, the greatest rascal, who will wield destruction to all, even those who will have been committed to its appearance. The churches will be restored as at first and the clergy reinstated to their original state, but will lapse again into vileness and lust to make and commit a thousand crimes. Nearing another desolation, whereby she shall be at her highest and most sublime dignity, the potentates and warlords will set themselves up against her. Her two swords will be taken from her and nothing will be left to her but her signs.

From which, by means of the bending which attracts them, the people causing it to go straight and not willing to comply to those by the end opposite to the pointed hand which touches the ground they shall arouse.

Until there shall be born to the branch so long sterile one who shall deliver the people of the universe from that benign and voluntary servitude, putting himself under the protection of Mars and stripping Jupiter of all his honors and dignities for the free city constituted and seated in another scanty Mesopotamia.

The one "born to the branch so long sterile" is believed to relate to a future great Pope who will be a descendant of the lost branch of the Bourbon family. The progenitor of this recovered royal line is said to be the former Duke of Normandy, Louis XVII, titular King of the French from 1793 to 1795. The second son of Louis XVI and Marie Antoinette, he was born at Versailles on March 27, 1785. In 1789, on his elder brother's death, the Duke of Normandy became heir to the throne which he never ascended.

At first the young Dauphin shared the imprisonment of his parents in the tower of the Temple, where he was taken in August, 1792, but, after the decapitation of his father, he was separated from his mother. Thereafter his history largely is conjecture. His death in his cell from ill-treatment and neglect was announced in June, 1795. Some think, however, that he escaped and that his legitimate descendants are living today.

His death often has been disputed because it was rumored that Barnave had taken the true Dauphin from the prison and substituted another in his place. Several impostors appeared, claiming to be Louis XVII, and many stories of his escape were spread abroad.

From wherever he comes, this future great pontiff will accept "the protection of Mars"—his Bourbon kinsman who will be the King of the French—and will strip "Jupiter of all his honors and dignities." Jupiter was the chief divinity of the Romans; his temple on Capitoline Hill was regarded as the heart of the Roman state. This is taken to mean that this Pope will leave Rome, abandoning his titles of "Bishop of Rome, Pontifex Maximus, Primate of Italy, Archbishop and Metropolitan of the Roman Province and Sovereign of Vatican City."

Like his predecessor, Clement V, driven from Rome in 1309, this future Pope will take refuge in Avignon, ancient walled city of France where the heads of the Church lived seventy years. Clement VI bought Avignon in 1348, and it remained papal property until its annexation by France in 1791. Avignon is "seated in another scanty Mesopotamia," being the capital of Venaissin, France's scantiest county, which is between the Rhone, Durance, and Eygues rivers. "Mesopotamia" means "the country between the rivers."

> The chief and governor shall be cast from their midst and put into a place of air, ignoring the conspiracy of the traitors with the second Thrasybulus, who for a long time had managed all this. Then shall the dirt and abominations be with great shame thrown out and manifest to the shadows of the beclouded light and shall cease toward the end of the changing of his reign. The heads of the church will be backward in the love of God, while many will betray the true faith.

"The chief and governor" who will "be cast from their midst and put in a place of air" may be whoever is the Nazi satrap at Vichy, with its principal henchmen, at the future time that France is liberated. Presumably prison confinement will be on a mountain, "in a place of air," somewhere in France.

Thrasybulus was an Athenian general, attached to the democratic party, who won the battle of Cynossema in 411 B.C. In 407 he subjugated most of the revolted cities of coastal Thrace and, about the same time, was elected, along with Alcibiades, one of the new generals. Banished on the establishment of the thirty tyrants, he seized the fortress of Phyle, occupied Piraeus, and finally delivered Athens, restoring democratic government in 403. He died in 390 B.C. Perhaps he is the prototype for General Charles de Gaulle, "who for a long time had managed" the Free French fight for democracy.

Of the three sects, that which is in the middle will be a little in decadence because of its own followers. The first totally throughout

Europe and the most part of Africa exterminated by the third by means of the poor in spirit who by insensate breeding and by lustful luxury will adulterate. The people will rise against those who oppress them and expel the supporters of the legislators.

"The three sects" are communism, democracy, and fascism. Democracy, "that which is in the middle, will be a little in decadence because of its own followers." Today, many nations which enjoyed democracy have been steam-rollered because politicians and citizens were unwilling to make sacrifices to maintain their free way of life.

Communism, "the first," has been "totally throughout Europe [Russia's has been greatly diluted, if not eradicated] and the most part of Africa exterminated by the third" system of fascism, which exhorts "the poor in spirit" to "insensate breeding" to provide more cannon fodder for the mechanized slaughters. The day of reckoning when "the people will rise against those who oppress them and expel the supporters of the legislators" who enslaved them is coming soon.

It will seem from the realms enfeebled by the East that God the Creator had loosed Satan from the infernal regions to give birth to the great Gog and Magog [Revelation, xx, 7, 8] which will make such a great and abominable breaking in churches that the reds [radicals] and the whites [reactionaries], without eyes and without hands [without foresight and capacity], cannot judge of it. Their power will be taken away from them. Then will come more of a persecution of the churches than ever had been.

During these events will be born such a great plague that two of the three parts of the world will be pulled down. So fiercely will this follow through that one will not know the ownership of fields and houses, and grass will grow in the city streets up to the knees. To the clergy there will be great desolation and the warlords will usurp whatever returns from the city of the sun [Paris], from Malta and from the Isles of Hyères [off the French Riviera] and the great chain of the port which takes its name from the marine ox [Bosporus] will be opened.

There will be made a new invasion by the seashores, willing to deliver the leap of freedom since the first Middle Eastern recapture. Their assaults will not be all in vain and the place where was the dwelling of Abraham [Ur] will be assailed by those who venerate the Jovialists [who worship Jehovah]. The city of Achem will be surrounded and assaulted from all sides by a most powerful armed force. Their maritime power will be weakened by the Occidentals [Americans]. Upon this realm [Japan] there will be wrought great desolation and the greatest cities will be depopulated. Those who enter therein will be taken in the vengeance of the wrath of God [earthquake].

Nostradamic commentators believe that Achem refers to Achin [Dutch, Atjeh], a province of northern Sumatra, in the Netherlands East Indies, whose capital is Kota Raja, a few miles from the mouth of the Achin River. Achin was visited in 1506 by a Portuguese of Tristan d'Acunha's expedition. Subsequently, Portugal, France, England, and the Netherlands tried to establish a colony there. The Dutch finally gained control in 1873. The natives are Muslim.

The Sepulcher [in Jerusalem], so long an object of great veneration, will lie open to all, under the sovereign vision of the eyes of the sun and moon. The holy place [Bethlehem] will be converted to a stable for cattle, great and small, and applied to profane uses. Oh what a calamitous affliction it will be for pregnant women! For, then, the principal Eastern chief will be conquered, chased for the most part by the northerners [Europeans] and westerners [Americans], who will put him to death, overwhelm him and put the rest to rout and his children by many women in prison. Then will come to its accomplishment the prediction of the royal prophet: "Let the sighing of the prisoner come before thee and preserve those that are appointed to die."

What great oppression then will be made to the princes and governors of kingdoms, even on those which are maritime [Britain and America] and oriental [Japan and China], their tongues intermingled in a great association of Latins and Arabs by the Punic communication!

This is taken to be the Nostradamic gloss upon the futility of the League of Nations before the outbreak of the Second World War, beginning in the "China incident." English, the "Punic tongue," was spoken by many delegates as the most understood language of those times.

These kings will be driven out, overwhelmed, and exterminated not at all by the forces of the kings of the eagle [Hitler and Mussolini], but by the proximity of our era [perhaps the Biblical times of the Gentiles], by means of the three united together secretly [Germany, Japan, and Italy], seeking out infidelity by ensnaring one another. The renewed triumvirate [League of Nations, deserted by Germany and Japan in 1933, died in 1940] will last seven years, the renown of this sect will spread universally and the sacrifice of the holy and immaculate Host will be sustained. Then will two lords in the number of the eagle [United States and Russia] be victorious over the East, and so great a noise and warlike tumult will be made by those that all the East will tremble in fright at those brothers, yet not brothers, of the eagle.

Because, Sire, by this lecture I almost turn these predictions into confusion as to the time when the advent of each shall be, for the enumeration of the time which ensues is very little conformable, if at all, to what I gave previously, that, indeed, could not be in error, being by astronomical as well as other methods and the same as the Holy Scriptures.

Did I so desire, I could determine the time for every quatrain; it could have been done easily enough, but it might be displeasing to some and still less easy to interpret, Sire, unless your Majesty give me power to do this in order not to give liars a chance to vilify me.

Always counting the years since the creation of the world up to the birth of Noah as being 1506 and from that birth of Noah to the completion of the building of the Ark near the universal flood as 600 (they may be solar or lunar years or mixed), I hold that the sacred Scriptures take them to be solar. At the end of these six years, Noah entered the Ark to escape the flood. The flood was world wide and lasted a year and two months. Since the end of the flood and up to the birth of Abraham there passed 295 years. From the birth of Abraham to the birth of Isaac there passed 100 and from Isaac to Jacob 60 years. From the hour that he entered Egypt up to his exit was 130 years. From the entry of Jacob into Egypt to his departure was 430 years and from the exodus out of Egypt up to the building of the Temple by Solomon in the fourth year of his reign elapsed 480 years. From the building of the Temple up to Jesus Christ, according to the reckoning of the sacred writing, there passed 490 years. Thus, by the reckoning which I have made, collecting it from the Holy Writ, there are approximately 4173 years and eight months, more or less.

Now from Jesus Christ, in that there is such a diversity of sects, I pass this date by and having computed these present prophecies in accordance with the order of the chain which contains its revolution, and all of it by astronomical doctrine, together with my own natural instinct and after some time and including in it the time which Saturn takes to turn between April seventh up to August twenty-fifth, Jupiter from June fourteenth up to October seventh, Mars from April seventeenth to June twenty-second, Venus from April ninth to May twenty-second, Mercury from February third to the twenty-fourth of the same month, and afterwards from June first up to the twenty-fourth of that month, and from September twenty-fifth up to October sixteenth, Saturn in Capricorn, Jupiter in Aquarius, Mars in the Scorpion, Venus in Pisces, Mercury in a month of Capricorn, Aquarius, and Pisces, the Moon in Aquarius, the Dragon's Head in Libra, the Tail in her opposite sign. Following a conjunction of Jupiter at Mercury with a quadrant aspect of Mars at Mercury, and the Dragon's Head will be in a conjunction of the Sun with Jupiter and the year will be peaceful without an eclipse.

Then will be the beginning of an era comprehending within itself that which long will endure [the French Revolution] and starting that year there will be greater persecution of the Christian Church than ever transpired in Africa, and this will last from the year 1792 [September 25, First French Republic], which they will think to be a renewal of the age. After this the Roman people will begin to rearrange things and to chase away the dark shadows, recovering a little of their original brilliance, but not without great division and continual change [unification of Italy, 1859–1870]. Venice [Italy] thereafter, in great force and power, will raise her wings very high, not far short of the might of ancient Rome. And in that time great Byzantine [Austrian] sails, associated with the Ligurians [Italians] by the alliance and power of the [German] eagle [Triple Alliance, 1882–1915] will hinder them so that the two Cretans [Franco–Russian Dual Alliance, 1891–1917] will not be able to maintain their faith.

The ships built by the ancient [British] warriors will accompany them to the waves of Neptune [Entente Cordiale, 1901–1940]. In the Adriatic there will be made such great discord that what was united [Italy] will be separated and that will be nearly reduced to a house which before was a great city [Rome], including the all-powerful one [Mussolini] and the Mesopotamia of Europe [Italy] to forty-five [degrees], and others to forty-one, forty-two and thirty-seven [from Sicily to Lombardy]. And in that time and in those countries [Germany and Italy], the infernal power will set the power of the opponents of its law [fascism] against the Church of Jesus Christ. This will be the second Antichrist, which will persecute the Church and its true vicar [the Pope] by means of the power of the temporal kings [dictators], who will be seduced in their ignorance by the tongues [propaganda] which will cut more than any sword [German army] in a madman's [Hitler's] hand.

The so-called reign of Antichrist will last only up to the finishing off of the one who was born near that era [the millennium] and of the other in the city of Plancus [Lyons], accompanied by the elect of Modena, Fulcy, by Ferrara, maintained by the Adriatic Ligurians, and by the proximity of great Sicily. Then [Henry V], the great Gallic Ogmius [Celtic Hercules] shall pass Mount Jove [Rome], accompanied by such a great number that from far away the empire will be presented with its great law and then and for some time thereafter the blood of the innocent shall be spilled profusely by the criminals recently upraised.

The sense of this paragraph is that the power of Antichrist will last only to the death of King Henry V of France and that Antichrist's sway will begin at Lyons. There will be schism in the Church, with the party of Modena electing an anti-Pope, designated by Fulcy, a Nostradamic anagram for Lucyf, the schismatic Bishop of Caralis, now Cagliari, in Sardinia, who died in 370. The similarity of this anagram to Lucifer, a traditionalist name for the fallen angel, heightens this allusion to a coming schism.

"Ferrara," who will be "maintained by the Adriatic Ligurians [Venetians and Genoese], and by . . . great Sicily," seems to indicate the true Pope. Ferrara came into the possession of the Este family in 1146 and was their capital until 1598, when it passed to the papacy, a land transfer making its identification with the regular papal candidate even more conclusive.

Then, by great floods, the memory of things contained in such instruments will receive innumerable loss, even to the letters themselves. This will be among the northerners [Europeans]. By the divine will and once again Satan will be bound [Revelation xx, 10] and peace will be made world wide among mankind and the Church of Jesus Christ will be delivered from all tribulation, though the Azostains [Sophists] would like to mix honey with the gall of their pestilential allurement.

This will be near the seventh millennium, when the sanctuary of Jesus Christ no longer will be harassed by the infidels who come from the north and the world then will be approaching the great conflagration, though by my reckonings and my prophecies the course of time will travel much farther along.

In the letter which several years since I dedicated to my son, Caesar Nostradamus, I have openly enough declared some points without omen. But here, Sire, are included many great and marvelous events which those who follow hereafter will see. During this astrological reckoning are included coordinated with the Holy Writ the persecution of the ecclesiastical nation [Italy], taking its origin in the power of the eagle-kings [Hitler and Mussolini], united with the Japanese. This persecution shall last eleven years, or somewhat less by the defeat of the principal eagle-king [Hitler].

French political analysts date the beginning of Adolf Hitler's power from September 14, 1930, when his National Socialists polled 6,406,397 votes to win 107 seats in the German Reichstag. Eleven years or somewhat less would be to September, 1941. However, Hitler came into complete power as a result of the March 5, 1933, Reichstag election, which date marks the beginning of his real authority through the Enabling Act conferring absolute authority upon him. Eleven years from that date would take us into 1944.

Which years being accomplished, a southerner will succeed him who will persecute still more severely the clergy of the Church for the space of three years by the apostate seduction of one who will take away all the absolute power of the Church Militant and the holy people of God who observe its law; and the whole order of religion will be persecuted greatly and so afflicted that the blood of true ecclesiastics will swim everywhere. To one of these terrible temporal kings [Hitler (?)] such praise will be given by his henchmen [Nazis] that he will have spilled more human blood of innocent ecclesiastics than anyone could have done with wine. This king will commit incredible crimes against the Church. Human blood will flow in the streets and temples like water after a furious rainstorm and will incarnadine the neighboring rivers and in another naval war redden the seas to such an extent that the report of one king to the other [Mussolini to Hitler] will say: "The sea blushed red with the blood of naval fights."

Then, in the same year and those following, there will ensue the most horrible plague, the more astounding because of the preceding famine, and such great tribulations that nothing approaching them ever had taken place since the foundation of the Christian Church. This also will take place throughout all the Latin regions, leaving vestiges in every country of Spaniards.

Then the third king of the [bald] eagle, hearing the cry of the [American] people, from whom he takes his principal title [President], will raise up such a mighty army [A.E.F. II] and pass beyond the confines [Western Hemisphere] of his last ancestors and predecessors to him who will put the greatest part into its original state [Anglo-American Atlantic Federation] and the great vicar of the hooded cloak [the Pope] will be put back into his former estate

[Rome], but, desolated and then abandoned by everyone, he will return to the Holy of Holies [Jerusalem], destroyed by paganism and the Old as well as the New Testament will be banished and burned.

After that, the Antichrist will be the infernal prince. Then, at this last time, all the realms of Christendom and all those of the infidels for the space of twenty-five years will be attacked and the wars and battles will be most grievous and towns, cities, castles, and all the other buildings will be burned, razed, and destroyed with a great gushing of virgin blood and violated wives, widows, and sucking children dashed against the walls of the towns and battered to pieces, and so many evils will be committed by Satan, the infernal prince, that nearly all the world will find itself defeated and desolated.

Before these events occur, certain unusual birds will cry in the air, "Now! Now!" and after a certain time vanish. After this has lasted a certain time, there almost will be renewed another reign of Saturn, a golden age. God the Creator will say, hearing the affliction of His people, that Satan will be cast into the abyss and bound at the bottom of the vast pit [Revelation xx, 2–5]. Then there will begin universal peace between God and men, while he [Satan] will remain bound the space of a thousand years and shall turn in her greatest force, the ecclesiastical power, then all is unbound.

How all these figures are adapted justly by divine writ to visible, celestial things, that is to say, by Saturn, Jupiter, and Mars and the others in conjunction with them, may be seen more plainly by some quatrains which the reader examines. I would have calculated more profoundly and adapted some to the others, but seeing, O most serene King, that some would find difficulty of censorship, I will take cause to retire my pen for my nightly repose.

Many events, O most powerful King of all, of the most astounding kind soon are to transpire, that I neither could nor would fit them all into this letter; but, to understand certain things, a few terrible facts must be set forth for examples, though your fullness and humanity toward all men and your piety toward the gods is so great, and that you only appear worthy of the great title of the most Christian King and to whom the whole authority in all religion should be bestowed.

But I shall only entreat you, O most clement King, by this your singular and prudent humanity, to understand most of all the desire of my courage and the guiding wish which I have to obey your most serene Majesty ever since my eyes approached so near to your sunny splendor, than greatness can attain or requite.

From Salon, June 27, 1558

Done by Michael Nostradamus Salon-in-Provence

5

"Like Unto a Leopard"

One of Great Britain's poets laureate, Alfred Lord Tennyson, is credited with more than poetic fancy in his Locksley Hall ballad, written in 1826 and published in 1842. Prophetically, he wrote:

> For I dipt into the future, far as human eye could see,
> Saw the Vision of the world, and all the wonder that would be;—

Ballooning then was a scientific experiment in the hot-air stage, attempted by daredevils to amaze the gowks at county fairs, yet Tennyson

> Saw the heavens filled with commerce, argosies of magic sails,
>
> Heard the heavens fill with shouting, and there rain'd a ghastly dew
> From the nations' airy navies grappling in the central blue.

Decades later the Italian General Douhet's theory of all-out aerial warfare was put into effect by Marshal Hermann Goering's *Luftwaffe*.

Not the Pyrrhonistic fatalist, as was Nostradamus, Tennyson bade the new Lord of Locksley to:

> *Follow Light, and do the Right—for man can half-control his*
>   *doom—*
> *Till you find the deathless Angel seated in the vacant tomb.*

The Poet Laureate wrote the above in recanting the frenzied judgments of his youth in *Locksley Hall Sixty Years After,* published in 1886, and showed his prophetic fires still burning luridly, confessing:

> *I myself have often babbled doubtless of a foolish past;*
> *Babble, babble; our old England may go down in babble at last.*

Nostradamus agrees with Tennyson, but spells it Babel.

Most Nostradamic prophecies appertain to the Latin and Catholic realms, particularly to the prophet's beloved France. Oracles affecting England and the world speaking its Anglo-Saxon tongue have been disentangled, however. Few Englishmen had heard of Nostradamus; and, to those who had, he was little more than a French charlatan, until the New York *Sun* and several other American newspapers recounted some predictions which might relate to the current war. Then, even the bluff Lords of His Majesty's Admiralty took notice.

The *Sun's* London correspondent, Gault MacGowan, on July 8, 1940, cabled:

> One of the most recent bits of Nazi propaganda here, according to British naval circles, is the resurrection of the prophecy of Michael Nostradamus, soothsayer of the sixteenth century, that the French will defeat "a lion opposing them from the sea."
>
> The most accepted interpreters of Nostradamus, whose predictions have been confirmed with uncanny frequency, always have assumed that the "lion" was Italy, but this has been

given a new meaning by the stories that are going around London. The lion is clearly the British Empire, the story goes, and the implication is clear that France's navy will turn to the aid of Germany and defeat the English fleet.

However much this is believed in Germany, it causes only smiles here. In fact it would not surprise the English very much to learn that Hitler, an avowed follower of astrology and other forms of divinations, is using Nostradamus as one of his advisers in planning his stroke against the British Isles.

It may be significant that the hundredth and last quatrain of the tenth and final complete Nostradamus *Centurie* is a widely quoted prediction anent the rise and fall of the British Empire. This terminal placing could be taken to indicate that this empire will last to the Day of Judgment:

Le grand empire sera par Angleterre,
Le Pempotam des ans plus de trois cens:
Grandes copies passer par mer et terre,
Les Lusitains n'en seront pas contens.

Pempotam is a hybridized word, possibly coined by the learned Nostradamus himself, from the Greek *pan* (all) and the Latin *potens* (English, potent). The Lusitani were the inhabitants, in the days of the Roman conquests, of what now is Portugal, whence the Lusitania of modern poets and the ill-fated Cunarder.

Without departing from the connotations of the original French, this quatrain has been turned into English doggerel:

An empire grand will be England
For three centuries most potent.
Great wealth will pass by sea and land,
The Portuguese won't be content.

Thus, Pempotam implies the all-powerfulness of the British Navy for more than three hundred years, but is this potency to be reckoned from the destruction of Philip of Spain's Invincible Armada in 1588 by Queen Elizabeth's sea dogs, or from the Dutch wars (1652–1667)? Since more than three centuries had elapsed at the turn of this century, the Elizabethan date must be too early.

A French commentator, Charles Nicoullaud, believes that the Navigation Ordinance of 1651, drafted by Oliver Cromwell to build up the shipping of England at the expense of the Dutch, whose enterprising traders had found the Portuguese colonies a pushover, is the significant date from which to reckon Britannia's hegemony over the waves. This would yield a date in the nineteen-fifties.

Study of the Portuguese portion of the prophecy evokes the historical fact that two centuries, 1380 to 1580, embraced Portugal's prosperity, but it was not until the Treaty of Methuen, in 1703, that England was assured of Lusitania's erstwhile place in the sun by getting this new dominance expressed in writing. Thus, Portugal is England's oldest ally. Adding 300 years gives 2003 for the fulfillment of *Centurie* X, quatrain 100.

A second Nostradamic quatrain, *Centurie* III, No. 57, helps in dating the previous stanza. In the seer's crabbed French, it reads:

Sept fois changer verrez Gent Britannique,
Taints en sang en deux cent nonante ans:
France, non poinct, par appuy Germanique;
Aries double son Pole Bastarnam.

Seven times you'll see the British rule change,
Bloodstained for 290 years:
France, not at all, because of Germanic support;
The ram doubles his Bastarnic pole.

It is the last line, seemingly obscure, which dates this quatrain as of today. The clues are in the last two words. The Bastarnae were a tribe inhabiting the territory between the Dniester and Pruth Rivers in the second century, their lands extending up to the headwaters of the Vistula. Thus, they dwelt in modern Bessarabia and in that part of erstwhile Poland seized by Soviet Russia in 1939. In 1940, Russia doubled this Bastarnic boundary, or "pole," by seizing Bessarabia from Rumania. The word Pole also gives a hint that Poland is involved while the word Aries, for the zodiacal sign of the ram, is close phonetically to the modern French rendition of the Union of Soviet Socialist Republics in initial form—U.R.S.S. Reckoned from the Navigation Act (1651), 290 years bring the year 1941.

Some commentators believe that the seven changes referred to in the first part of the quatrain chronicle the mutations of the British Crown. After the death of Nostradamus, these were:

1. The accession of the Scottish dynasty of Stuarts on March 24, 1603.

Three years before she died, Queen Elizabeth Tudor showed positive recognition of James VI of Scotland as her successor when she said that "the King of Scotland would become one day King of Great Britain."

"The fact is deeply interesting that it was from the lips of this last and mightiest of England's monarchs that the style and title by which her royal kinsman and his descendants should reign over the united kingdoms of the Britannic Empire was first pronounced. It surely ought not to be forgotten that it was Queen Elizabeth herself who gave that prospective empire the name of Great Britain," wrote Agnes Strickland in *The Queens of England*. Nor should it pass unnoticed that Nostradamus uses the then rare Britannique rather than the current old French form of Anglois for the neighbors across the Channel. He called attention clearly to the first change. Other changes were:

2. Revolution and Civil War, with Charles I, a royal blockhead, losing his royal head on the block on January 30, 1649. The Commonwealth which followed the headsman's ax-time on December 16, 1653, made Oliver Cromwell the Lord Protector, kingship having been declared "unnecessary, burdensome and dangerous to the liberty, safety and public interest of the people."

3. Restoration of the Stuart kings, Charles II returning from his enforced travels on May 29, 1660, his thirtieth birthday.

4. The Glorious Revolution of November 5, 1668, Guy Fawkes Day, anniversary of the celebrated Gunpowder Plot, bringing over William III, of the House of Orange, and his wife, Mary Stuart, from The Netherlands. Her succeeding sister, Queen Anne, should be included as within this transition.

5. Enter the Germans, in the person of the Hanoverian George I of the House of Guelph on May 21, 1714.

6. Edward VII, son of Queen Victoria, last of the Guelphs, and of her Prince-Consort, Albert of Saxe-Coburg-Gotha, whose surname was Wettin, ascended the throne of a Greater Britain on January 22, 1901. His son, King George V, dropped German names and titles in 1917, during the First World War, for himself and his family to set up the British House of Windsor.

7. An ancient prophecy has it that England's greatness will be from Elizabeth to Elizabeth.

Nostradamus first published his vaticinations in 1555. The first of these directly affecting England apparently was quatrain 94 of the Eighth *Centurie* reading:

Devant le lac ou plus cher fut getté
De sept mois, et son ost desconfit
Seront Hispans par Albanois gastez,
Par delay perte en donnant le conflict.

Before the lake where much wealth was anchored
After seven months and its host discomfited,
Spaniards will have the English as guests,
Lost by delay in giving battle.

This describes the attack by the English privateers under the Earl of Essex on the Spanish treasure galleons, seven months out from South America, anchored in the Bay of Cadiz in June, 1596. Thirteen Spanish warships were destroyed and forty argosies sacked, then the English burned the town. Had the galleons been unloaded betimes by the mañana-loving Spaniards, their cargoes could have been saved. Had they attacked the English sea rovers first, they might have saved themselves. Cadiz inlet well may be described as a lake, since it is a dozen miles long and half that width, almost entirely enclosed by land.

Now it is time to ring the seven changes on the refrain, "There'll Always Be an England." Nostradamus goes further—he tells what kind of England, too.

1. The Royal Stuarts

That the change-over from England to Great Britain marked a new era in Nostradamus' opinion is evidenced by *Centurie* III, quatrain 70:

La Grand Bretagne comprinse l'Angleterre,
Viendra par eaux si fort à inonder:

La Ligue neusve d'Ausonne fera guerre,
Que contre eux ils se viendront bander.

Great Britain, absorbing England,
Shall become flooded by high waters.
The new League of Ausonia shall make war
Against any who'll band together against them.

As England's Gloriana foretold before her death, her native land became Great Britain with the accession of Scotland's James VI in 1603, though actually he assumed the title of King of Great Britain seventeen months later, on October 24, 1604.

The floods mentioned in this quatrain began in January, 1607, when the port of Bristol and the Somersetshire hinterland were inundated along a thirty-mile coastal stretch for six miles inland. The East Anglian area of the English eastern shore also was flooded, but not so extensively.

In 1606, the Holy League of 1526 was renewed by the French King, the Papal States, and the Venetian Republic as a defensive alliance, but this pact had no apparent effect upon Britain. The original Holy League also had included the Florentine Republic, the Swiss Confederation, and England, which may be why Nostradamus tied its renewal with the proclaiming of Great Britain, the principal theme of this stanza.

Nostradamus uses the word Ausonia as French poets have employed Ausonie for Italy. The Ausones were one of Italy's most ancient tribes, from whom southern Italy was called Ausonia.

2. Bloody Rebellion

This erstwhile country doctor had a positive flair for predicting revolutions. The soothsayer who died in 1566 foretold not only the French

Revolution of 1789, but also England's Great Civil War of 1642–1651. The number of quatrains involved in the spilling of the blood royal in these two internecine slaughters shows his horror of regicide.

His cycle on the Great Rebellion begins with the birth of him who caused all the trouble, Charles I, born a prince of Scotland at Dunfermline Castle on November 19, 1600, and succeeding to the British Crown in 1625. This is quatrain 93 of the Fifth *Centurie*:

Soubs le terroir du rond globe lunaire,
Lors que sera dominateur Mercure:
L'isle d'Escosse fera un luminaire,
Qui les Anglois mettra à déconfiture.

On his native heath, when Mercury will govern
The full lunar globe:
The island of Scotland will bear a light,
Who will put the English to discomfort.

The first two lines of the quatrain detail the astrological auguries attendant upon the birth of Charles I; these have been verified with that ill-destined autocrat's horoscope. That his idea of the Divine Right of Kings caused the English acute discomfort is a matter of history known to every schoolboy.

The fortieth quatrain of the Tenth *Centurie* describes the accession and fall of Charles I:

Le jeune nay au regne Britannique
Qu'aura le père mourrant recommandé,
Iceluy mort, LONOLE donra topique,
Et à son fils le regne demandé.

The young heir to the British realm
Whose dying father will have recommended,

Whereafter dead, Ole Nol will give the cue,
And wrest the kingdom from his son.

By dropping the anagram LONOLE into the quatrain, Nostradamus perplexed many interpreters. Transposition of letters turns it into Oliver Cromwell's nickname. For a decade the creator of the New Model Army stomped all over the British Isles in his jackboots, ruling under the high-sounding title of Lord Protector. Today, we'd say dictator, but among his friends the austere, hymn-humming Puritanical gerent was "Noll" or "Nollie," while the Republican Commonwealth he bossed was known affectionately as "Old Puss."

Historians have noted certain parallel lines in the shaping up of both the English and French revolutions. A comparison of Nostradamic *centuries* bears out the old saw that history repeats itself. As was Louis XVI's Marie Antoinette in France, Charles I's Henrietta Maria was extravagant and fond of gaiety. The youngest daughter of the Henry of Navarre who turned Catholic to become Henry IV of France because "Paris is worth a Mass," Queen Henrietta's partiality for the Roman Catholics governed almost all she did in English politics.

To the indignation of the populace, she gave countenance and more to her coreligionists, and just before the outbreak of the Civil War her activities did much to fan the flames of the popular discontent. Quatrain 22 of the Tenth *Centurie* tells this story:

Pour ne vouloir consentir au divorce
Qui puis apres sera cogneu indigne,
Le Roy des Isles sera chassé par force,
Mis à son place qui de Roy n'aura signe.

For unwillingness to agree to a divorce
Which thereafter would have been deemed unworthy,

The King of the Isles will be hunted by force,
Replaced by one without a sign of royalty.

Charles, to his eternal credit, refused to divorce his consort; future generations uphold his action. He was hunted from pillar to post by Cromwell's Roundheads and brought to the block, and the Huntingdonshire brewer with the wart-studded face became king in all but style and title.

The eightieth quatrain of the Third *Centurie* carries on this action thus:

Du regne Anglais le digne dechassé,
Le conseiller par ire mis à feu,
Ses adherans iront si bas tracer,
Que le bastard sera demy receu.

The rightful ruler of the British realm dethroned,
The counselor put to the stake amid wrath,
His adherents will lie so low,
That the bastard will become viceroy.

When Charles, needing funds urgently, summoned the Long Parliament in 1640, the Commoners met in no uncertain temper. They denounced his chief advisers and, finally, on May 12, 1641, arrested Thomas Wentworth, Earl of Strafford, upon whose good counsel and abilities the throne's strength depended. When the impeachment proceedings failed, the Long Parliament passed a bill of attainder against Lord Strafford. Charles sealed his own doom when he assented to this act, urged thereto by his wife. Charles's political support melted away with Strafford's beheading, presaging the loss of his own royal head. When that was gone, only time lay between Cromwell and the gaudy trappings of his Protectorate.

In the Ninth *Centurie*, quatrain 49, Nostradamus predicts roundly:

> *Gand et Bruxelles marcheront contre Anvers,*
> *Senat de Londres mettront à mort leur Roy,*
> *Le sel et vin luy seront à l'envers,*
> *Pour eux avoir le règne en désarroy.*

> *Ghent and Brussels will march upon Antwerp,*
> *The London Senate will put to death its King,*
> *Salt and wine will put him in wrong*
> *With those who have the realm in disarray.*

The Peace of Westphalia, October 14, 1648, ended the war in the Spanish Netherlands, today's Belgium, in which Philip IV's troops from Ghent and Brussels marched against Antwerp to seize that vital port. The so-called Rump Parliament convicted "the man Charles Stuart" as "tyrant, traitor and murderer" to die on the headsman's scaffold on January 30, 1649. Nostradamus never is clearer than in forecasting the shedding of the blood royal.

Salt and wine symbolize wisdom and force, Charles having neither wisdom nor a standing army to defend his Divine Right theories, and he certainly had been constantly at odds with the Parliamentarians. Details of his execution were foretold in the Eighth *Centurie*, quatrain 37:

> *La forteresse auprès de la Tamise*
> *Cherra par lors, le Roy dedans serré,*
> *Apres du pont sera veu en chemise*
> *Un devant mort, puis dans le fort barré.*

> *The fortress overlooking the Thames*
> *Will fall at that time, the King being beset,*

Afterward on the bridge will be seen the shirt-front
Of the dead one, then to be barred in the fort.

Most Nostradamian interpreters have believed that this stanza foresees the doom of the Tower of London, forgetting that there's another fortress on the Thames higher up the river—Windsor Castle. From December 23, 1648, until January 19, 1649, while the Rump's high court of justice was being set up, Charles I was imprisoned at Windsor. On the scaffold in Whitehall, he handed an orange stuck with cloves and his kerchief to the masked headsman, who stripped him to his white shirt. In a trice after the King had knelt to the block, the royal noggin plopped onto the rough boards.

Though Cromwell is said to have regarded Charles Stuart's decapitation as "cruel necessity," the regicides of the high court seemed to glory in the bloody deed of January 30, 1649. There was much the same elated frenzy of self-glorification over this beheading that France's Jacobins displayed just 144 years later, though the short-memoried English shuddered when Louis Capet, better known as Louis XVI, met the Red Widow.

Charles' bloody shirt was displayed by a pike on London bridge, a grisly rite usually reserved for the heads themselves. He was buried secretly and without any funeral service in the tomb of Henry VIII in St. George's Chapel at Windsor Castle, from whence he had been taken to London for trial and punishment. In 1813 an unidentified coffin was opened. It contained the King-Martyr's skeleton.

Though their King was dead, sold to his butchers by his ain folk, the Scots, the Royalists carried on with true-blue doggedness under the Prince of Wales, the future Charles II. The Catholic Highlanders and some praying Covenanters remained faithful to their Stuarts. Yet, the free mountaineers and marauding moss-troopers were worsted in the Battle of Dunbar, September 3, 1650, as the Eighth *Centurie*, quatrain 56, tells:

La bande foible le tertre occupera,
Ceux du Hautlieu feront horribles cris:
Le gros trouppeau d'estre coin troublera,
Tombe pres DINEBRO descouvers les escrits.

The feeble band will occupy a knoll,
Those of the Highlands will raise horrible yells:
The great troop will be worried into a corner,
Falling near Edinburgh, their writings discovered.

Cromwell had only 11,000 of his New Model Army to oppose 20,000 Scots. From his higher position on a hillock near Dunbar, Cromwell attacked before daybreak. The Scots weren't ready and began giving ground.

The sun was just rising when Cromwell called out "Let God arise, let His enemies be scattered!" The Scots were followed as they fled and, altogether, 3,000 of them were slain. About 10,000 more Scots, with their arms, artillery and baggage, were taken prisoner. Many poor Highlanders, unable to ransom themselves, were shipped off to the American colonies as bondsmen, indentured for seven years. The English losses were slight.

DINEBRO is one of the more obvious Nostradamic anagrams, becoming EDINBRO, Scotland's capital. The discovered writings were the Scottish War Office's papers which, along with Scotland's Great Seal, were captured and shipped off to London as mementoes of the triumph of orderly totalitarian discipline over that many-headed hydra, individual freedom.

Yet, their crushing defeat couldn't erase Scottish loyalty to their Stuarts. Scotland's last coronation ceremony was on New Year's Day of 1651 at Scone, without the sacred stone, stolen by England's Edward I, Hammerer of the Scots, in 1296, but with the Prince of Wales, heir of the Bruce, of the Great Stewards, of the high Plantagenets, and of the upstart Tudors, becoming Charles II, King of Scots.

After his coronation, Charles II essayed one more sally south of the border. This resulted in the Battle of Worcester on September 3, 1651, a year to the day after the crushing defeat at Dunbar. The King's subsequent storied flight from Worcester half across England has been chronicled romantically in the Boscobel Tracts; the Eighth *Centurie*, quatrain 58, embellishes this story:

Regne en querelles aux frères divisé,
Prendre les armes et le nom Britannique:
Tiltre Anglican sera tard advisé,
Surprins de nuict mener à l'air Gallique.

The realm in quarrels with brothers divided
To assume the arms and Britannic name:
The titular Anglican will be advised too late,
Surprised by night to take the Gallic air.

There's a good deal of history crammed into this quatrain. The realm certainly was divided, with the Scottish Covenanters fighting their coreligionists, the English Puritans. Like our War Between the States, families were divided, brother actually battling with brother. There were peers of the realm as generals and colonels in both armies.

At first glance "prendre les armes" would appear to imply the taking up of arms, one against the other, but that had been done by the opposing sides almost a decade previously. The rest of this line, "le nom Britannique," points to the real meaning—"to assume."

Even a commonwealth of shopkeepers must have a great seal, but the significant fact is that the flamboyant heraldic trappings of royalty were not jettisonèd in their entirety. Unlike the United States a century and a quarter later, the Britannic Republic continued the lucrative practice of heraldry, with the Levelers, who succeeded the royal kings-of-arms, issuing grants of skillful armorial composition.

Since the golden leopards of England and flowers of the French quartered by the Plantagenets and Tudors, plus the ramping ruddy lion of the Scots added to the old shield by the Stuarts, were identified too closely with the Divine Right of Kings, the new state forthwith adopted the cross of St. George for England and the harp of Tara for Ireland. After the submission of the turbulent Scots, the X-shaped white cross on a blue field of their patron, St. Andrew, was adopted in their behalf.

In 1655 a new great seal came into being for the Commonwealth with a new national shield of arms: St. George's cross in the first and fourth quarters, where the English leopards were and again are; St. Andrew's cross in the second quarter, where now the Scottish lion roars defiance; while the third quarter bore Ireland's harp unwillingly then and to this very day.

As Lord Protector, Cromwell supported this quartered shield by the British lion, wearing his regal crown, and the Welsh dragon of ruddy gold, the twin emblems of Elizabeth, last of the mighty Tudors. Surmounting the shield was the six-barred helm of monarchy with the same royal crown that was lopped off the Stuart head, a crowned leopard cresting its bejeweled arches.

These blent emblems of the old and new, heraldically unharmonious, typify the chaotic Commonwealth and the muddled mind of its Lord Protector. The retention of the external ornaments of royalty around the simple arms of the new republic suggest forethoughts of a revival of monarchy. At the feast of Lupercal in 44 B.C., Julius Caesar, when offered a kingly crown by Mark Antony, refused it, just as did Oliver Cromwell. Yet, according to Sir Bernard

Burke, when Old Noll's coffin was opened, a copper plate was found, graved with England's three golden leopards on crimson impaling the Cromwells' ramping silver lion on black. Thus a king in all but name had taken the arms and name of Britannic Majesty.

The titular king, Charles II, ill-advisedly had invaded his English domain and, surprised by the Parliamentary generals, escaped under the cover of darkness, eventually reaching France's more hospitable shores, as the last two lines explain.

Had Charles Stuart known of the fourth quatrain of the Tenth *Centurie*, his hope of ending his travels might have been stronger:

> *Sur la minuict conducteur de l'armée*
> *Se sauvera, subit esvanouy;*
> *Sept ans après la fame non blasmée;*
> *A son retour ne dira t'on qu'ouy.*

> *At midnight the leader of the army*
> *Will save himself, suddenly vanishing;*
> *Seven years thereafter his fame is not dimmed;*
> *To his return no one will demur.*

This quatrain, covering nearly a decade, relates Charles' escape after the ill-starred descent into England, culminating in the Battle of Worcester on September 3, 1651. Seven years from then, to the very day, on September 3, 1658, the Commonwealth's uncrowned king died, some say brokenhearted because he had not wangled the crown. His addlepated son, Richard, succeeded as Protector but fled to the Continent just before Charles II returned amid universal acclaim.

Three Nostradamic quatrains subject Old Noll's character to searching analysis, not exactly flattering. The first, quatrain 76 of the Eighth *Centurie*:

Plus macelin que Roy en Angleterre,
Lieu obscur nay par force aura l'empire:
Lasche sans foy, sans loy saignera terre.
Son temps s'approche si pres que je souspire.

More butcher than king in England,
Born in humble station, he will seize the empire by force:
Cowardly, without faith, without law, he will bloody the land.
His time draws so nigh that I sigh.

By paternal descent, Cromwell was a member of a Welsh family named Williams. He derived his surname from his great-grandfather, Sir Richard Williams, who took the name of Cromwell from his mother, sister of Thomas Cromwell, the Earl of Essex, who acted as Henry VIII's vicar-general in the despoiling of the monasteries, but who was beheaded for treason. Thomas Cromwell was the son of a Putney blacksmith, unrelated to the ancient baronial house of Cromwell. Sir Richard Williams, however, retained the Williams coat of arms—the silver lion on black used by Oliver. That his name forever is execrable to the Irish because of his massed slaughters is sufficient explanation of the last two lines of this stanza. These thoughts are carried out with quatrain 41 of the Eighth *Centurie*:

Esleu sera Renard, ne sonnant mot,
Faisant le saint publique, vivant pain d'orge;
Tyranniser auprès tant à un coup,
Mettant à pied des plus grands sur la gorge.

The fox will be elected, saying nothing,
Feigning public sainthood, living on barley bread;
Tyrannizing afterward by such a coup,
Putting his foot on the throat of the greatest.

Cromwell and his musketeers turned themselves into a permanent oligarchy, dismissing the Rump Parliament on April 20, 1653. Praise-God Barebones' Parliament drew up the Instrument of Government appointing the general "Lord Protector of the Commonwealth of England, Scotland and Ireland" with almost unlimited executive power.

Cromwell's really was a military rule, a despotism greater than Charles I ever attempted. Royalists he put to boot, many of them fleeing to the American colonies, where they founded some of the First Families of Virginia. The Eighth *Centurie*, quatrain 65, carries on the story:

> *Le vieux frustré du principal espoir,*
> *Il parviendra au chef de son empire:*
> *Vingt mois tiendra le regne à grand pouvoir.*
> *Tiran, cruel en delaissant un pire.*

> *The old one, frustrated in his main hope,*
> *Will reach to the chieftaincy of his empire:*
> *Twenty months he will hold the realm in great power.*
> *Tyrant, cruel in making affairs worse.*

After Parliament bickered five months, Cromwell, on January 22, 1655, dismissed it to rule as dictator. He placed the country, divided into eleven military districts, under the regime of major generals. Twenty months later, he dismissed the generals (August, 1656), thus fulfilling the prophecy.

In March, 1657, Cromwell's new Parliament proposed to revise the Constitution, presenting the Humble Petition and Advice, offering the dictator the crown, which he refused, not without reluctance, but compelled by the sentiment of the army. Like Caesar, he hoped for another chance at the diadem.

3. Restoration

London played a most important part in the defeat of Charles I in the Civil War, its Trained Bands forming the nucleus for Cromwell's New Model Army. The British metropolis suffered much during the Great Plague, approximately 70,000 persons, a tenth of the population, perishing. This pestilence, coming from The Netherlands, whence Charles II had landed to avenge his father's execution, was followed in 1666 by the Great Fire, when about five-sixths of the area within the ancient city walls was reduced to ashes. Nostradamus recounts these two events in the Second *Centurie*, quatrains 51 and 53, respectively:

> *Le sang du juste à Londres fera faute*
> *Bruslez par foudres de vingt trois les six*
> *La dame antique cherra de place haute,*
> *De mesme secte plusieurs seront occis.*

> The blood of the just shall be appeased at London
> Burnt by fireballs in three score and six;
> The ancient lady will fall from the high place,
> Of the same creed many others will be done for.

> *La grand peste de cité maritime*
> *Ne cessera, que mort ne soit vengée*
> *Du juste sang par pris damné sans crime,*
> *De la grand dame par feincte n'outragée.*

> The great pestilence of the marine city
> Shall not diminish until Death has been avenged
> For the just blood, condemned blamelessly for a price,
> And the great lady outraged by faint hearts.

Nostradamus warned London that it must pay dearly for reg-icide. He appears to note precisely that the fire will come in the 666th year of the second millennium after Christ.

The Great Fire broke out at the shop of the king's baker, one Farynor, in Pudding Lane, Eastcheap. A pile of faggots beside the overheated oven caught fire, igniting near-by flitches of bacon, which flared greasily into the lane, one of the narrowest in the city. The houses had projecting stories, with their woodwork coated with pitch, the stuff from which fireballs are made. The flames spread slowly until they reached the cellars and warehouses along the Thames. At 8 A.M. on September 2 London Bridge was ablaze.

St. Paul's Cathedral, "the great lady," as parish church of the British Empire, was destroyed, along with the Guildhall, the next day. Two days thereafter only a sixth of the city within the walls was standing and 100,000 people were homeless. However, not more than a dozen persons were burned.

In addition to St. Paul's, eighty-four parish churches "of the same creed" were "done for." However, though their great lady of old was gone, Londoners weren't long fainthearted. Despite terrible tribula-tion, the Cockneys never lost their resilience. It was not until 1668 that rebuilding was taken thoroughly in hand and within a few years a flourishing commercial community had arisen, phoenix-like. Sir Christopher Wren lived to see his masterpiece, the new St. Paul's, finished; started in 1675, it was completed in 1710.

Thus ended a most interesting century in English history, spanned by the reigns of monarchs who, though possibly not great, certainly were remarkable characters, and including the interregnum of an uncrowned monarch who, though without a remarkable char-acter, certainly was great. England under the Stuarts was bestudded with the names of men whose influence on humanity well may be as permanent as that of the Athenians of the Golden Age. The name of James I, Shakespeare's patron, lives in that literary masterpiece, the King James Version of the Bible. Milton began his poetic career under

Charles I and continued it under the latter's foeman, Cromwell, who made England a world power.

Charles II, patron of science, founded the Royal Society, whose members included Isaac Newton and Dr. Harvey. As Lord High Admiral, the Duke of York, who became James II, built up the Royal Navy, which seized Dutch New Netherland and New Amsterdam, renaming them for the royal admiral. The faults of the Stuarts do not blind their glories to the eyes of Nostradamus.

James II, who succeeded his brother in 1685, was the narrowest and least competent of the Stuarts. In three short years he made enemies of almost all his subjects. He appointed Catholics, who could not hold office under Parliament's laws, to the army, church, and universities. In 1688, he issued a declaration granting further favors to Catholics.

4. Bloodless Revolution

When a son was born to James by his second marriage to a Catholic princess, under-cover revolt started. Hitherto it had been expected that James would be succeeded by his Protestant daughter, Mary, wife of William of Orange, the Dutch Protestant leader of Continental Europe against Louis XIV. Since James's son would be brought up a Roman Catholic, a number of prominent noblemen united in inviting William and Mary to England.

When Dutch William accepted, James was deserted everyone—colonels, courtiers, and councilors. He tried to leave England and was captured, but William made his escape easy. England had learned the consequences of regicide. This so-called Glorious Revolution is recounted in quatrain 89 of *Centurie* IV:

Trente de Londres secret conjureront,
Contre leur Roy, sur le pont l'entreprise:

Luy, satallites la mort degousteront,
Un Roy esleu blonde, natif de Frize.

Thirty of London shall conspire secretly
Against their King, an undertaking on the bridge:
His satellites, they will dislike bloodshed,
Elect a blond King, native of Friesland.

Just how many peers of the realm instigated the plot to bring over William and Mary is not a matter of recorded history, conspirators being notoriously lax in keeping minutes of their meetings. That there were those who played with both sides both before and after the Glorious Revolution is a fact, however. It is said that the plotters frequently met in an inn on London Bridge. That they wished to avoid bloodshed already has been noted. Dutch William was a blond, though not a native of Friesland. However, the Duchy of Friesland formed a prominent part of his Netherlandish dominions, providing many sailors of the navy which he used to ferry him into his kingdom.

5. Guelphic Georges

The century from England's Glorious Revolution of 1688 to the inauguration of George Washington as first President of the United States in 1789 as the result of our Glorious Revolution is colorless and humdrum, as dull as Britain's German Georges, so far as Nostradamian centuries are concerned. Four quatrains have been translated and interpreted as appertaining to the Hanoverians, but these redactions appear to be just the flattery of the king's henchmen.

Nostradamus' prophetic *Centuries* had been translated into English and edited by Theophilus de Garencières in London in 1672.

Furthermore, the Nostradamic oracles were brought to the attention of George III in 1775 by an anonymous subject of that stubborn Guelph who dwelt in his German appanage of Hanover. This pamphlet interpreted several Nostradamic quatrains as warnings of impending revolution in those confounded colonies across the sea. He told his sincere, but obstinate, King who would be a real king, that he was about to lose his American dominions, citing the Nostradamic *Centurie* X, No. 66, or putting it in Arabic numerals, *Centurie* 10–66, the year George's remote ancestor, William the Bastard of Normandy, carried out the last successful invasion of England.

> *Le chef de Londres, par règne l'Américh,*
> *L'Isle d'Escosse t'empiera par gelée;*
> *Roy rebauront un si faux Antichrist,*
> *Qui les mettra trestous dans la meslée.*

> *The chief of London, out of the American realm,*
> *The island of Scotland will be glazed with frost;*
> *They will reverse the King as such a false Antichrist*
> *Who will put them all in the thick of the fight.*

When, during the winter of 1776, Scotland underwent what still is known locally as the Great Freeze, George III should have taken warning. Scottish lochs, tarns, rivers, and burns were frozen solid, even straits separating the nearer Western Isles being frozen over sufficiently to enable the Highlanders to cross to the mainland afoot.

Nostradamus also notes the beginning of American sea power and forecasts the infant republic's future glories in the eightieth quatrain of the Seventh *Centurie*:

> *L'Occident libres les Isles Brittaniques*
> *Le recogneu passer le bas, puis haut*

Ne content triste Rebel. corse. Escotiques
Puis rebeller pas plus et par nuict chaut.

The West freed of the British Isles,
The oppressed to pass low, then high;
Scottish corsairs, dissatisfied with the dismal revolt,
Then to rebel all the more and make the night hot.

Never was Nostradamus' crabbed and abbreviated French more difficult of translation than in this quatrain, yet the intent of his stanza seems obvious enough. The last two lines point to the naval aid of John Paul Jones, born in Arbigland, Scotland, the son of a laborer named John Paul. The younger John went to sea at twelve and was the mate of a Whitehaven slaver at nineteen. Later he settled in Virginia and on the outbreak of the Revolution became a privateer. He cruised the Irish Sea in 1778, harassed the coastal trade of Scotland, and made a bold attack on his erstwhile home port of Whitehaven, landing forces to dismantle the fort there. He led a similar exploit in Kirkudbright Bay, then passed along the coast of Scotland in 1779, taking many prizes.

Other sails than those of the Scottish-American freebooter were to make the English tremble, but this was to be more than two decades later, when Napoleon Bonaparte was as much the master of Europe then as Adolf Hitler is now. This is related in the Second *Centurie*, quatrain 68:

De l'Aquilon les efforts seront grands,
Sur l'Ocean sera la porte ouverte:
Le regne en l'Isle sera réintégrand,
Tremblera Londres par voiles descouverte.

The efforts of the Eagle will be vast,
The portals of the ocean wide at last:

The reign in the island will stand fast,
Though trembling London fears its die is cast.

This quatrain has been turned into a stanza of English doggerel, without losing the implications of the Nostradamic phraseology. If it be objected that the Eagle equally could be that of Adolf Hitler, critics should remember that the Nazi Fuehrer's chief insignia is the swastika, rather than the German imperial eagle. Furthermore, the last line, literally "London shall tremble, discovering sails," marks this quatrain as in the era of sailing navigation. First Consul Bonaparte became Napoleon I, Emperor of the French, on May 18, 1804. He jettisoned his quite ordinary family coat of arms, modeling his new device on the eagle of the Caesars as it figured on the head of the Roman legions' standards. In terms of blazon, Napoleon's shield would be: azure, an eagle displayed with wings inverted, the head to the sinister, standing upon a thunderbolt, all gold.

Napoleon's struggle with Britain in 1803–1805 was entirely naval. The English did not send troops to the Continent, which, with its ports, was entirely held by the French Emperor. So Napoleon planned to invade England. At Boulogne, in 1804, he assembled 180,000 men and a flotilla of 2,400 transports—very many sails, indeed. The English forgot their political squabbles and rallied to the defense of the motherland, even as today.

Napoleon, however, unable to cross the strait of Dover without control of the sea, disbanded his troops that year, but he gathered a grand army for the invasion of England again in 1805. His admiral, Villeneuve, was ordered to entice Lord Nelson, the English commander, across the Atlantic and to return immediately with the French fleet to convoy the Grand Army across the Channel. Villeneuve failed to outwit Nelson, who returned to British waters before the French knew what he was doing. Later in 1805, Nelson utterly destroyed the combined French and Spanish fleets off Cape Trafalgar. From that victory, Britannia has ruled the waves.

6. "Come the Three Corners"

It was not until the turn of this century that England's commanding position again was challenged, and again it was a land power, Imperial Germany, which threw down the gage of battle. The culmination of this challenge was the indecisive battle of Jutland, May 30–June 1, 1916. Britain had a John Paul Jones leading the battle cruisers, but the commander in chief of the Grand Fleet lacked the Nelson touch. Consequently, Germany claimed Skagerrak as a victory, though the High Seas Fleet never again went out against Britain's might. Let us see what Nostradamus has to say in the Tenth *Centurie*, No. 2 and the Ninth *Centurie*, No. 100:

> *Voila galère voile de nef cacher*
> *La grande classe viendra sortir la moindre.*
> *Dix naves proches, tourner repoussera*
> *Grande vaincue, uni à soi conjoindre.*

> There is a man-of-war disguised as a merchantman,
> The grand fleet will sally forth against the feebler.
> Ten ships near by turn to repulse the foe;
> A great victory had one man joined battle.

> *Navalle pugne nuict sera supérée,*
> *Le feu, aux navez à l'Occident ruine;*
> *Rubriche neusve, la grand nef colorée;*
> *Ire à vaincu, et victoire en bruine.*

> Night will be superfluous in the naval battle.
> Fire ruins the ships on the west;
> A new trick, the great vessel colored;
> Woe to the vanquished and victory in a drizzle.

What apparently was a Danish tramp steamer but what, in the belief of many naval experts, really was a German naval auxiliary disguised as a harmless merchantman, tipped off the Kaiser's men-of-war that the British fleet was out in force. The British Grand Fleet had left its bases on the night of May 30, acting on Admiralty intelligence that the German fleet was coming out the next day.

Vice-Admiral Beatty's six battle cruisers, supported at long range by four battleships of the Fifth Battle Squadron, rushed to attack the German vanguard under Hipper. There came this message to Jellicoe from Beatty: "Submit van of battleships follow battle cruisers. We can then cut off whole enemy battle fleet."

It clearly was Beatty's purpose to hold the enemy until Jellicoe's main battle force could come nearer. It was the main German fleet, however, which came nearer. Beatty's little squadron was badly mauled and the over-cautious Jellicoe lived up to the first two syllables in his name, as Nostradamus indicates.

The second quatrain carries on the story of this futile action. Later in the day, mist and fog began hampering operations. The lowering of the mists broke up formations, the action resolving itself into a series of small engagements, with the Germans taking every opportunity to slip away in the darkness. Night settled about 9 P.M. and throughout the first half of the dark hours there were intermittent outbursts of gunfire, with searchlights stabbing the skies on the lookout for Zeppelins and seaplanes. The British ships, which were west of the Germans when the casualties were inflicted, suffered most, three battle cruisers and three armored cruisers being lost because shells striking the turrets exploded the unprotected magazines below. Thus fire ruined the ships on the west.

Furthermore, the Germans had developed a new stratagem, as Nostradamus says, a clever maneuver called *Kehrtwendung*, a simultaneous swing-around of all the ships to turn the course in the opposite direction. Of this new trick, Jellicoe himself said: "Nothing but ample time and superior speed can supply an answer and this means that unless the meeting takes place fairly early in the day, it is most difficult, if not impossible, to fight the action to a finish."

The great colored ship about which Nostradamus spoke was camouflage, used by both sides at Jutland. The German fleet's escape was unfortunate, Ludendorff's memoirs giving rise to the belief that had the Navy been destroyed, Germany might have collapsed in 1916 or early in 1917. Thus, the vanquished went through two more years of woe because the British victory was amid the drizzle and fog of more war, winter, and discontent, rather than in the new light of a glorious summer sun which should have shone on June 1.

So the Great War wore on to its sorry end, related by Nostradamus in quatrain 77 of the Tenth *Centurie*:

> *Trente adhérants de l'ordre des quirettes,*
> *Bannis, leurs biens donnés ses adversaires;*
> *Tous leurs bienfaits seront pour démérites,*
> *Classe espargie, délivré aux Corsaires.*

> *Thirty members of the order of quitters,*
> *Banished, their wealth given to their enemies;*
> *All their good deeds will be discredited,*
> *The fleet dispersed, booty for the freebooters.*

While Germany pounded to pieces on the jagged reefs of defeat with dishonor and discredit in November, 1918, Wilhelm II, the world's most powerful emperor for three decades, fled in a motor car for exile in Holland. Germany's kings, crown princes, princelings, and dukelings, to a round number of thirty, quit summarily, their estates being seized by the ensuing socialistic republic. Whatever good the Hohenzollerns and their feudatories had done in uniting Germany, making her strong, proud, and productive, was forgotten in a wave of revulsion and revolution. The German fleet was surrendered under the watchful eyes of a mighty Anglo-American armada at Scapa Flow in November, 1918, and the greater part of the High Seas Fleet was scuttled by its officers and crews on June 22, 1919, but it seems rather unfair for Nostradamus to call the English-speaking sea dogs corsairs.

The evils men do live on.

"There is no boasting in sturdy John Bull, but his sleeves are rolled half back and his steady eye looks about him," Stephen Leacock once wrote. "For all his advancing years and his heavy feeding, there is a terrible punch left yet in that right arm."

Yet, there were Britishers aplenty who did not care a hoot what the Canadian professor said back in the tortuous 'thirties. Along troubled Whitehall, where it would be unthinkable to roll up the sleeves, Britishers felt assured of their place in the midday sun while a mad dog rearmed. Heavy feeding on doctrines of pacifism and disarmament curtailed all three British defense services—Navy, Army and Air Force—as Nostradamus relates in quatrain 78 of his Second *Centuric*:

> *Le grand Neptune du profond de la mer*
> *De gent Punique et sang Gaulois meslé:*
> *Les Isles à sang pour le tardif ramer,*
> *Plus nuy nuira que l'occult mal celé.*

> *The great Neptune of the ocean deeps,*
> *Of Punic race mingled with Gallic blood:*
> *The Isles amid bloodshed because of the slow rearming,*
> *Shall harm him more than the poorly concealed secret.*

Until Colin de Larmor, Breton commentator on the Nostradamic *Centuries,* pointed out fifteen years ago that the last word in the third line of this quatrain probably was a typographical error for *armer,* the French verb for "to arm," this phrase was translated "because of the slow rowing." True, it also makes sense, at least metaphorically, with such a translation, but "slow rearming" fits the facts much more sensibly. Written history of the British Isles tells us that the first peoples were tribal offshoots from the Celts of Gaul; while Phoenician traders and seamen, who ruled the waves with Punic faith before Rome humbled Carthage, knew of the "Pretonnic Isles." Hanno, the navigator, brought tin from Cornwall to Carthage.

Even now these same Isles are amid bloodshed because of the slow rearming and the Punic faith of Munich. The poorly concealed secret was the weakness of the British armed forces, which Adolf Hitler well knew, but what will harm the *Fuehrer* more is that terrible punch left in Britain's right arm—the same sea power which served Phoenicia and her colony, Carthage, until Rome outbuilt the Punic state.

To oppose a resurgent Germany on the Continent, Britain began seeking allies early in 1938. Nostradamus tells of this checkmate diplomacy in two quatrains, the hundredth of the Second *Centurie*, which is almost self-explanatory, and No. 51 of the Fifth *Centurie*:

> *Dedans les Isles si horrible tumulte,*
> *Rien on n'orra qu'une bellique brigue,*
> *Tant grand sera des préditeurs l'insulte,*
> *Qu'on se viendra ranger à la grand ligue.*

> *Inside the Isles such a horrible tumult,*
> *Nothing is heard but a warlike clamor,*
> *So great will be the insult of the brigands*
> *That a great league will be ranged against them.*

When it turned out that the umbrella mended at Munich leaked badly, the British clamored, though too late, against those who sold them down the river. Neville Chamberlain had to mend political fences both at home and abroad.

La gent de Dace, d'Angleterre, Polonne
Et de Boësme feront nouvelle ligue.
Pour passer outre d'Hercules la colonne,
Barcins, Tyrrens, dresser cruelle brigue.

The nations of Dacia, England, Poland
And Bohemia will form a new league.
To pass beyond the pillar of Hercules
Barcelonians and Tyrrhenians will prepare a cruel plot.

Dacia was the name of the Roman province conquered by Trajan which is coterminous with the postwar Rumania before the recent Russo-Hungarian amputations, while Bohemia was the Czech backbone of modern Czechoslovakia. That England guaranteed the integrity of these three countries and what happened to them is a matter of contemporary history.

The second half of this stanza is a bit more esoteric. Barcins for the people of Barcelona is derived from the name of the city's Carthaginian founder, Hamilcar Barca. Incidentally, Barca means lightning, from the Hebrew word *barak*. Thus that Punic faith bobs up again.

Tyrrhenia was the Greek name for Etruria, or modern Tuscany. The Etruscans, or Tuscans, who called themselves Rasena in their own tongue, were absorbed by the ancient Romans, but not before their lucumo, their chief rulers, progenitors of the *Duce* idea, became the terrible Tarquin kings of the new Latin realm. The Etruscans also are blamed for the gladiatorial cruelties of those days.

Florence, the chief city of present Etruria, was the home of the man whose name is a synonym for intrigue—Niccolo Machiavelli. Restless Barcelona, center of revolutionary, socialistic, anarchistic, Carlist, and republican movements, typifies the Spanish flair for plotting. Combining these terms which Nostradamus uses by poetic license, it appears that the Spaniards and Italians will try their fine Latin hands at outwitting John Bull in his Gibraltar fortress, the pillar of Hercules guarding the Mediterranean lifeline.

Predicting an attack on Gibraltar by the Axis powers, our Secretary of the Navy, Colonel Frank Knox, speaking last November before the New England Council at Boston, said that the aggressors, if successful, might attempt to move along the African coast to establish an air base 1,500 miles from South America, where they could patrol sea traffic, adding that "a good deal of the sea traffic there is our own." He expressed the opinion that Britain's hope of success rested upon the blockade, because "this war is a war of food and oil." He insisted that the American position regarding this blockade "must not be deterred by the ghastly conditions and the black starvation for helpless people in a savage war conducted by a fanatic, greedy for world domination."

Almost four hundred years ago Nostradamus put it this way in the Third and Fourth *Centuries*, quatrains 71 and 15. Both have been turned into doggerel without sacrificing their real meaning:

Ceux dans les Isles le long temps assiegez,
Prendront vigneur force contre ennemis,
Ceux par dehors morts de faim profligez
En plus grand faim que jamais seront mis.

Those in the islands, long at bay,
Will wield mighty force against the foe,
The pangs of hunger will join their fray
In the greatest famine we'll ever know.

D'ou pensera faire venir famine,
De là viendra le rassasiement:
L'oeil de la mer par avare canine,
Pour de l'un l'autre donra huille froment.

Whom they think they'll starve
Will have meat to carve
As the sea dog, with his mighty fleet,
Patrols the lines of oil and wheat.

Even as Secretary Knox was speaking in Boston, the Nazi Government promulgated for 1941 a new law in Berlin legalizing the meat of dogs, foxes, bear, and beavers for human consumption, but neutral observers doubted that this measure would augment the Reich's food supplies greatly, since such meats already had been on the German bill of fare in large quantities. At the same time, it was said that the hardest hit of any Europeans would be the French, whose northern provinces were depopulated during most of the growing season. However, Denmark, Belgium, Poland, and The Netherlands also were on restricted diets. Thus modern warfare boils down to its subhuman essential element—dog eat dog.

When the massed Nazi air raids upon the British Isles began in the summer of 1940, the fulfillment of another Nostradamic prophecy began. This was quatrain 64 of the Eighth *Centurie*:

Dedans les Isles les enfans transportez,
Les deux de sept seront au desespoir:
Ceux du terroüer en seront supportez,
Nom pelle prins des ligues fuy l'espoir.

From within the Isles the children will be transported,
Two out of seven will be in despair:
Those of the soil shall be supported by it,
The name of shovel being taken by the leagues, hope flees.

London children continually have been evacuated to the greater comparative safety of the country, while many others have been sent to the colonies and the United States. Perhaps two out of every seven, at least in London, already are homeless, though reports insist that British morale has held up well under the merciless rain of bombs. However, if one's home is gone, a feeling of despair might well be the rule.

Under the Ministry of Agriculture, there is a return to the soil for noncombatants not needed in the defense industries. Many hitherto unused plots of ground are being tilled. The last line is a puzzler, but may indicate merely that Adam is reduced to his pristine delving and Eve her spinning, an existence hopeless to the "civilized" urbanite.

The first quatrain of the Third *Centurie* gives the result of a future naval battle:

> *Après combat et bataille navale,*
> *Le grand Neptun à son plus haut beffroy*
> *Rouge adversaire de peur deviendra pasle*
> *Mettant le Grand Océan en effroy.*

> *After the combat and naval fight*
> *The Great Neptune will be on his tower.*
> *The bloody foe from fear will glower,*
> *By the vast ocean put in affright.*

This, however, indicates only a future battle of Jutland in this current world war. There must be yet another battle of the Marne, too. Just as there were Americans in that second battle of 1918, it may be that there will be Americans in the coming Armageddon of the fighting forties, if the Fifth *Centurie's* quatrain 34 is read aright:

> *Du plus profond de l'Occident Anglois*
> *Ou est le chef de l'Isle Britannique*
> *Entrera classe dans Gyronde, par Blois*
> *Par vin et sel, feux cachez aux barriques.*

> *From the vast reservoir of the English West*
> *Where is the chief of the British Isle*
> *A fleet shall enter into the Gironde; by Blois,*
> *By wine and salt, fires hidden in the hogsheads.*

Some interpreters of the Nostradamic oracles believe that the leadership of the British Empire will escheat to a United North America, whose sea power will compel Europe to cease its eternal war. The Gironde is the great estuary leading to the Bay of Biscay formed by the junction of the Garonne and Dordogne rivers of Aquitaine. Bordeaux is the principal harbor.

The reference to Blois can mean nothing but the historic seat of the French kings in the chateau country, the Windsor of the Bourbons. Wine and salt symbolize force and wisdom and are part of the ceremonial in the anointing of a king. This pertains to the predicted restoration of the French throne, dealt with more fully elsewhere.

The meaning of fires hidden in the hogsheads is obscure, but if the nearest English word to the French *barriques*—barracks—is substituted, this could mean that a sixth column of patriots will liberate France by roasting to death the German army of occupation.

There is one more reference to this army from overseas, in quatrain 68 of the Tenth *Centurie:*

> *L'armee de mer devant cité tiendra,*
> *Puis partira sans faire longue allee:*
> *Citoyens grande proye en terre prendra,*
> *Retourner classe prendre grande emblee.*

> *The army of the sea will hang on before the city,*
> *Then leave without making a long voyage:*
> *Citizens will take a great prey on land,*
> *The fleet return to take over at the very outset.*

Apparently, then, a France, aflame with revolt against its conquerors, will be helped by a great army from overseas which will restore liberty in that harassed land.

7. "Her Ashes New Create Another Heir."

It is with six-lined rhymes that Nostradamus summarizes an era. These are called *Predictions* but this one, his fiftieth, doesn't lend itself to doggerel. Nostradamus characterizes Hitler as a wolf, the name Adolf in Old Teutonic, incidentally, meaning "noble wolf."

Un peu devant ou apres l'Angleterre
Par mort de loup mise aussi bas que terre,
Verra le feu resister contre l'eau
Le ralumant avec telle force
Du sang humain, dessus l'humaine escorce
Faute de pain, bondance de couteau.

Soon after England slays the wolf,
She also must bite the dust,
You will see fire resist water.
They'll rekindle the lamps so brightly
That flesh and blood will pay—
For when bread is gone, knives are handy.

Thus, win, lose, or draw, it appears that England must go through a seventh revolution after this war is over. A great British statesman already has hinted as much.

On April 6, 1776, several days after the redcoats had evacuated Boston, *The Craftsman,* London newspaper, printed a gloomy article forecasting that by 1944 imperial London would be a heap of ruins with the world ruled by a "great North American empire." Unlike

Nostradamus, the soothsayer of 1776 didn't trouble to tell why London was doomed.

Instead, he described the Cook's tour of two Americans around the rubble of "this once-famous city, which was the mistress of Europe, the seat of the arts, learning, trade and power . . . but, alas, her glory is now vanished and her sun is set!"

Of the Houses of the Mother of Parliaments, only a wall was left standing, while turnips grew along the Whitehall whence an empire on which the sun never set once was ruled. The vast dome of St. Paul's Cathedral had vanished, but enough remained of the walls built by Sir Christopher Wren to prove that he had designed "a most stupendous and expensive building."

The Craftsman's prophet of the wrath to come remarked that all this ruin had come to pass because of "the depravity of rulers" and "the mistakes of the ministers of former ages who had tried to fight all the battles of Europe, keeping great standing armies."

6

"Three Unclean Spirits like Frogs"

France, like ancient Egypt, often has been plagued by the unclean, impudent foes which frogs represent in the Biblical sense. In Revelation xvi, 13, which provides the heading for this chapter, frogs represent uncleanness. The frog early became identified with France. A toad was the emblem of the conquering fifth century Franks.

One suggestion as to the origin of France's royal fleurs-de-lis is that they are a corrupted, though conventionalized, form of the three toads in the arms of Pharamond, a legendary Frankish king during the fifth century, to whom medieval armorists attributed the coat: "azure three toads gold," or "silver three toads sable."

This long-since exploded legend of heraldic pundits perhaps gave rise to the nickname *Crapaud Franchos* bestowed on Frenchmen by their Flemish neighbors and revived by English-speaking sailors in the last century in the form "Johnnie Crapaud," or plain "Froggy." The popular theory that this name came from the alleged penchant of French gourmets for the frog as a table delicacy is unfounded.

In any case, "three unclean spirits" have bedeviled the French from the days of Nostradamus. These are Bourbon absolutism, Bonapartist imperialism, and Parisian communism. Nostradamus devotes many quatrains to eliciting the failings of these three isms.

The quatrains also are studded with the names of famous French cities and towns to which disasters have happened in the course of their long histories. One of these is particularly in keeping with Nostradamus' reputation as an accurate clerk of the weather and with his interest in the history of his own south of France. It is the sixth quatrain of the Tenth *Centurie*:

> *Gardon, Nyme eaux si hault desborderont,*
> *Qu'on cuidera Deucalion renaistre,*
> *Dans le colosse la pluspart fuyront;*
> *Vesta, sepulchre, feu esteint apparoistre.*

> *Keep watch, Nîmes, the waters will overflow so high,*
> *That it will be feared the Deluge has returned,*
> *The greatest part will flee into the amphitheater;*
> *Vesta, a sepulcher and extinct fire to appear suddenly.*

The architectural monuments from the Roman period which Nîmes contains are of the highest interest. Its amphitheater, because of careful attention, is in an excellent state of preservation. The Roman vaults, which resemble a natural cavern, are notable, and the stadium is said to have held more than 20,000 persons.

This quatrain appertains to the events of only eight or nine hours on September 9, 1557, at Nîmes, when there fell such a great rain of cloudburst intensity, mixed with hail and accompanied by thunder and lightning, from between 1 or 2 and 8 P.M., that the ancient city was nearly flooded. It was thought that Nîmes would have been filled to its topmost tower had the rainstorm lasted another six or seven hours.

Lightning struck many homes. The velocity of the flood, which rolled down the roads in sheets from the hills northwest of Nîmes, breached the walls of the city at several points. A mill built over the moat at the entering gate of Madeleine was knocked down, along with a near-by tower. A bridge over the moat, through which entry was gained into the city, was demolished, and the water rose six feet in the college quadrangle.

The fields about Nîmes were strewn with the rubble and ruins of the buildings battered by the storm, and vineyards were choked with sand. The water covered a great number of ancient Roman monuments, tombs, and columns. After the flood receded, the townsfolk recovered long-buried ancient sepulchral lamps, urns, and metal medals. Pavements, mosaics, and some baths built under Agrippa also were laid bare.

Nîmes is renowned chiefly for its *Maison Carrée* (Square House), a rectangular building considered as among the finest survivals of Roman architecture. This temple, during Roman days, had contained a shrine to Vesta, the goddess of the hearth in Roman mythology. Vesta was not represented by any image in her temples, but a perpetual fire burned upon her altars. The worship of Vesta was a recognition of the supreme importance of fire in primitive communities and each city throughout the Roman Empire had to raise an altar to her, no matter who the local deities might have been. This Nostradamic quatrain tells how the flood of 1557 revealed the long-extinct vestal fire on the altar of the goddess of the home.

One of the most spectacular of the fulfilled predictions of Nostradamus was that which foretold the manner of the death of his patron, Henry II of France, four years before it took place. The words of the seer, in quatrain 35 of the First *Centurie*, are:

Le lyon jeune le vieux surmontera
En champ bellique par singuliere duelle:
Dans cage d'or les yeux luy crèvera,
Deux classes une, pour mourir mort cruelle.

The young lion will surpass the old one
In martial field by a single duel:

He will pierce his eyes in a golden cage,
Two blows at once, to die a grievous death.

This may sound, offhand, as of quite general application, if not on the ridiculous side; but the prediction, unforeseen in such detail by anybody except Nostradamus, actually came true.

The sinister significance of this obscure quatrain became only too apparent when, in July, 1559, Henry II gave a tournament to celebrate the betrothal of Princess Marguerite of France, his sister, to the Duke of Savoy. The King invited Gabriel de Lorge, the young Count of Montgomery, a captain in his bodyguard, to match lances with him. The young nobleman tried to decline the dubious honor, but, on the sovereign's insistence, he put on his armor and entered the lists. In crossing the second lance, the young officer spurred his horse and struck Henry's "golden cage" of a helm, raising the visor. The guardsman's tilting spear broke and a splinter pierced the King's right eye, cutting several veins. The monarch lingered ten days in terrible agony, then died an excruciatingly painful death.

Other quatrains deal in the same symbolic language with the extinction of the royal house of Valois, the rise of Henry IV, first of the Bourbons, the greatness of Louis XIV, and the bloody end of Louis XVI. The prediction concerning the blinding and death of Henry II is just one of two hundred quite as explicit.

For the ten days that the Seer of Salon's patron survived after being fatally wounded, he was a one-eyed king ruling over France. This was the only time in French history that a one-eyed monarch held sway. Here, then, is the prophecy of the fifty-fifth quatrain of the Third *Centurie*:

En l'an qu'un oeil en France regnera,
La court sera en un bien fascheux trouble:
Le grand de Bloys son amy tuëra,
Le regne mis en mal et doute double.

In the year when One-Eye will reign in France,
The court will be in most vexatious trouble:
The great one of Blois will kill his friend,
The realm thrown into evil and double distrust.

The mortal wounding of King Henry II brought many trials and tribulations to France. His eldest son and heir, Francis II, husband of the beauteous Mary, Queen of Scots, was only sixteen and afflicted with a chronic illness. His reign, which lasted only a year and a half, was taken up with a renewed persecution of the Huguenots and court intrigues, the Queen-Mother, Catherine de' Medici, and the Valois family's kinsmen, the Guises, struggling for the mastery which the dowager finally obtained just before her boy-King fell into a swoon on November 17, 1560, dying the following December 5.

The second half of this quatrain refers to King Henry III, third son of Henry II and Catherine de' Medici, who succeeded to the French throne after the death of their second son, Charles IX, in 1574. Henry III's reign is memorable chiefly for the assassination of Henry, third Duke of Guise and head and soul of the league against the Huguenots.

The King had found a dangerous enemy in the league's leader and all but lost his crown on the Day of the Barricades, May 12, 1588, when the Guise party engineered a rising in Paris, which the Duke entered in triumph in April, virtually imprisoning the King in the Louvre. At this point the Duke's courage failed him and Henry III left Paris for Blois, where he invited Guise to attend the States-General, which he had convoked there.

Despite warnings of intended treachery, the Duke followed the "Great One" to Blois and Guise was assassinated by the King's arrangement and almost in his presence on Christmas Day, 1588. Excommunicated, Henry III tried to retrieve his power by an alliance with the Huguenots and Henry of Navarre, whom he recognized as his heir, but he was stabbed mortally at St. Cloud by Jacques

Clément, a Guise partisan, dying on August 1, 1589, the last of the Valois line.

All these deaths gave rise to this couplet among the Huguenots:

Par l'oreille, l'espaule et par l'oeil,
Dieu a mis trois rois au cercueil.

By the ear, the shoulder and by the eye,
God has put three kings in the grave.

This refers to Henry II, who was pierced in the eye in the tourney of 1559; Francis II, who died of a gathering in the ear at Orleans in 1560; and Anthony of Bourbon, King of Navarre, who was mortally wounded in the shoulder at a siege of Rouen in 1562.

Thus, the last days of the one-eyed King Henry II had ushered in an era of "most vexatious trouble" for France, just as Nostradamus had warned four years before the titled guardsman's blow had forged this chain of dire events. The treacherous murder of Guise touched off a civil war between the league and the Huguenots over the succession of the Protestant Henry of Navarre. The Guise murder was the first "distrust," becoming "double distrust" because Henry III, being childless, was bound to have the Navarrese as his successor. When Henry III fell under Clément's dagger, France's popular cry was:

"Rather die a thousand deaths than obey a Hugenot king."

This prediction covers rather more ground than most Nostradamic prophecies, so the stream of history must be retraced to Francis II and Mary of Scots. When that boy King died, Michael Suriano, the Venetian ambassador, wrote from Paris to his sovereign Doge, Girolamo Priuli:

"Every courtier recalls the thirty-ninth quatrain of the Tenth

Centurie of Nostradamus and comments thereupon under his breath." Here is the quatrain:

> *Premier fils de la veusve malheureux mariage,*
> *San nuls enfans, deux Isles en discord:*
> *Avant dix-huict incompétant âge,*
> *De l'autre près plus bas sera l'accord.*

> *The first son of the widow, unhappily married,*
> *Without any children, two islands in discord:*
> *[Dies] before eighteen, incompetent in age,*
> *He will agree on the second, next in rank.*

Francis, then Dauphin and heir to the French throne, was married to Mary, Queen of Scots, niece of the Guises, in 1558, though against his will, since he was sick unto death. Thus was the widow's first son unhappily wed. They had no children, as Nostradamus had forecast. Queen Elizabeth of England, to promote the stability of the Anglican throne which she had just ascended (1558), helped the Protestant insurgents of Scotland, France, and The Netherlands with money and troops. Thus were the two Queens of the Isles in discord. Francis II, born on January 19, 1544, died on December 5, 1560, before he was eighteen, the royal age of competence. He was succeeded by his brother, Charles, who, as second son, bore the title "next in rank"—Duke of Orléans.

When this ten-year-old became Charles IX, the power was shared by his mother, Catherine de' Medici, and Anthony of Bourbon, King of Navarre. In 1563 the royal lad was declared of age by an assembly at Rouen, but this declaration made no change in his position under the regency. Civil and religious wars between the Catholics and the Huguenots had begun in 1562. Bloody conflicts were suspended several times by treaties, but renewed through the perfidy of the court.

In 1572, Charles IX was induced to agree to the massed slaughter of St. Bartholomew's Eve by his mother and Henry, third Duke of Guise, leading spirits of the crusade against the Huguenots. This massacre of his Protestant subjects preyed upon the mind of Charles IX, his health gave way and he died at Vincennes on May 30, 1574.

Fortunately, Nostradamus was safely dead and buried, beyond the torturing punishments which the fine Medici hand might have devised for the Seer of Salon, who had predicted that all her sons would ascend a throne which happened to be the same throne. At that, the Sphinx of Issachar was one-third right, since Catherine's youngest son, Henry, Duke of Anjou, in 1573 was elected, despite his reluctance, king of Poland, making presage 58 of the Nostradamic almanacs all the more noteworthy:

> *Le Roy-Roy n'estre, du Doux la pernicic,*
> *L'an pestilent, les esmeus nubileux.*
> *Tien'qui tiendra, des grands non leticie:*
> *Et passera terme de cavilleux.*

> *The King-King to be no more, destruction by the mild one,*
> *The year pestilent, the disturbers marriageable.*
> *Let him who holds carry on, to the displeasure of the great-*
> *ones:*
> *And he will pass the boundary of cavilers.*

At first brush this is mere gibberish, were it not that Henry III was the Polish king before acceding to the French throne, making himself "King-King." As heretofore mentioned, he was assassinated by Jacques Clément. This yields another Nostradamian pun, since both "Clément" and *doux* mean mild. It was in the pestilent year of 1572, after the peace of Saint-Germain and just before the massacre of St. Bartholomew, that Henry, nonconformist and schismatic son of Anthony of Bourbon and Jeanne d'Albret, Queen of Navarre, married Marguerite of Valois, licentious and extravagant sister of Charles IX. So two disturbers of the peace were wed.

Henry, the White Plume of Navarre, was brought up as a Protestant and spent part of his youth at the French court, where he was educated, the Bourbons being a junior branch of the royal family. In marrying the King's sister, Henry was compelled to abjure his faith. Six days later, the slaughter of the Huguenots began, but the White Plume's life was spared because of his promise of conformity to Roman Catholicism.

The absence of children to succeed the Valois kings made Henry of Bourbon an important person in France and for the next thirteen years he held on, deep in various intrigues. The Guises and their Catholic party were determined to prevent his succession, but, perhaps because he followed Nostradamus, the White Plume carried on until, much to "the displeasure of the great ones" of Guise, the first of the Bourbons was recognized as the heir of Henry III, last of Valois, thus passing the limits set on his career by the caviling Pope Sixtus V, who had excommunicated the Navarrese in 1585, declaring him incapable of the succession.

In 1563, when the first of the Bourbons was ten, Nostradamus saw the future Henry the Great and urged the lad's teacher to undress him so that the physician-prophet could examine him better. The young prince declined stubbornly to be disrobed, fearing that an unmerited whipping was in the offing and, as he related much later, cowed by the Sphinx of Issachar's waggling, forked beard. Next morning, when the royal lad was opening his eyes drowsily for the first time, the teacher, before giving the boy his clothing, led Dr. Nostradamus into the bedroom so he could see his charge naked. After studying the child, the clairvoyant prophet turned to the royal mentor and predicted:

"If the good God spares you until then, you will have for your liege-lord one who will be both King of France and Navarre."

That was nine years before the White Plume became king of

Navarre and twenty-six years before he became titular king of France on August 1, 1589. Nostradamus also paid heed to the memory of Henry of Navarre, whose goodness and greatness have become merged in a kind of nationalized myth. He is the most human and friendly of that quartet which also includes Charlemagne, Joan of Arc, and Napoleon Bonaparte, being at once rugged, firm, and awe inspiring, as well as mild, beneficent, and winsome. This is set forth in the seventieth quatrain of the Sixth *Centurie:*

Un chef du monde le grand Chiren sera:
Plus oultrè après aymé, craint, redoubté:
Son bruit et los les cieux surpassera,
Et du seul titre Victeur, fort contenté.

The great Henry will be a chief of the world:
More greatly beloved afterward, awesome and redoubtable:
His renown and portion will soar to the heavens,
And with the sole title of Victor he is well contented.

Chiren is a Nostradamian cipher for Henric, Frankish form of Henry. This name means, appropriately, "prince of the house."

Henry IV had to conquer his own kingdom, which he did by a wise admixture of diplomacy and force. He won the battles of Arques (1589), and Ivry (1590), captured Paris after a siege and beat off a Spanish invasion under the Duke of Parma in a long and varied war in which Henry, with small means and the ineffectual support of the English, performed prodigies of valor and activity.

Equally potent was his politic conversion on July 25, 1593, when he decided cynically that Paris was "worth a Mass," and he became both a Roman Catholic and king of France in fact as well as name. In 1594 he was anointed king at Chartres and entered Paris. In the course of four years he had expelled the hated Spaniards and brought all France to subjection. In 1598 Philip II of Spain, who had helped Henry's enemies, made peace; and France, granted the Edict of Nantes, restoring religious toleration, was more than ready to accept its first Bourbon monarch.

Henry's reign was a period of comparative prosperity for his country. Under Sully's direction much was done for industry; the burdens on the people were reduced and the evils of the civil war remedied to some extent. Henry owed his popularity to the circumstances of his reign and the relief it brought from civil strife, as well as to his own qualities of courage, gaiety, frankness, and amiability. He was assassinated on May 14, 1610, by one Ravaillac, a fanatic.

Though Nostradamus does not name places and give dates often, such combinations do occur in the *Centuries*. Some Nostradamians insist that had the Sphinx of Issachar been so inclined, he could have specified every place and described every leading character in his prophetic quatrains. "Did I so desire," he wrote King Henry II, "I could determine the time for every quatrain."

Quatrain 45 of the Eighth *Centurie* is proof of this pudding:

> *La main escharpe et la jambe bandée,*
> *Longs puisnay de Calais portera,*
> *Au mot du guet la mort sera tardée,*
> *Puis dans le temple à Pasques saignera.*

> *The rugged hand and bandy leg*
> *Long will take junior rank at Calais,*
> *Death will be delayed by the watchword,*
> *Then in the temple they will bleed at Easter.*

This cryptic stanza describes the Spanish capture of Calais by a surprise raid during Henry the Great's war with Philip II. Christian de Savigny, Lord of Rosne, a French renegade from Lorraine, to prove his fidelity to the Spanish cause, which he had embraced, spied on Calais. This gateway port commanding the English Channel had been recaptured from Queen Mary Tudor's pitiful garrison by the Duke of Guise in 1558. Thereafter, French troops had been quartered at Calais.

Savigny, who rose to high command in the French Army by his ruthlessness ("rugged hand") in warfare, had served in Calais as a bowlegged captain of horse, a "junior rank." He discovered that Francis de St. Paul, Lord of Bidossan and governor of Calais, had neglected the fortifications and maintained a garrison of only six hundred. The Cardinal-Archduke Albert of Austria, when he was put in command of the forces in the Spanish Netherlands, found that he lacked generals of repute, so he called upon the renegade Savigny.

They planned a sudden attack upon Calais. Because absolute secrecy was the "watchword," there was little resistance to the defenders of Calais, and "death" was "delayed"—took a holiday, in other words. Savigny took the greater part of the Spanish troops, four thousand foot and four hundred horse, making a swift onslaught on the positions covering the approaches to the walls on Easter Sunday, April 14, 1596, and taking the castle on Easter Monday. The unprepared city quickly surrendered to the renegade and his Spaniards before Henry IV could arrive to make a defense.

In *mot du guet* (watchword) Nostradamus makes another *jeu de mots*. A landmark of Calais is the *Tour de Guet* (Watch Tower), built in 1214 and manned by sentinels during the many wars which swept Flanders. In latter days the tower was used as a lighthouse until 1848.

Meticulous attention to minor details stamps Nostradamus as a clairvoyant of rare acumen. None of the quatrains recording past history shows his facility more clearly than No. 58 of the Fifth *Centurie*:

De l'aqueduct d'Uticense, Gardoing,
Par la forest et mont inaccessible:

Emmy du pont sera transché au poing,
Le chef Nemans qui tant sera terrible.

By the aqueduct from Uzes to Gardon,
Through the forest and inaccessible mountain:
The middle of the bridge will be cut short by hand,
The chief of Nîmes who will be so terrible.

Uzes, when founded by the Romans, was called Ucense Castrum, becoming Ucetia in the Late Latin tongue. Gardoing is Old French for the town of Gardon, which takes its name from the River Gard, a tributary of the Rhone. Nemans is an adjectival form of Nemansus or Nemausus, the Latin name of ancient Nîmes, capital of the Department of Gard. In the time of the Reformation, Nîmes was a Protestant stronghold and the scene of considerable bloodshed.

This quatrain has to do with that period. It refers to a military exploit of Henry, first Duke of Rohan (1579–1638). When the decree for the restitution of the Church property in the south of France threw the Bearnese and Gascons into open revolt, Rohan appeared as a rebel. His ability and constancy contributed to the happy result of the war for the Huguenot cause and brought about the Treaty of Montpellier (1623). Rohan renewed the war when the Montpellier pact was broken. Again a shallow peace was patched up, but it lasted only a short time and Rohan undertook a third campaign (1627–1629), the first events of which, including the feat chronicled here, are recounted in the Duke's celebrated *Mémoires*.

The sense of the stanza is that the Huguenot leader will be so redoubtable that he will recognize no obstacle to his plans. To aid his besieged coreligionists at Nîmes, in September, 1627, he moved his artillery through a forest and mountain, supposedly impassable, over the aqueduct which carried water from Uzes across the Gardon valley. His pioneers cut away part of the arcade props supporting a bridge over the Gard to widen a path for his cannon. After compelling King Louis XIII to maintain the Edict of Nantes, Rohan convoked the Huguenots at Nîmes. In gratitude, they made him general of the party—"chief of Nîmes," their stronghold.

One of the Seer of Salon's predictions stands out above all others because of its singularly explicit fulfillment. It is the eighteenth quatrain of the Ninth *Centurie*, running as follows:

Le lys Dauffois portera dans Nansi,
Jusques en Flandres Electeur de l'Empire.
Neufve obturée au grand Montmorency,
Hors lieux prouvez delivré à clere peyne.

The lily of the Dauphin will be carried into Nancy,
And into Flanders an Elector of the Empire:
A new prison for the great Montmorency,
Away from the customary place, delivered to public punishment.

It must be conceded that this particular prophecy, as it stands, is not very enlightening. In view of actual events, however, it is curt, clear, and quite complete. The two halves of the stanza are not connected and appear together only because, as will be explained, they occurred between 1632 and 1635.

On September 24, 1633, King Louis XIII of France, who had been the first heir to the French throne to bear the title of Dauphin as eldest son since the death of Nostradamus half a century before, entered Nancy at the head of his troops. The flag carried by the French Guards was "blue, powdered with yellow fleurs-de-lis, with a large white cross in the middle." Nancy was the capital of the Duchy of Lorraine, not then a French province, which had supported rebels against Louis XIII's authority.

Two years later, the Archbishop-Elector of Trier having been imprisoned in Brussels by the Spaniards, then rulers of Flanders, Louis XIII declared war (March 26, 1635) on Spain, marched into Flanders and besieged Louvain. Thus is the first half of this quatrain clarified.

The next two lines are even more strikingly perfect. On October 30, 1632, Henry, fourth and last Duke of Montmorency, taking part in the first rebellion of Gaston of Orléans against Louis XIII, was beheaded at Toulouse by order of Cardinal Richelieu. While awaiting trial there, Montmorency had been kept under guard in the newly built prison of the *Hôtel de Ville*. As a concession to his high rank (when sixteen years old he became Admiral of France and Viceroy of Canada), the execution took place in the courtyard of that prison and not in the "customary place"—the gallows in the public square of Toulouse.

In many Nostradamic quatrains it is not unusual to find minute details set forth as a pun or similar play upon words. This is especially true here. The phrase *clere peyne* (Latin, *clara poena*) signifies a public or notable punishment, but in relation to Montmorency's beheading it has another and closer application. Private execution was not the only concession made to his ducal status. Richelieu granted another, permitting Montmorency to be beheaded rather than hanged, the customary method of dispatching traitors. Nor was the headsman the usual Monsieur de Paris or a local "Performer of the High Tasks of the King," but a common soldier, chosen from the ranks by lot. The soldier's name was Clerepeyne!

All these facts are vouched for by two contemporary chroniclers, the Chevalier de Jant (1637) and Étienne Joubert (1656). A pamphlet by Motret, published at Nevers in 1806, also summarizes the data bearing upon this particular quatrain. Remember that this prophecy most assuredly was in print in 1566 and that its deadly accurate fulfillment occurred in 1632.

There is such specific exactitude in many Nostradamic quatrains.

One particularly striking one, No. 68 of the Eighth *Centurie*, concerns Cardinal Richelieu:

> *Vieux cardinal par le jeune deceu,*
> *Hors de sa charge se verra desarmé,*
> *Arles remonstres double soit aperceu;*
> *Et liqueduct et le Prince embaumé.*

> *The old cardinal deceived by the youngster,*
> *Beyond his burden he will see himself foiled,*
> *Pointed out at Arles, let the duplicate be perceived;*
> *And led by water and the Prince embalmed.*

Even in his sacerdotage, Richelieu had to defend himself perpetually against the intrigues of the nobles, which he invariably succeeded in crushing. This particular quatrain refers to the Cinq-Mars conspiracy. Henry Coiffier de Ruze, Marquis of Cinq-Mars, went to the French court in 1639, as a protégé of Richelieu, who intended to make him the favorite of King Louis XIII, then use him as a spy. At nineteen, the young nobleman entered court life and attracted the King's notice, various offices being bestowed upon the youth.

The clever old cardinal, however, had mistaken his man. Cinq-Mars, proud, noble, and brilliantly gifted, had ambitions of his own; and a deadly hatred soon sprang up between the favored courtier and the exalted prelate. In 1642 Cinq-Mars became involved in an intrigue against Richelieu, who originally had befriended him. Gaston of Orléans, the King's brother, was the nominal head of the plot. In conspiring to overthrow the cardinal, the Orléanists concluded a secret alliance with Spain.

While "the old cardinal" was at Arles, resting from the "burden" of his office as prime minister, he began to pick up the threads of the web Cinq-Mars was weaving. The key to the plot

NOSTRADAMUS SPEAKS | 129

came into his skillful hands when he received a copy (un double) of the treaty which the young Cinq-Mars treacherously had negotiated with Spain. Richelieu made the last use of his strength and intelligence in unraveling the clues and punishing the rebels. Cinq-Mars and his friend, De Thou, were arrested at Narbonne on June 13, 1642.

The triumphant, but failing, Minister ascended the Rhone on a state barge, reclining on his bed, since he was desperately ill, and towing his two prisoners behind him, all three going to certain death. On the arrival of the aquacade at Lyons, the finishing-off process was short and fatal for Cinq-Mars, who died on September 12, 1642.

Richelieu died at Paris on December 4, 1642. His body, as required by the canon law, was embalmed properly. Though Richelieu held a French dukedom, Nostradamus calls him "Prince," since the cardinalatial dignity is considered superior to any other except the Papal and royal, cardinals being "Princes of the Church."

What strikes the imagination most is the use by the Sphinx of Issachar, nearly ninety years before the event, of the very strange word *liqueduct*, compounded from the Latin *ille aqua ductus* ("he who is conveyed by water").

Many Nostradamic stanzas are equally difficult to interpret, but numberless past interpretations, though seemingly inexplicable for a long time, become comprehensible following the happenings mentioned. For example, there is a quatrain which goes:

Quand le fourchu sera soustenu de deux paux,
Avec six demy-cors, et six sizeaux ouverts:
Le très puissant Seigneur, héritier des crapaux,
Alors subjuguera sous soy tout l'univers.

When the fork will be supported by two pillars,
With six half-horns and six scissors opened:

The very powerful Lord, heir of the toads,
Then will bring the whole world into subjection to himself.

After the death of Nostradamus, Jean de Chavigny, his first Boswell, worked twenty-eight years editing and interpreting the dozen *Centuries,* though he was unable to find all the necessary hundred quatrains for the seventh, eleventh, and twelfth series. The above stanza was added to the Tenth *Centurie* from among these manuscripts and published in the edition of 1605; thus, it was in print fifty-five years before the event it recounts.

Though they sound nonsensical, the first two clumsy lines yield the date 1660 in this wise: When a fork, or V, is put between two pillars it becomes an M, the Roman symbol for one thousand. Six half-horns are CCCCCC, or six centuries, and the opened scissors are XXXXXX, sixty.

A year after Richelieu's death, Louis XIV, a lad of five years, became king of France, being the heir of a long line of sovereigns who traced back to the mythical Pharamond, whose shield was supposed to have been blazoned with three toads. During the King's boyhood, the real ruler was the Italian, Cardinal Mazarin, who tried to carry out Richelieu's policies. In 1660 Louis really began to rule, in the same year marrying Maria Theresa, daughter of Philip IV of Spain, whose ancestor, Charles V, had adopted the "Pillars of Hercules" to support his royal coat of arms. Thus was Louis XIV "supported by two pillars."

Mazarin died on March 9, 1661, and the King suddenly assumed the reins of governance as his own prime minister. Louis the Great reigned seventy-two years, one of the most glorious periods in French history. For much of it the royal armies were invincible, but the era was more notable for its art and literature, while the influence of the court on manners and customs scarcely can be overemphasized. Louis was the focal point of all national activity, his energy being tremendous. The character of his absolute rule is indicted in that often-quoted phrase, which Louis himself probably never used, "I am the State." To govern absolutely, to enlarge the boundaries of France, to be the center of the most distinguished court in Europe, to be the most prominent figure in world politics—these were the ambitions of the *Grand Monarque,* the first personage of Europe.

His reign was a period of display. He spent vast sums on his court. He erected at Versailles a magnificent new palace which cost more than a hundred million dollars. This was the first truly royal palace of the French kings, as Nostradamus shows in quatrain 89 of the Tenth *Centurie:*

> *De brique en marbe seront les murs réduicts,*
> *Sept et cinquante années pacifiques,*
> *Joye aux humains, renoüé l'aqueduict,*
> *Santé, grands fruits, joye et temps mellifique.*

> *Walls of brick will be converted into marble,*
> *Seven and fifty peaceable years,*
> *Joy to humans, the conduit resumed,*
> *Health, great fruits, joy, and times of milk and honey.*

The first line refers to the magnificent construction of the Sun King's era—Versailles, the Invalides, Gobelins, Savonnerie, and the like. The second line is more difficult of interpretation. If the many foreign aggressions by Louis are disregarded, applying "peaceable years" merely to the banishment of the civil and religious wars which had wracked France, then some sense is made. The Peace of the Pyrenees, by which Louis obtained his bride, was signed on November 7, 1659. From that date to Louis's death on September 1, 1715, is not quite fifty-six years.

Under the royal leadership, great enterprises were undertaken successfully. Commercial treaties were concluded; manufactures of various kinds were established; and, while the condition of the people was improved, the revenues increased and the King grew rich. Colbert, an expert financier and economist, doubled the royal exchequer without adding to the taxes paid by the people. The canal of Languedoc, uniting the Atlantic with the Mediterranean, was built, and other canals were improved—"the conduit resumed."

No less successful was Louis XIV in the organization and development of the intellectual life of the French people, encouraging literature and art. It was an age of splendor—on the surface—but Nostradamus saw the trouble of France beginning in the reign of Louis XIV.

The Sun King's death gave another boy the throne, his great-grandson, Louis XV, third son of Louis, Duke of Burgundy. The fifteenth Louis's long reign was one of misfortune for France, marking the beginning of the end for the Bourbon monarchy and the concomitant rise to political power of the baseborn Third Estate—the "vulgar advent," says Nostradamus. Most commentators point to the fifteenth quatrain of the Third *Centurie* as a pen portrait of Louis XV:

> *Cœur, vigueur, gloire, le règne changera*
> *De tous points, contre ayant son adversaire:*
> *Lors France enfance par mort subjuguera,*
> *Le Grand Regent sera lors plus contraire.*

> *Heart, vigor, glory, the reign will change*
> *At all points, opponent having his adversary:*
> *Then a child will subjugate France because of a death,*
> *Then the great regent will be more injurious.*

Louis XV's long reign contrasts with his great-grandfather's at every point. He was five when he succeeded to the throne. He became king in September, 1715, and in 1723 he was declared of age, but the conduct of affairs was not in his hands until 1743, and then only partially. During his minority, the country was governed by Philip, Duke of Orléans, as regent appointed by Parliament, which recovered its right to remonstrate, the first crumbling of the powers the Bourbons had winnowed during the long age of absolutism.

During the regency, France was plunged into the deepest financial embarrassment by the bursting of the great Mississippi bubble. Thereafter, the popular opposition to the Regent's abuses of his authority began to show itself in the Parliament of Paris, which had the privilege of countersigning the royal tax edicts, but which refused to do so. This resistance, however, was curbed with violence; Parliament was broken up; its members were punished and more willing tools put into their seats.

Without ability or industry, Louis XV did nothing to avert the approaching cataclysm, as quatrain 38 of the Fifth *Centurie* explains:

> *Ce grand monarque qu'au mort succedera,*
> *Donnera vie illicite et lubrique:*
> *Par nonchalance à tous concedera,*
> *Qu'à la parfin faudra la loy Salique.*

> *He who will succeed the great deceased monarch*
> *Will carry on an illicit and lustful life:*
> *By carelessness he will yield in everything,*
> *So that finally the Salic law will fail.*

After the Regent's death in 1723, Cardinal Fleury, who had been the King's tutor, became prime minister. His parsimony restored some order to the finances, which had been brought to the very verge of bankruptcy by the prodigality of Louis XIV and the wild schemes of the Duke of Orléans. The profligacy of the court became the scandal of Europe. The King had a succession of mistresses, of whom Madame de Pompadour and Madame du Barry are the best known, while stories are told of Louis's seraglio in the Parc aux Cerfs.

The King's private life generally is regarded as having been more than usually scandalous. When Cardinal Fleury died in 1743, Pompadour rose to power as Louis's mistress. Her authority, well-nigh absolute, lasted twenty years. Thus was the Salic law, forbidding the succession of women to the throne, supposedly based on the ancient Frankish rule and adopted by France, broken in the spirit, if not literally. When a needed reform was mentioned, Louis would say: "Well enough of that, things will last as long as we do."

Undeservedly, the King won the title of Louis the Well-Beloved because, during an illness in 1744, before matters grew so bad, a good deal of anxiety was shown for his recovery. This feeling was not in evidence when he died on May 10, 1774. He was succeeded by his grandson, who became Louis XVI. The saying attributed to the elder Louis, "After us the deluge," characterizes the man and the age.

Nostradamus did predict that deluge, the French Revolution, which he said would bring great misfortunes to France from which she never would recover fully. He also foresaw the appearance of Napoleon Bonaparte, declaring that the Revolution also would create the man who next would rule France. His character sketch of Louis XVI in quatrain 43 of the Tenth *Centurie* is well-informed and accurate:

Le trop bon temps, trop de bonté royale,
Faicts et deffaicts prompt, subit négligence.
Léger croira faux d'espouse loyale.
Luy mis à mort par sa bénévolence.

Too good the times, too much of royal kindness,
He does and undoes, hasty, unexpected neglect.

He will believe the falsehoods of his thoughtless, loyal spouse.
Put to death by his own kindness.

Louis the Headless was a good-natured, well-meaning, honest man, of pure morals, and capable of making a sacrifice for the public weal, but his will was weak and his intellect narrow. Lacking entirely in political instincts, knowledge, and judgment, he was unable to comprehend the situation. For fifteen years he ruled, while the condition of the country grew steadily worse. Thus he hastened the approach of the Revolution.

There were two remedies—restriction of the expenses, which his "thoughtless, loyal spouse" and the court opposed, and taxing the privileged classes, which the Parliament opposed. The King hoped to find a third expedient by appealing to the people; thus it came to pass that he himself appealed to the Revolution.

There was an undercurrent of unrest. Times had been easy, but Louis XVI was too good natured, and trouble makers took advantage of him. The King could have escaped from his dilemma if he had used his head—but he didn't, except to lay it on the block, when many loyal subjects perished with him.

When he summoned the States-General, which had not met for many years, he afforded the opportunity for an outbreak. The representatives of the Third Estate (commoners), refused seats with the other estates, determined to take matters into their own hands. The Assembly became a prey to faction. The hopelessness of the situation led to all manner of excesses. The King finally was tried, condemned, and executed, "put to death by his own kindness" in trying to find the way out.

That last line in the Old French yields yet another Nostradamic pun. Spell *Luy* the modern way, *Lui;* it is pronounced Louis!

It must have taken great prophetic insight to peer two centuries and a generation more ahead to a French king's execution, then give the name of Louis the Headless. Yet Nostradamus did even better than that, telling the details of the King's flight and naming the place of his recapture in the twentieth quatrain of the Ninth *Centurie*:

> *De nuict viendra par la forest de Reines,*
> *Deux pars vaultorte Herne la pierre blanche:*
> *Le moine noir en gris dedans Varennes,*
> *Esleu cap. cause tempeste, feu, sang, tranche.*

> *He will come by night through the forest of Rheims,*
> *Two parties wheeled around, the Queen a white gem:*
> *The black monk in gray at Varennes,*
> *The elected Capet causes a tempest, fire, blood, slice.*

Early in the summer of 1791, Louis XVI and his Queen, Marie Antoinette, a Hapsburg princess to whom he was married in 1770, decided to join their friends, who had emigrated. On June 21 they left Paris, the Queen being dressed expensively as Baroness Korff, a Russian lady, and Louis as her be-wigged valet. The Queen could not forget her rank and they proceeded in the great coach by easy stages. At one town Louis put his head out of the carriage and was recognized. At Varennes they were stopped, taken prisoner, and finally sent back to Paris. From that time the people had even less confidence that Louis was playing the game squarely.

By January, 1793, it was decided to try Louis XVI for conspiracy or treason. Unanimously, the members of the National Convention voted that the King was guilty of conspiracy, but, despite the raving of the radicals in the gallery, his death was decreed by only a bare majority. On the twenty-first of January, 1793, Louis Capet, as he was called, was taken from his cell and guillotined in the presence of an enormous crowd.

Readers may remember that Louis XVI and Marie Antoinette

made a swift nocturnal flight through the forest of Rheims as they neared the French border, fearing that the King had been identified. When the eye strikes the word Varennes, curiosity is aroused immediately, since it must be conceded that Varennes has come into history on only one particular occasion and perhaps is unlikely to do so again.

The villagers of Varennes, warned that something was amiss, had blocked the road for the heavy royal carriage by placing across the bridge, over the Aire, a cart laden with furniture, which they found there by chance. Then, four or five citizens armed with muskets stopped the "two parties" near the bridge and their coach was "wheeled around," pointed back toward Paris.

"Herne" is cryptogrammatic for *Reine* (Queen) while the "white gem" is a double reference to her costly white gown and the fact that when the Tuileries later was invaded, the mob heaped such abuse on Marie Antoinette that her hair turned white in the night. The mention of "the black monk in gray," according to Nostradamian commentators, is supposed to refer to the King's subfusc disguise of a valet, an attire not unlike a Grayfriar's.

When they were brought back to Paris, the King took an oath to reign as a constitutional monarch, but in September, 1792, the kingly office was abolished. "Esleu cap." (it is printed with a period after it in the original text) is interpreted as meaning "the elected Capet," the first king of the French owing his position not to divine right, but to the vote of a constituent assembly. Thus the flight to Varennes caused political storms and tempests, leading to the bloody guillotine. If all that be conceded, the word *tranche* leaps to the eye, and almost to the ear, like the whish of the weighted knife blade of Dr. Guillotine's pain killer.

There are some stanzas which are even better—when untangled. In some ways, the Ninth *Centiirie's* quatrain 34 is even more explicit and perhaps more amazing in its exposition of the afflictions of the ill-fated Louis:

Le part soluz mary sera mitré,
Retour conflict passera sur la thuille:
Par cinq cens un trahyr sera tiltré,
Narbon et Saulce par contaux avons d'huille.

The quite exceptional only husband will be mitred,
Return journey; conflict will pass over the tile
By five hundred; a traitor will be titled
Narbonne and Saulce with his grandsires' oilcans.

Louis XVI was temperamentally unfit to cope with serious problems. Well-meaning and indolent, he would have preferred to be a locksmith rather than a king. Unlike his predecessors of Bourbon stock, he had a bourgeois locksmith's idea that one wife was enough. That, apparently, is what Nostradamus means by "the quite exceptional only husband" who was devoted to his "thoughtless, loyal wife" (X, 43).

By the time of the return from Varennes, the nation, as well as the Assembly, was thoroughly aroused against royalty. Throughout France was sung the Marseillaise, the song of the Red revolutionaries from Marseilles, who had marched to Paris urging extreme measures. The Assembly was ordered to depose the King. When it failed to do so, "five hundred" hotheads from Marseilles on August 10, 1792, stormed and ransacked the Tuileries, where the King was in residence. This former royal palace in Paris was named from the tile yards (*tuileries*) once on the site. Designed by Philibert de l'Orme for Catherine de' Medici, construction was begun in 1564, but the palace was not finished until long after Nostradamus died, Jean Bullant completing the structure.

The Swiss Guards offered resistance, but the mob sacked the palace and killed its defenders almost to the last man. The members of the royal family first were removed to the assembly hall, then were kept prisoners in the temple. When the Marseilles mob stormed the erstwhile tile yard, Louis XVI, wearing a scarlet Phrygian cap of liberty, was treated with cold contempt. The liberty cap resembles the Gothic form of bishop's miter, which often was of red silk. So he was "mitered," only to be martyred later.

Nostradamus showed remarkable acumen when he cited the names of the two traitors. "Narbon" is Count Narbonne-Lara, Louis XVI's minister of war. He was the son of an illegitimate daughter of Louis XV and had been brought up in the court. In those difficult times he chose to be a mugwump on a fence, playing the game with both royalists and republicans and suspected of double-dealing by both parties. With the rise of Napoleon Bonaparte, he threw in his hand with the First Empire upstarts.

Saulce, too, was an upstart made famous by the French Revolution. He was the Proctor of Varennes who, recognizing the fleeing Louis XVI, detained the royal cavalcade and had its principal parties arrested. Saulce's ancestors had been shopkeepers and the proctor had inherited his grocery, later building a tavern to swell his income. After the capture, Marie Antoinette sat in the back parlor between two boxes of candles, chatting with the Saulces among their "grandsires' oilcans." The upshot of all this was sauce for the grocer, and the ax for the two royal geese.

France's States-General always had consisted of the three estates—clergy, nobility, and the Third Estate. From all parts of France demands were made that the Third Estate have as many deputies as both the others. This was granted.

The Abbé Sièyes, later the constitution maker of France, said of the *Tiers État*:

"What is the Third Estate? The nation. What is it now? Nothing. What ought it to be? Everything."

In the seventeenth quatrain of the Ninth *Centurie*, Nostradamus tells how the Third Estate became everything:

Le tiers premier pis que ne fit Néron,
Vuidez vaillant que sang humain respandre:
R'édifier fera le forneron,
Siecle d'or, mort, nouveau Roy grand esclandre.

The Third became first, did worse than Nero;
See how much brave human blood it sheds:
It will re-install the scaffold,
The golden age dead, a new king and great to-do.

One of the exciting causes of the French Revolution was the dispute which arose in 1789 between the bourgeois Third Estate and the nobles and clergy as to whether the commoners had a right to sit with the two upper houses. Against a single national assembly, King, nobles, and higher churchmen protested vigorously. On June 20, 1789, the doors of the hall where the Third Estate held its meetings were closed by royal orders. Immediately the bourgeois delegates adjourned to a near-by tennis court. There the deputies, with upraised hands, amid intense excitement, swore that they would not separate until they had made a constitution for France.

The King called all the estates together and asked them to vote separately. Most nobles and some clergy obeyed. The representatives of the nation kept their seats, whereupon the majordomo said: "Gentlemen, you have heard the King's orders."

The huge, brainy Count of Mirabeau, the new leader of France, rising, thundered in reply: "Go tell your master that we are here by the will of the people and that we shall be removed only at the point of the bayonet." The French Revolution had begun. Soon thereafter the guillotine seemed never idle and the blundering "ancien régime," a Golden Age to Nostradamus, perished in a pool of blood.

The "new king" who will make a "great to-do" is, naturally,

Napoleon I, whose imperial adventures hither and yon Nostradamus has predicted in entire sets of verses.

The emergence of Napoleon Bonaparte and his attacks on the papal authority and the Holy Roman Church were historic material for quite a large number of succeeding quatrains of prophetic significance and remarkable lucidity. The first of these, the sixtieth quatrain of the First *Centurie,* notes the birth of Napoleon and sums up his character:

Un Empereur naistra près d'Italie
Qui à l'Empire sera vendu bien cher,
Diront avec quels gens il se ralie
Qu'on trouvera moins Prince que boucher.

An Emperor will be born close to Italy
Who will pay a most costly price for Empire,
They will say with such cattle he rallies to himself
That one will find him less Prince than butcher.

Napoleon was born in Corsica, an island off Italy's shores. We now are able to see that despite outstanding qualities, there were mingled petty traits—devouring egotism, a hard view of life as a series of calculated risks and golden opportunities. Above all, he had a profound contempt for the average man and a disbelief both in religion and in the higher capabilities of the human race for progress. Napoleon's mechanical view of life, shown abundantly in Gourgaud's journal, discloses inner reasons why Bonaparte failed to attain the peak of the great possibilities offered in the years following the French Revolution.

Napoleon sought to surround himself with an elaborate court similar to that of the well-established monarchies. Since most imperial noblemen were of comparatively humble origin, Bonaparte sought among the old nobility for instructors in the proper conduct of court procedure. Nostradamus was quite correct in calling the Emperor a "butcher." He carved up his enemies and their countries, too!

Bonaparte tried his fine Italian hand not only at butchering but at patchwork, too. That feudalistic crazy quilt labeled the Holy Roman Empire for want of a better name was reduced from 418 principalities, ecclesiastical holdings and free cities to fewer than 50 petty states. Thus there no longer was any plausibility in maintaining the pretense that there was one imperial head of Christendom. The Hapsburg yielded his imperium to the upstart Little Corporal. The fortieth quatrain of the Sixth *Centurie* puts this pithily:

Grand de Magonce pour grande soif estaindré
Sera privé de la grand dignité:
Ceux de Cologne si fort le viendront plaindre
Que le grand groppe au Rhin sera jetté.

The great one of Mainz for slaking a great thirst
Will be deprived of the great dignity:
Those of Cologne will come to begrudge it so strongly
That the great group will be cast into the Rhine.

Mainz is the Celtic and Roman Moguntiacum. Its Late Latin name was Maguntia, the old French was Magonce, while the modern French is the softer Mayence. The Archbishopric of Mainz, dating from 747, was one of the seven electorates of the Holy Roman Empire and became a powerful state during the Middle Ages, retaining some importance until that empire's dissolution. Its archbishop was president of the electoral college, archchancellor of the empire, and primate of Germany as the successor of St. Boniface, the apostle to the Teutons. The feudatory lands of the princely archbishops lay around Mainz and were on both sides of the Rhine; their area at the time of the French Revolution was about 3200 square miles.

Mainz had welcomed the French revolutionaries in 1792, the republicans entering the city almost without a blow. The joined forces expelled the archbishop. Subsequently, Mainz changed hands several times. The primatial archbishopric was abolished on February 25, 1803, two years after the lands along the left bank of the Rhine were seized finally for France by Napoleon. This signified the end of the rule of archbishops who had abrogated individual freedom, suppressed civic liberties, and grabbed territory right and left, "slaking a great thirst" for power. The archiepiscopal see itself was transferred to Regensburg (Ratisbon). The modern diocese of Mainz is a new foundation. Thus was "the great one of Mainz . . . deprived of the great dignity."

Cologne once had been one of the most populous and wealthy cities of the Hanseatic League, deriving much prosperity from the navigation of the Rhine. After the sixteenth century, Cologne declined and, in common with the other Hanseatic cities, its commerce lost its former importance. In the seventeenth and eighteenth centuries a variety of causes led to Cologne's further commercial decay.

When, in 1794, Cologne was occupied by the French revolutionaries, it was a poor city of some forty thousand inhabitants, of whom only six thousand possessed civil rights. Incorporated into France in 1801 by Napoleon, it was not then important enough to be more than the chief town of an *arrondissement*. The last electoral archbishop died in 1801 and the see was left vacant. In 1803 the remainder of the electorate was secularized, an inglorious end for the ancient archbishopric of Cologne. The loss to the Roman Catholic Church in Germany was great. The territory which the archbishop ruled as a temporal power included in its Rhenish possessions alone sixty square miles with 199,000 inhabitants.

In 1815 the lands of the electorate were given to Prussia, and Cologne soon began its recovery, which became more marked after the next patchwork reconstruction of the German Empire in 1871.

The venerable metropolis of the Rhineland now is Germany's third largest city, the residence of a cardinal-archbishop, and a most important commercial center. Yet, in 1796 its then unfinished cathedral was converted by the French into a hay magazine. No longer do "those of Cologne" begrudge once-golden Mainz its long-vanished gilded era.

This resurgence of Cologne could not have transpired so long as the primatial archbishop up the Rhine maintained his dead-handed authority in the fictitious state which Voltaire wittily said was neither holy nor Roman nor imperial. It was necessary for the anachronism of the Middle Ages to vanish. When the left bank of the Rhine was annexed to the French Republic, Görres wrote his celebrated obituary which began: "On December 30, 1797, at three in the afternoon, the Holy Roman Empire, supported by the Sacraments, passed away peacefully at Regensburg at the age of 955, in consequence of senile debility and an apoplectic stroke." Görres concluded that the last Emperor "bequeathed the left bank of the Rhine to the French Republic."

So was "the great group . . . cast into the Rhine" while another imperial dictatorship was built up across the river of changing fortune.

The thirteenth quatrain of the Seventh *Centurie* tells of the rise and duration of the Napoleonic tyranny and First Empire:

> *De la cité marine et tributaire,*
> *La teste raze prendra la satrapie:*
> *Chasser sordide qui puis sera contraire,*
> *Par quatorze ans tiendra la tyrannie.*

> *From the marine and tributary city*
> *The shaven head will seize the satrapy:*
> *To chase out the sordid, who then will be contrary,*
> *During fourteen years he will maintain the tyranny.*

The tributary port in question is Toulon, the siege of which made Bonaparte famous. In 1793 young Bonaparte went as a captain with the forces sent to regain royalist Toulon from the English, to whom it had surrendered. By the proper placing of the siege guns, Napoleon contributed largely to the evacuation of the port.

There is no doubt that "the shaven head" corresponds to Bonaparte's nickname of *Le Petit Tondu* ("The Little Shaveling"). Before the failure of his Egyptian campaign was known, Bonaparte, evading the British cruisers, landed in the south of France on October 9, 1799. He found that the French Directory (*La Satrapie*) had not maintained order at home or repelled invasion from abroad. Hastening to Paris, he was met with universal acclaim. Accordingly, he found it easy to concert with some associates in the overthrow of the Directory.

On the Eighteenth Brumaire (November 9, 1799) the famous *coup d'état* took place which gave Bonaparte the satrapy. Upon the ruins of the republic, Napoleon and his cronies constructed a strongly personal system in which he, as First Consul, held all the executive and much legislative power. By sweeping away the "sordid" directors, the First Consul ended the strife of the "contrary" factions and effected much-needed changes by placating all but the irreconcilable royalists. Napoleon's tyranny crashed about his ears in the long run, and he was forced to abdicate on April 16, 1814, having held absolute sway "fourteen years" and five months.

In 1802 Napoleon was proclaimed consul for life and in 1804 he had himself crowned emperor, as Nostradamus foresaw in quatrain 57 of the Eighth *Centurie*:

> *De soldat simple parviendra en empire,*
> *De robe courte parviendra à la longue:*
> *Vaillant aux armes, en église ou plus pyre,*
> *Vexer les prestres comme l'eau faict l'esponge.*

From simple soldier he will attain to an Empire,
From short gown he will succeed to the long:
Valiant in arms, whence much worse in the church,
To vex the priests as water does the sponge.

Napoleon Bonaparte was born on the island of Corsica in 1769, about the time that Corsica became part of France. The Bonapartes were a poor but noble Genoese family. Especially from his mother, a woman of little education but great force of character, did Napoleon inherit those qualities which afterward made him famous. Even in boyhood he showed himself passionate and domineering; as he grew older, his egotism and ambition became more pronounced.

At ten he obtained a free cadetship at the military school of Brienne, in eastern France. His poverty, as well as his inability to speak French fluently, kept him from making friends and he did not excel as a scholar, though his work in mathematics was good. In 1784 he was transferred to the military academy at Paris, where he told the officers how to reorganize their system of instruction. Naturally these suggestions from a little shaver of fifteen did not meet with the approval of the faculty. During his year in school at Paris, Cadet Bonaparte attracted attention chiefly by his mathematical talents, by the clearness and power of his perception, and by the imperturbability of his temper.

In 1785 Napoleon Bonaparte became a sublieutenant in the La Fère artillery regiment. The new republic badly needed able officers, so Bonaparte attained his captaincy in 1793, but acted as a major at Toulon, as we have seen, where his ability brought his promotion to brigadier in 1794. He began the Italian campaign of 1796 an almost unknown general, received with murmurings by his subordinates. By the end of 1797 he had generals and troops absolutely at his disposal, and France acknowledged him as her greatest strategist.

First consul for ten years in 1799, in August, 1802, he obtained the consulate for life, with power to name his successor. An obsequious Senate begged him to reestablish hereditary rule "to defend public liberty, and maintain equality." On May 18, 1804, he became emperor of the French. The Pope was brought to Paris for the coronation, on December 2, in the ancient cathedral of Notre Dame, where the pontiff poured on the holy oil, showing that all the splendor and prestige of the old monarchy was to reappear.

Thus the simple soldier rose from a subaltern's blue cutaway tunic to a coronation mantle of imperial purple, powdered with golden bees. That the Pope might not maintain, as had his predecessors, that emperors were of right crowned by him, Napoleon I completed the ceremony by seizing the crown from the pontiff's hands and placing it on his own head.

By this independent attitude toward the papacy, the *parvenu* Emperor was following the practices of Gallicanism, which aimed at a vindication of the national position of the French Church against the encroachments of the Roman court. Napoleon's position was: "Render to Caesar the things that are Caesar's."

Such Pilatial reasoning is not for Nostradamus; for the Sphinx of Issachar, all roads lead to Rome. Napoleon realized fully that at heart the French were both Catholic and religious. For political, rather than for religious, reasons he wished to reestablish cordial relations between the papacy and France. Healing the schism in the Church by what was known as the Concordat of April 18, 1802, Napoleon earned the title of "Restorer of the Altars."

For his part, Pope Pius VII accepted suppression of the monasteries and the secularization of other church properties. Napoleon was to nominate the bishops, who were to be appointed by the Pope; the bishops, in turn, were to appoint the priests. Perhaps this concordat vexed "the priests as water does the sponge." Catholicism was recognized as the religion of a majority of the French people.

This arrangement lasted with slight changes until 1905. Thus, from the long view, Napoleon's ecclesiastical policy, like his famous body of laws from the same period, far outlasted his military conquests.

Napoleon the Great took something in addition to his crown from Rome—his imperial eagle, which had little in keeping with the then existing heraldic types of the king of birds. There can be little doubt that the model upon which the French eagle was based was the Roman emblem of the Caesars as it figured on the head of the legionary standards. This Napoleonic eagle is the metaphorical basis for quatrain 44 of the Second *Centurie:*

> *L'aigle posée en tous des pavillons,*
> *Par autres oyseaux d'entour sera chassée,*
> *Quand bruit des cymbres, tubes et sonnaillons*
> *Rendront le sens de la dame insensée.*

> *The eagle borne on all the colors*
> *Will be chased by the other surrounding birds,*
> *When the noise of cymbals, trumpets, and bells*
> *Will bring an unconscious lady back to her senses.*

The remainder of Napoleon's story must be told briefly. In 1812 the Emperor-General met with his great disaster in Russia. Thus, the first eagle, the two-headed bird of the Czars, got in its pecks. The fumbling of the Russian campaign seemed to precipitate distrust and discontent everywhere. Thenceforth, Austria and Prussia began to hope, taking measures to oppose him, and in 1813 formed a new coalition. Austria's emblem was the double-headed eagle; Prussia's the familiar German bird of prey.

It is not strange that the collapse of the Muscovite invasion should have caused every nation in Europe to rise against Napoleon; but the Comet of 1811 had not yet faded entirely from sight. With remarkable skill, the Emperor raised new levies of troops, this conscription making a total of nearly a million and a half soldiers furnished by France since Bonaparte's accesion to power in 1800. Fighting began anew in east Germany, where a "War of Liberation" was preached by Prussia, the nationalistic spirit of the German people being fully aroused.

The campaign which followed for a long time was without definite result. The battles of Lützen, Bautzen, and Dresden gave Napoleon some advantage, but they were not decisive. Finally, at Leipzig, on October 19, 1813, the "Battle of the Nations" was fought by the French against the allied forces of Austrians, Bavarians, Prussians and Swedes. Nearly three-quarters of a million troops were engaged in the three-day conflict. Napoleon was beaten, but he succeeded in withdrawing his army.

After this disastrous battle, Napoleon moved slowly back to the Rhine, fighting a defensive campaign. Gradually he was "chased" farther and farther west "by the other surrounding birds." When the masses of the Allies closed in on Paris, "the noise of cymbals, trumpets, and bells" brought "an unconscious lady back to her senses" and *La belle France* deserted the beaten conqueror. Overwhelmed by the combined armies of his enemies, the Senate proclaimed that he had forfeited his crown.

The return from Elba, the Hundred Days, and Waterloo merely mark an anticlimactic full stop to Napoleon's career, giving the powers the satisfaction of declaring him an outlaw for disturbing the peace of Europe.

The Nostradamic use of "the eagle borne on all the colors" is particularly neat. Since the flags of the Napoleonic armies were borne on staves surmounted by a golden eagle, the term "eagle" often was applied to these colors.

Nostradamus predicted that the years following the great Napoleon would be an era of instability. He foresaw the name of one successor as "Philip," the citizen-King Louis-Philippe of Orléans (1830–1848). This jittery period also evoked another Nostradamic prophecy, in which the Seer of Salon accurately dated his prediction. This is quatrain 96 of the Third *Centurie:*

> *Chef de Fossan aura gorge couppée,*
> *Par le ducteur du limier et levrier:*
> *Le fait paré par ceux du mont Tarpée,*
> *Saturne en Leo treziesme Février.*

> *Chief of Fossano will have his throat cut*
> *By the leader of the bloodhound and greyhound:*
> *The deed done by those of the Tarpeian rock,*
> *Saturn in Leo February thirteenth.*

Charles Ferdinand, Duke of Berry, younger son of King Charles X of France and second in succession to the crown, was mortally wounded on February 13, 1820, while leaving the Paris Opera House. The assassin was a fanatical saddler named Louis Pierre Louvel. This frightful crime stupefied the French generally and produced an outburst of royalist fury.

The Duke's mother was Maria Theresa of Savoy, daughter of King Victor-Amadeus III of Sardinia. Fossano is an imposing, four-towered castle in Piedmont begun in 1314 by Filippo d'Acaia. His successor handed it over to the House of Savoy, whose dukes long made it their residence, much as Windsor is the seat of the English royal family. By synecdoche, *Fossan* refers to the half-Savoyard prince whose French title was Duke of Berry. Louvel cut the ducal throat with his saddler's knife.

A variety of readings can be given to the second line. The most logical seems to be a reference to the bloodthirsty saddler's sideline—making the dog collars by which bloodhounds and greyhounds were led about. At one time the assassin had served as a white-liveried Bourbon lackey and, as a groom, well may have led the royal hounds around on their leashes.

"Those of the Tarpeian rock" forms an analogy with Rome's Tarpeian Rock, for centuries the scene of the execution of political criminals and traitors. Others see in this phrase a synonym for the Mountain (French, *La Montagne*), the name given to the most savage of the political parties which arose in France during the revolution. This appellation was due to the fact that this bloc, about a hundred strong, sat on benches raised above those occupied by other groups. The assassin's trial elicited the view that he believed in terrorism akin to the Mountain's. Louvel's name, incidentally, is akin to *louve* (she wolf).

Whether the *en* in the last line means Saturn "into" or "out of" Leo on February 13, 1820, is a matter left to the astrologers.

Though this identification with the ducal assassination appears to be well enough documented to satisfy all but the most captious, modern mystagogues have twisted the quatrain into an attempt to forecast the sloughing off of Adolf Hitler. To do this it is necessary to treat the third word of the first line as an anagram, turning the perfectly good place name of Fossan (Old French for Fossano) into Ossanf. This is mere weasel-wording (*fossane* is French for a species of civet cat).

Ossanf in this tergiversation then becomes the German abbreviation for Oberste Sturm Scharon an Fuehrer, said to have been a title by which Hitler was known to his followers before he became Chancellor of the Third Reich. This is close to Osaf, which Hitler did use as an abbreviated title for Oberste Sturm-Abteilungens Fuehrer (Supreme Leader of Storm Battalions).

To ascertain Hitler's assassin, we may translate the second line two ways: "Keeper of the bloodhound and greyhound," alluding to "Master of the Hunts and Forests," one of Marshal Goering's many titles; or "Leader of the spy and courier." The latter meaning would point to the Gestapo chief, Heinrich Himmler; translating *limier* into its figurative sense of police spy or detective and *levrier* as courier or courser—he who brings in secret information.

"Those of the Tarpeian rock" is regarded as a clear warning to

Hitler to keep out of Rome if he doesn't want his jugular slit by a stiletto, while the binding argument is said to be that the Nazi *Fuehrer's* horoscope shows sudden death from an injury to the throat. Astrologers claim that the most direct identification, however, is the reference to "Saturn in Leo 13," since this is the exact degree in the zodiacal sign of the Lion which is occupied by the planet Saturn in the House that Hitler Built.

The "Words of Warning to Inept Critics" ending Chapter 2 well may be reread at this point.

Occasionally the eye is caught by a similar line or a quatrain of double meaning such as the eighth of the Fifth *Centurie:*

Sera laissé feu vif et mort caché,
Dedans les globes, horrible espouvantable.
De nuict à classé cité en poudre lasché,
La cité à feu, l'ennemy favorable.

He will drop live fire and hidden death
Inside the globes, horrible, frightful.
At night by a crash, the city fired by powder,
The city by fire, the enemy favorable.

This might pass for a prophecy of current aerial bombardment had M. le Pelletier, one of the most scholarly Nostradamic commentators, not annexed it (writing during the Second Empire) for Count Felice Orsini's attempt to assassinate Napoleon III. Regarding the second Emperor of the French as the incarnation of the spirit of reaction and the principal obstacle to Italian independence, Orsini made his way to Paris. On the evening of January 14, 1858, the Count and his three accomplices threw three bombs under the imperial carriage, which was nearing the Opera House.

Happily, the brutal attempt failed, neither Napoleon III nor Empress Eugenie being injured by the explosions, but their carriage was wrecked and one horse was killed. Ten bystanders were wounded mortally and the bursting of the projectiles injured 150 Parisians who happened to be in the street, Count Orsini himself being one of those hurt. Cries of grief and horror arose from all sides. A tense anxiety filled the Opera House when the royal pair entered their box to show themselves uninjured.

The horrible outrage created indignation in France, which was heightened when it became plain that the conspiracy had been hatched in England by refugees living there and that the bombs had been manufactured in Birmingham. The importance of Orsini's plot lies in the fact that it terrified Napoleon the Little, who came to believe that unless he took up the Italian cause of unification, other attempts would follow and that sooner or later he would be assassinated. This fear contributed quite a little to the Emperor's subsequent Italian policy. Thus, the effect of the bombs came in reverse English, making "the enemy favorable."

According to the Sphinx of Issachar, Napoleon III, whom he does not name but places quite exactly, would be the worst monarch ever to reign over France. Through him, the Seer warned, France would be deprived of territory (Alsace-Lorraine) and a third of a million of her soldiers would be incapacitated (in the Franco-Prussian War). Quatrain 38 of the Third *Centurie* tells of the outbreak of this disastrous conflict:

> *La gent Gauloise et nation estrange,*
> *Outre les monts, morts, prins et profligez:*
> *Au moys contraire et proche de vendange*
> *Par les Seigneurs en accord redigez.*

> *The Gallic folk and the alien nation*
> *Beyond the mountains, dead, seized, and destroyed:*
> *In the unfavorable month and near to the vintage*
> *By the Lords drawn up in accord.*

On July 19, 1870, "the Gallic folk" found themselves at war with Germany, "the alien nation beyond the [Vosges and Alps] mountains." In August, the French regular armies were bottled up or destroyed: Nostradamus said, "dead, seized, and destroyed." July was an "unfavorable month" for Napoleon, who believed his ministers' assurance that his army was "ready to the last gaiter button." July also bulks critically in French history making. On September 3, this dispatch was received from the Emperor: "The army has been defeated and is captive; I myself am a prisoner." This was "near to the vintage," Vendémiaire being the first month in the year as rearranged during the French Revolution. This month of vintage (Latin, *vindemia*) actually begins on September 22. The day after Napoleon's message was received, the Third French Republic was proclaimed.

The further unification of Germany was brought about as a by-product of this war. Prussia had the hegemony of the North German Confederation, but lacked the support of the south German states—Bavaria, Baden, Württemberg, and parts of Hessia. Their kinglets and dukelings joined the northern alliance by the force of a natural Teutonic instinct when the war drums rolled. Thus were "the lords drawn up in accord." As a result of their happy warfare together, the German princes agreed to create a larger political organization to be known as the German Empire.

On January 18, 1871, King William of Prussia was proclaimed German Emperor in the palace of Louis XIV at Versailles. When President Raymond Poincaré of France opened the Paris conference after the First World War, he wrote the epitaph of that German Empire:

"It was born in injustice; it has ended in opprobrium."

This uncannily close prophecy of the Franco-Prussian War is carried along in quatrain 92 of the First *Centurie*:

Sous un la paix partout sera clamée,
Mais non long temps, pille et rebellion,
Par refus, ville, terre et mer entamée,
Mort et captifs le tiers d'un million.

Under one, peace everywhere will be claimed,
But not a long while, pillage and rebellion,
By a refusal, city, land, and water encroached upon,
Dead and captives a third of a million.

When Napoleon III proclaimed himself Emperor, his rallying cry was: "L'Empire, c'est la Paix" ("The Empire, it is Peace").

Instead he sought three wars—in Mexico, the Crimea, and northern Italy—and was tricked into the fourth by Bismarck. Thus it is seen readily that peace did not last very long. Details of the advance of the German veterans into France, looting as they went, read like records of the subsequent campaigns of their Teutonic sons and grandsons. Rebellion came on Sunday, September 4, 1870, when a Parisian mob invaded the legislative halls shouting "Down with the Empire! Long live the Republic!" The "Terrible Year," as the French call it, of 1870–1871, had greater horrors in store when civil war followed the battles with the Germans, shorter but exceeding that conflict in ferocity and concluding with the last "Bloody Week" of the Paris Commune, May 21 to 27, 1871.

The new republican government of France began negotiating for an armistice on September 19, 1870. Bismarck and Jules Favre almost concluded arrangements, but the Iron Chancellor demanded the surrender of Strasbourg, Toul, and Verdun; these harsh terms of peace the provisional government would not accept. This refusal cost France dearly, since the military position was hopeless. The final terms of peace granted by Bismarck were extraordinarily severe and humiliating. They were laid down in the Treaty of Frankfort, signed on May 10, 1871. France was forced to cede Alsace and a large part of Lorraine, including the important fortress of Metz, and to pay an absolutely unprecedented war indemnity of a billion dollars in three years. In this way France was excluded entirely from the valley of the Rhine, "city, land, and water encroached upon by a refusal."

Nostradamus embellished his clairvoyant art with accurate mathematical computations. Run-of-the-mill prophets of the crystal-gazing variety give whatever soothsaying senses they have free rein to follow the natural human inclinations to exaggerate for the sake of producing a sensation. None of that for Nostradamus: he double checked his visions with statistics and figures of comptometric accuracy. The last line of the above quatrain is a case in point.

It will be observed that the Franco-Prussian War falls into two periods—the imperial and the republican. During the first, in which the fighting and the surrendering was limited to August and September, 1870, except for one isolated later example, the regular armies, as has been seen, were destroyed or bottled up. Then the Empire collapsed and the little Napoleon was imprisoned in Germany. The regulars who wore the imperial eagle fought in five major engagements and were trapped in three great capitulations. The French casualties in the following table include killed, wounded, and captured, both officers and men:

BATTLES			
	Place	Date	Casualties	
(1)	Spichern (Forbach)	August	6	4,000
(2)	Worth (Froschweiler)	"	6	14,000
(3)	Courcelles	"	14	4,000
(4)	Vionville (Mars-la-Tour)	"	16	16,000
(5)	Gravelotte (St.-Privat)	"	18	13,000

CAPITULATIONS				
(6)	Sedan (Bazeilles)	September	2	84,333
(7)	Strasbourg	"	27	19,000
(8)	Metz	October	27	179,000
	"Dead and captives a third of a million."			333,333

Naturally, the casualty statistics in a war of the magnitude of this one do not agree either for single actions or for grand totals. Official French and German figures do not correspond individually or collectively. No given set would vary widely, however, if the Nostradamic round number of "a third of a million" is borne in mind. Those who wish to check up on the source material for the individual battles yielding the total 333,333 may read: (1) *New International Encyclopœdia,* Vol. IX, page 172; (2) the same; (3) Appleton's *New Practical Encyclopedia,* Vol. II, page 447; (4) same as 2 and 3; (5) *New Larned History,* Vol. IV, page 3440; (6) same as 3, and (7 and 8) *Fifty Years of Europe,* by Charles Downer Hazen, page 30.

For both the imperial and republican phases of the war, the French dead totaled 156,000, while the wounded and disabled added up to 143,000, or 299,000 all told, according to the *Encyclopœdia Britannica,* Vol. IX, pages 683 and 684. The total number of Frenchmen slaughtered during the Paris Commune, that metropolitan civil war within the framework of the Franco-Prussian conflict, has been estimated as high as 36,000, the *Britannica* remarks in Vol. VI, page 129. Adding 299,000 and 36,000 yields 335,000 dead and wounded, or "a third of a million," in round figures.

There is imperial irony in the fact that Strasbourg and Metz, capitals of the lost provinces of Alsace and Lorraine, held out for the Emperor after fickle France deserted the tinsel eagle. Nor was that the end of the desertion, as Nostradamus relates in the eighteenth quatrain of the Seventh *Centurie:*

Les assiégés couleront leurs paches,
Sept jours après feront cruelle issuë,
Dans repoulsez, feu sang. Sept mis à l'hache
Dame captive qu'avait la paix tissuë.

The besieged will slide out of their compacts,
Seven days afterward they will make a cruel way out,
Repulsed in fire and blood. Seven put to the ax
The lady captive who had the tissue peace.

The German siege of Paris, one of the most famous in history, began on September 19, 1870, lasted four months, and astonished Europe. The Germans began the bombardment of the city early in January. Food was so scarce that rats sold for forty cents each. Wood was exhausted, though many trees were cut down; and most of the fires in the city during one of the coldest winters on record were started by the bursting of German shells. Wine froze in casks. On January 28, 1871, with famine knocking at the door, Paris capitulated after heroic resistance.

The "besieged" Parisians slid "out of their compacts." Paris had proclaimed the republic upon the Emperor's capture, but in the early spring of 1871 the city organized its own government, known as the Commune, refusing to take further orders from the Thiers Government at Versailles. Before many weeks the Commune was controlled by extreme radicals and the leaders of the Paris mob. This necessitated a regular siege of Paris, the second for that unhappy city within a year.

This time the siege was conducted by Frenchmen, the Germans, controlling the forts to the north of the capital, looking on. For two months the Communards fought the troops of the republic, finally in the streets of Paris. At last, on May 21, Marshal MacMahon's army forced its entrance into the city by the Porte St. Cloud. Then followed seven days' ferocious fighting with the rank and file of the mob, now at bay, battling with the frenzied courage of cornered rats, the Versailles army more and more vengeful and bloodthirsty.

Those Communist leaders who were not already taking refuge in cowardly flight gave their last desperate commands for the slaughter of sixty-seven hostages, mostly priests, in their prisons, and for the firing of all the great public buildings which had been the glory of the French capital. A long line of conflagrations stretched across the center of Paris on both banks of the Seine. Parisians have not yet banished the horrors of the "Bloody Week"—seven days of "fire and blood . . . a cruel way out."

The Commune was almost as rough on its generals as the Steely One of the Kremlin. General Cluseret, one commander in chief, was an American. With an average of one commandant sacked every fortnight, the Parisian grim wits revived this quatrain from the 1848 revolution:

> *On sait c'une facon réelle*
> *Combien elle croque de gigots,*
> *Mais nul ne sait encore ce quelle*
> *Dévorera de généraux.*

> *One knows quite well the number*
> *Of legs of mutton it [the Commune] consumes,*
> *But no one yet can say*
> *How many generals it will devour.*

Had they troubled to read Nostradamus, the Communards would have learned the answer—seven. The names and faces of the Commune's Jacks-in-office were forgotten long ago. Some ringleaders escaped, others died on the barricades, but seven kingpins lasted long enough to be executed summarily after drumhead courts-martial pronounced rough-and-ready justice.

They were: Charles Thèophile Ferré, apothecary and professional revolutionist who became the Commune's Chief of Police; Raoul Rigault, the anarchistic fop who, as Commissioner of Public Safety, seized the venerable Archbishop Darboy and ordered the firing of the Tuileries; Pascal Grousset, the Foreign Minister, who tried to escape in the clothes of his mistress; Rossel, the cashiered army officer who had held the chief command of the besieged Reds for a time; Assi, the politician of the workshops; Millière, the turncoat who had been a deputy; and Louis Pyat, who raised the white flag surrendering the last barricade.

The Government's revenge was heavy. It punished right and left summarily. Many Communards were shot on the spot without any trial. Arrests and trials went on for years. The rage of the monarchical Assembly was slow in subsiding. It was not until May, 1877, that *Madame la République,* "the lady captive who had [made] the tissue peace" with Germany, came into her own, as was shown in Chapter 4.

Nostradamus disposes lightly of less sanguinary eras of human history. He calls the more peaceable years between 1870 and 1914 a "longish rain of milk" in the eighteenth quatrain of the Third *Centurie:*

> *Après la pluye laict, assez longuette,*
> *En plusieurs lieux de Reims le ciel toucher,*
> *O quel conflit de sang près d'eux s'appreste!*
> *Peres et fils, Roys n'oseront approcher.*

> *After the longish rain of milk*
> *To touch the sky in several places of Reims,*
> *Oh what a bloody conflict prepares itself around them!*
> *Fathers and sons, Kings will not dare approach.*

That first line was epitomized by Léon Bailby, writing in *Le Jour* on Armistice Day, 1937: "The war of 1914 broke out after forty-four years of a truce wherein one actually had tasted the sweetness of life." Use of Reims as a symbol of the wrath to come is the key to reading this stanza. From A.D. 987 onward, Reims was the scene of the coronation of all French kings except six. St. Joan of Arc recaptured it from the English.

The beautiful cathedral city is the capital of Champagne province, whose chalky soil weltered in the blood of the First World War. From September 14, 1914, the Germans bombarded the city continuously from the hills to the north and east until October, 1918. Most inhabitants left, "fathers and sons, Kings" not daring to approach.

Around Reims, the pivotal center of two battles of the Marne and ceaseless combat, the constant artillery duels developed such clouds of smoke that the very skies seemed to hug the earth. These were much easier for the Seer of Salon to espy than the scrapped "Scrap of Paper" he spotted in the thirtieth quatrain of the Sixth *Centurie*:

> *Par l'apparence de faincte saincteté,*
> *Sera trahy aux ennemies le siege.*
> *Nuict qu'on cuidoit dormir en seureté,*
> *Pres de Brabant marcheront ceux de Liege.*

> *By the appearance of false sanctity,*
> *The siege will be betrayed to its enemies.*
> *The night when one had hoped to sleep in security,*
> *Those of Liège will march close to Brabant.*

Belgian neutrality had been guaranteed in 1839 by all the great powers of that era, and France and Germany reaffirmed this is 1870. On August 2, 1914, Germany abandoned "the appearance of false sanctity," demanding that Belgium permit German armies to cross the territory. Albert I, King of the Belgians, rejected Berlin's peremptory ultimatum.

During "the night when one had hoped to sleep in security," the lightning struck. The thundering German herd burst into the lowlands, determined to reach Paris by the valley of the Meuse, the shortest path. Well-fortified Liège barred the way. Heavy German artillery answered the stout, but futile, Belgian resistance. "The siege" was "betrayed to its enemies" when most of the Germans crossed the Belgian plain by way of Brussels and into Brabant before the fall of Liège on August 7. Thus "those" who had been besieging Liège marched "close to Brabant" while the forts to the rear still were being defended.

The Allies were in for a long, hard fight. Russia of the Czars was torn apart by a mighty revolution and quit the alliance, plunging Britain and France into extremity. Then Nostradamus looked across the water in quatrain 48 of the Eighth *Centurie*:

> *Saturne en Cancer, Jupiter avec Mars,*
> *Dedans Février Chaldondon saluterre.*
> *Sault Castallon assailly de trois pars,*
> *Pres de Verbiesque conflit, mortelle guerre.*

> Saturn in Cancer, Jupiter with Mars,
> In February the Chaldean gives the Earth safety.
> The stronghold falls, assailed from three sides,
> With a conflict of Five over Serbia, mortal war.

The first line is mere astrological rigmarole for warring powers in an era of misery, which 1914–1918 certainly was. The second has much fact crammed into it. On February 3, 1917, answering Germany's declaration of total submarine warfare, the United States severed diplomatic relations with Berlin. Chaldean is a deft, Nostradamic touch epitomizing Woodrow Wilson, architect of the League of Nations, that modern Leaning Tower of Babble at Geneva. The clairvoyant word-twister added *don* (gives) to *Chaldon*, making another pun, President Wilson having been a college don before he entered politics.

The last word of the second line, *saluterre,* is telescoped from the Latin *salus* (safety) and *terrae* (of the earth). The first word of the next line, *sault,* has been taken as deriving from the Latin *saltus* (fall), while the next, *castallon,* is cognate with *castallum* (strong point).

Verbiesque is a typical Nostradamic anagram which is unraveled into three parts, as he hints slyly in the preceding line. These are V, the Roman numeral for five; *erbies,* transformed into Serbie by transposing the terminal *S* to the front of the cryptogram, making the perfectly good French name for Serbia; and *que* ("what").

The "stronghold" of the third line is Germany, chief of the Central Powers, which occupied such a naturally defendable position, but which had to fight a war on three fronts—eastern, southern, and western, a nightmare for any general staff. The V, or five, stands for the five powers originally involved in the dispute over Serbia in 1914—France, Belgium, Russia, Germany, and Austria-Hungary.

All that seems a bit cryptic, but clarified somewhat.

That victory might be achieved, it was necessary for a sixth power to take up arms, replacing Russia. The twentieth quatrain of the First *Centurie* has been accepted generally as portraying the American Expeditionary Force, first in its training behind the lines, then moving into the battle zone for the push to victory:

> *Tours, Orléans, Blois, Angers, Reims et Nantes*
> *Citez vexez par subit changement,*
> *Par langues estranges seront tendues tentes*
> *Fleuves, dards, renes, terre et mer tremblement.*

> *Tours, Orléans, Blois, Angers, Reims, and Nantes*
> *Cities vexed by sudden change,*
> *Tents will be pitched by foreign speakers*
> *Rivers, darts, reins, land, and sea trembling.*

Reims here is in the same key position which it occupied in the eighteenth quatrain of the Third *Centurie,* while all the other cities mentioned are in the valley of the Loire. St. Nazaire, where the first A.E.F. contingent landed, is at the mouth of the Loire, not far from Nantes. The "sudden change," probably annoying to the French, was when those cities became headquarters for various activities of the ever-growing A.E.F.

"Tents" were "pitched by foreign speakers" when the arriving Americans set up encampments in the Loire Valley preparatory to establishing training centers. When they moved up into the line, it frequently was in the Champagne sector, in the neighborhood of Reims, that the Americans were stationed. The last line symbolizes the multifarious military and naval engagements culminating in the final drive against the German invaders.

The work of the restoration of Reims Cathedral, destroyed by the German bombardments, took many years to complete. American contributions to the rebuilding of this cathedral form an additional link in this quatrain to the United States. A million dollars of the restoration cost was borne by John D. Rockefeller.

When Nostradamus looked across the Atlantic Ocean to see the New World called in to redress the balance of the Old, he also seems to have seen death's visitation at Halifax on the morning of December 6, 1917. This was in quatrain 97 of the Sixth *Centurie:*

Cinq et quarante degrez ciel bruslera,
Feu approcher de la grand cité neuve.
Instant grand flamme esparse sautera
Quand on voudra des Normans faire preuve.

At the forty-fifth degree the sky will burn,
Fire approaching the great new city.
A driving great flame will blow up and scatter
When one will wish to prove the mettle of the Normans.

The only new city which the forty-fifth parallel approaches is Halifax, Nova Scotia, scene of the most horrible explosion in world history. When the *Mont Blanc*, a French munitions ship from New York, entered the Narrows leading to Halifax, a Norwegian grain ship, the *Imo*, was heading for the open sea. Because of confused signals, the *Imo* headed directly for the *Mont Blanc*. In the collision, the *Imo's* bow sliced into the munitions ship, overturning a barrel of benzol. Apparently the friction of steel on steel generated sparks, which ignited the benzol fumes.

The French crew, mostly Norman and Breton sailors, didn't lose an instant in getting out the lifeboats and rowing furiously for shore. Seventeen minutes after the blue flames began licking about the munition ship's forecastle, a beam of saffron light about as thick as the *Mont Blanc's* mast shot upward from the deck, zooming a mile high. It twirled about a moment like a waterspout. Then the top blew out and the entire column of flaming death scattered into a gigantic purple cloud. Four thousand tons of T.N.T. exploded in the greatest blast the world ever had heard.

There was a vast, white, boiling torrent, soaring aloft, where the munitions ship had been. Then death advanced and roared across the bay in a great ball of fiery gas. Ships of war and peace were smashed into splinters and fragments of iron. Fires, started in hundreds of places, were joined into one roaring inferno. A tremendous tidal wave followed the explosion. The death list was two thousand, with ten times that number injured. Five hundred people were never found; they had been swept off the face of the earth.

The last line of this quatrain is not clear. It can be read two ways: one is that the Frenchmen of the munitions ship might have scotched the flames had they fought them properly from the start, instead of deserting immediately. The other, which requires reading Normans as Northmen or Norwegians, suggests that the *Imo* and her crew were not all that they seemed. The first interpretation seems the more acceptable.

Nostradamus saw that once the Allies had the Germans on the run, they would give what then was the world's greatest army no rest. In the twelfth quatrain of the Fourth *Centurie* he seems to see many towns and villages, some of them in German possession since 1914, recovered:

Le camp plus grand déroute mis en fuite,
Guères plus outre ne sera pourchassé:
Ost recampé et région réduicte,
Puis hors de Gaule le tout sera chassé.

The greatest army sent fleeing in rout,
Scarcely any farther will it be pursued:
The East reconquered and the region brought back,
Then all will be chased out of Gaul.

An endless string of triumphs filled the days and weeks after the initiative and the offensive were seized by the Allied High Command on the fateful July 18, 1918. Without haste, but without rest, throughout August, September, and October the terrific assaults continued. The victorious troops progressed steadily over ground which had been abandoned not so long before. Verdun was liberated, then Reims and Ypres. Then the stronghold of the Hindenburg Line was smashed along a twelve-mile front in three days.

The story of territory regained became a daily continued serial and the world's greatest army rapidly was demoralized. The terrible Teutons, being driven back toward their own soil, were facing the unheard-of necessity of fighting on the defensive. The Kaiser's gang of international looters fell apart, each taking cover as he might from the advancing whirlwind.

Monday, November 11, 1918, Americans were awakened by the screaming of whistles and clangor of bells. They thought "the war to end war" was over; it was only an armistice—the Great General Staff of Germany saw to that. The basic plans laid down by Helmuth Karl Bernhard, Count von Moltke, in 1858, for such future wars as seemed likely, and dedicated to the proposition that might makes right, were revised in the light of four years' experience.

The greatest army had been sent fleeing in rout. At that time, Allied generals said that it was a mistake not to pursue the beaten horde any farther. Alsace and Lorraine, the eastern borderlands, were reconquered when all were chased out of Gaul; and in 1919 the wrong of 1871 was righted, the two lost provinces again becoming part of France.

Attempts have been made to link no fewer than forty-seven other Nostradamic stanzas with the First World War. None are identified so accurately as those given here. After the comparatively incisive description of the war in the twentieth century's teen age, the Nostradamic visions grow more shadowy. Though he does not contradict his own statements, he seems to backtrack, hedge, and correct himself. The era following the 1914–1918 war is not limned with clear-cut strokes, but even in this portion of his prophesying there are plenty of amazing predictions, some of which have just come true, some seem to be shaping themselves even now, and others can be discerned dimly beyond the horizon.

Nostradamus wrote a six-lined prediction, No. 36, which epitomizes the last decade of the Third French Republic whose fall he dated so accurately in the Letter to Henry II, translated and interpreted in Chapter 4:

> *La grand rumeur qui sera par la France*
> *Les impuissants voudront avoir puissance,*
> *Langue emmiellée et vrays Chaméléons,*
> *De boutefeux, allumeurs de chandelles,*
> *Pyes et geys, rapporteurs de nouvelles*
> *Dont la morsure semblera Scorpions.*

The great uproar which will be in France
The powerless will wish to have power,
Honeyed tongue and true turncoats,
With firebrands, lighters of candles,
Magpies and jackdaws, reporters of news
Whose stings will seem scorpions'.

Twenty-three and a half centuries ago, Aristophanes put the same thought in even terser Greek: "Brekekekex, co-ax, co-ax"— *Ranae*, 209 [The Chorus of Frogs].

7

"Who Is Like Unto the Beast?"

When battle rages and totalitarian ax-grinders begin lying themselves purple about alarms and excursions, the armchair strategist feels inclined to seek elsewhere for the truth about victory or defeat. Then the voice of Nostradamus, prophet extraordinary of the ages, speaks its cryptic piece. One may read what the so-called military experts have to say in the newspapers, or he may puzzle over the thousand and two prophets.

When war comes, the soothsayer has his day. Seers of all sorts, with their partisans, leap avidly into the fray with bleak forebodings of what's around the corner. At that, their auguries often appear to be about as valuable as those of many military analysts of the situation. The names of the riddlers are legion and one takes his pick of these, according to his own nationalistic and factional bias.

Far and away above the writings of all these are the prophecies of Nostradamus, who, his followers maintain, has been calling the turns of fate for almost four centuries. Wedged between the burblings of the wishful thinkers and the pontifications of the expensive columnists, both those of the black-and-white newsprint and the blue ether-waves, appear, here and there, in our times of trouble, reproductions of the broad, sweeping, oracular writings of the Sphinx of Issachar. These appear to fit in with many strange things which currently are happening throughout the world.

Apparently the divinatory system employed by Dr. Nostradamus was to set up his magical gadgetry, whereby he wooed the guardian spirit which brought him his revelations, then to write out his prognostications in rough prose. In those turbulent days it was not politic to be too explicit with names and dates, so he would transmute the prose into mystifying quatrains compounded of old French interlarded with Latin, Greek and a number of words which he just made up out of his "thin flame."

Yet, as the years roll on, more and more of these prophecies are being borne out, in many cases giving the correct names of persons involved or anagrams and plays upon words which students are able to decipher into names. In this twentieth century, royalist pretenders and roundhead commoners, scholars and occultists, have endeavored to decipher the vague, abstruse wording of the *Centuries*. The antique, beclouded rhyme foretells fire and flood, plague and monster, war and earthquake, but generally at quite unspecified times.

It stands to reason that Nostradamus could not have used the words, for example, for the United States, submarine, tanks, airplanes, and the like. What he appears to have seen was a trend of events, though now and again he did cite more explicit details; when he saw such things, his symbolic language waxes amazingly descriptive. It is as if he regarded time's shadowy wings without troubling himself to count pinion feathers.

Two truisms arise from the *Centuries*: first, successive generations continually remodel these time-worn auguries to the shape of contemporary happenings; second, every new analysis of the fruitful stanzas is a certain barometer of another day of stress and strain. In 1907 French peasants were saying that there would be a war within a decade because Nostradamus had foretold one. Probably because some veiled prophecies may be twisted about to mean almost anything, the Germans, during the First World War, used Nostradamus to prove that they were sure to win, while the French foresaw an Allied victory equally clairvoyantly.

The Nostradamic parables are not always easy to unscramble, but the names are the most difficult problem. In the interpretation of these, it usually is necessary to rely either upon flat guesswork or the frequently bigoted opinions of French commentators. There are no stock interpretations, and both common-sense intuition and active imagination must be employed in understanding the quatrains. However, there does appear to be a certain recognizable affinity in the phrases, words, and symbols which the Seer of Salon adopted to depict persons, places, and occurrences.

It had been understood by French interpreters of the Sphinx of Issachar's riddles that he had predicted a Franco-German war in which the eternal enemy would invade Gaul through Switzerland, reaching nearly to the Bay of Biscay, then be defeated at Poitiers, in the valley of the Rhone and in the Jura Alps, to be forced into flight by the coming of a great French king named Henry. This may be another war in the immortal coil of time, or a later and perhaps final phase of current conflict.

Nostradamus certainly did exhort the French to stand firm, since they would emerge from the second war into another era of glory, though temporarily German prey. The Franco-Jewish prophet insisted that "the Germans will succumb wholly," that Germany ultimately will be thrown back in great distress: "the barbarian sect will be defeated soundly and driven out by all the nations." There is great comfort for the Allies in many verses, though doubtless the Nazis—Hitler is said to have great respect for the "astrologers, fools, and barbarians" Nostradamus has warned against—have developed their own totalitarian methods of prophecy to satisfy themselves.

Finally, the Sphinx of Issachar foretold that Italy would be plunged into revolution. The oracular doctor, peering into the future as into a glass, though darkly, made several very creditable stabs at identifying Adolf Hitler and his callous crew, but in other examples prophecies mentioning a gerent who rises from the ranks to dictate might be applied with clarity to Oliver Cromwell or Napoleon Bonaparte.

As a matter of fact, Nostradamians elicit thirteen predictions regarding the Second World War and its outcome and imply that the United States is the eventual winner. Those who believe in such things as numerology say that America's national number (lucky, of course) is thirteen. There are thirteen stripes in our flag, standing for the original thirteen colonies. The crest above the eagle of our national coat of arms is thirteen stars encircled by thirteen cloudlets. The emblematic eagle is drawn correctly with thirteen feathers upon each member, holding thirteen arrows in one talon and an olive branch with thirteen leaves and thirteen olives in the other, while the shield on the eagle's breast is composed of thirteen heraldic pallets. The Confederate battle flag, moreover, also contained thirteen stars.

Now for the thirteen predictions:

1. Though the war will be long and hard, the Anglo-American backbone to the free way of life is elastic enough to bend without breaking, but the French will be rent and riven by internecine warfare, the Gallic way.

2. Germany faces inevitable defeat because of Nazism's brittle and brutal structure, with Hitler unable to win decisively on land, or sea, or in the air.

3. The Allies will achieve aerial supremacy, just as they have it on the seas, bombing the daylights out of Germany.

4. Though Britain will fare badly at the outset, the Empire will not be overwhelmed, nor will England be invaded.

5. Soviet Russia will sap the strength of the German horde just as Czarist Russia destroyed Napoleon's Grand Army.

6. The United States also will be forced into open warfare, possibly through a declaration of war against Japan, within the next twelvemonth.

7. Japan will join the war on the Axis side by attacking the East Indies, where they will meet crushing defeat.

8. Latin America will be greatly affected by Italo-German intrigue, with governments there becoming more totalitarian.

9. Mussolini, shoved into this war by Nazi threats, will find Hitler an Old Man of the Sea, never to be shaken off.

10. France will be completely occupied by the German army and stripped of all its treasures, goods, and chattels.

11. The Nazi army of hobnailed submen, spread too sparsely in occupying all Europe, will crack and disintegrate when revolt flames in Germany.

12. The British Empire will be reorganized, with more and more of the white portions of the commonwealths being colonized from the Isles. There is a hint of Rauschning's coming Anglo-American Atlantic empire.

13. It is certain that an era of bloody wars and revolutions lies ahead, with great and devastating changes to things as they are now.

Among the Nostradamic quatrains there are many predictions which have not come true in the past, but which will give the clairsentient reader some amusement in applying to modern times. By using the imaginative faculties elastically, some of these predictions may be made applicable to current and future events. Readers may see in many stanzas what shapes of things to come they may envision, or what their more specifically accurate knowledge tells them may be there.

Bearing all that in mind, a plunge may be made into the sixteenth quatrain of the Ninth *Centurie* wherein Nostradamus accurately names and places General Francisco Franco, Spain's *El Candillo*, with:

De castel Franco sortira l'assemblée,
L'ambassadeur non plaisant fera scisme:

Ceux de Riviere seront en la meslée,
Et au grand goulphre desnier ont l'entrée.

From Castile Franco will issue the assembly,[1]
The ambassador, not pleasing, will cause a schism:
Those of the Riviera shall be in the fight,
And shall deprive the entry to the great gulf.

This is the Seer of Salon's first prediction of Fascist victory. The revolt of General Franco's Melilla garrison in Spanish Morocco on July 18, 1936, touched off the general assault upon the Spanish Second Republic, but it was not until the following October 1 that the insurgent generalissimo was proclaimed the head of the Nationalistic Government at Burgos, Castile's ancient capital.

Fascist Italy and Nazi Germany were rallied openly to his side by General Franco; the French and British democracies, spinelessly forgetting their pledges and even their interests, threw republican Spain to the Roman and Teuton wolves. Edward Daladier, the French Premier, went so far as to appoint Marshal Pétain, Franco's military mentor, as Ambassador to Burgos.

Franco's response was "not pleasing." He declined to receive Marshal Pétain until the republican fleet interned at Bizerte was turned over to him. Though it would have been simpler to recall the trembling tribune from Burgos, the French Government gave the fleet to Franco, who promptly appended himself to the Rome-Berlin Axis, a schismatic movement to say the least. "A schism" also was created in public opinion in the democratic nations by the Spanish Falangist slogan: "Saving Western Civilization."

Many French Popular Frontists trooped into Loyalist Spain from the Riviera to volunteer in the international brigades, thus getting "in the fight." The last line of the quatrain appertains to

---

1. In military terminology, the signal calling troops to form ranks.

the only tangible achievement of the western democracies in all 1937—the Nyon agreement—which, though it did not end Axist piracy in the Mediterranean, did prevent a regular Italo-German blockade of Spain's Mediterranean coast, depriving the enemy of "the great gulf" of Valencia for Franco-bound troopships and munitions cargoes.

Because of the key-word Melilla, used similarly to Reims in the First World War segment of Chapter 6, quatrain 45 of the Sixth *Centurie* is cited here, though its details await a more lucid clarification of history:

Le gouverneur du regne bien sçavant,
Ne consentir voulant au fait Royal:
Melille classe par le contraire vent,
Le remettra à son plus desloyal.

The well-informed governor of the realm
Not wishing to consent to the royalist action:
The fleet at Melilla by the contrary wind,
He shall remit it to his most disloyal one.

In *Terror in Our Time*,[2] Richard Wilmer Rowan tells how the Spanish "Republican secret service was equally amateur and some of the best of it impromptu . . . One of the self-appointed secret agents was a radio engineer attached to the marine relay station at Ciudad Lineal." He continues:

The Admiralty had, of course, been in touch with the plotters and was working to hand over the entire Spanish navy to the insurgent faction. The radio station at Ciudad Lineal was instructed to send out corresponding "mobilization" orders to the

---

2. Longmans, Green and Company, New York, 1941, pages 253–254.

whole fleet; but before this message of official betrayal went on the air, the radio engineer got ["a contrary"] wind of the Fascist conspiracy and realized the insurgents' design to use Spanish war vessels to safeguard the passage of the rebel legion from [Melilla] North Africa to the Peninsula. The engineer at the risk of being shot down—as many others who attempted to resist the plotters were instantly executed—sent out an immediate warning to the sailors of the various ships:

"ARMADA, THE REPUBLIC CALLS YOU! S.O.S. TREACH-ERY—FASCIST UPRISING—FORWARD—ACTION—TAKE COMMAND!"

Two hours later he had his first response:

"CRUISER JAIME I REPORTING. OUR OFFICERS AT-TEMPTED RESISTANCE. WERE SUBDUED AFTER HARD FIGHTING. STANDING BY FOR ORDERS—WHAT IS TO BE DONE WITH THE BODIES?"

[Apparently an old Spanish custom!]

In the next hour other ships reported. Their crews, together with some officers mindful of their oaths, were declared to be standing "enthusiastically behind our Republic and the working class." Which declaration signaled the onrush of that most sanguinary of internecine conflicts, a class war. But the Fascists and reactionary classes had begun it.

Spain's civil war offered a testing field for the German General Staff's chrysalis of blitzkrieg, emerging from the cocoon stage. Hitler found there a model proving ground for his grim gear of war and tactics of terror. Backing Franco's Fascists, he proved his new weapons and strategy while democracy's carpenters played oysters to the walrus. The result was another democracy destroyed and a new strategic Nazi ally on France's undefended flank.

There was a striking parallel, too, with the Napoleonic Peninsular War. Spain's Loyalists adopted the same guerrilla tactics against the Fascists that their forefathers had employed against Bonaparte's marshals, but the result was different, perhaps because Britain failed to send a Wellington to Iberia. There were Russians, both active and observing, in the Loyalist trenches to witness guerrilla warfare. Their ancestors had used those "scorched earth" methods to decimate Napoleon's Grand Army over the same terrain where Hitler now plunges, perhaps, to another Red hell.

History is a taut coil, springing back into a fool's hand. It began uncoiling in 1933, the beginning of what mystagogues call a seven-year cosmic cycle of paramount importance. The failure of the World Economic Conference, the disarmament deadlock, the beginning disintegration of the League of Nations, the inauguration of Soviet Russia's second five-year plan (*Pyatiletka*), Adolf Hitler's rise to the chancellorship of Germany and the inauguration of Franklin D. Roosevelt in the presidency of the United States all occurred in the fateful year 1933.

Another seven-year cycle began in 1940 with the German conquest of France and the blitzkrieg which failed against England, followed by the resultant rearmament, conscription, and a measure of war hysteria in the United States. Certainly drastic changes have taken place in Europe, and great alterations have occurred in America's national policies during the last nine years. Everything going on in Europe, Asia, and the Americas presages even greater changes in these fighting forties.

Many of those changes spring from the coil lashing out from the hand of one whose advent Nostradamus foresaw in quatrain 58 of the Third *Centurie*:

Aupres du Rin des montagnes Noriques
Naistra un grand de gens trop tard venu,
Qui descendra Saurome et Pannoniques,
Qu'on ne sçavra qu'il sera devenu.

Close to the Rhine in the Noric mountains
A great one of his race will be born much too late,
Who will descend upon Sarmatia and the Pannonias,
But one could not know what he was to become.

Adolf Hitler was born on April 20, 1889, in the Gasthof zum Pommer, Braunau am Inn, in Upper Austria, on the Bavarian frontier. The infant Rhine, at its nearest point as the crow flies, is 160 miles away. Braunau is in a land of romance, twenty-five miles from where the glaucous Danube foams from Passau to Linz through the gloomy, forest-clad Noric Alps. The culture of this upland is as old and its history is as significant as that of the Rhine Valley.

Had Adolf Hitler been born in the Middle Ages, he would have reveled as a Danubian robber baron or a Rhenish *raubritter* in the anarchy which disgraced the Holy Roman Empire. In Nostradamus' own sixteenth century, the Noric nobles drenched the province with the blood of rebel peasants. Heads bit the dust and entrails were nailed to the boles of trees.

Religious warfare blazed while princely bishops stood with their "nieces" to watch heretics writhe in agonized death at the stake. One titled prelate who had quarreled with his houri dangled her outside his castle window in an iron cage. She stripped herself while the yokels watched, whereupon milord the Dom speedily hauled her back into his stronghold. How plastically the atavistic Adolf would have molded himself into such times!

Noricum takes its name from the Noric Alps, stretching through the center of the province when it was part of the old Roman Empire. Noricum is the district south of the Danube, including part of

Bavaria and both Upper and Lower Austria, Salzburg, Styria, and Carinthia. A southern outpost of its warlike, barbarian inhabitants, it was the starting point of their attacks upon Italy, as it will be again, if Nostradamus has seen clearly.

Sarmatia is a vague and ancient name for the vast regions extending from the Baltic to the Black Seas and from the Vistula to the Volga Rivers, the territory coveted by the gormandizing Germans in their very real and modern *Drang nach Osten*. In the fifth century B.C., the Sarmatians lived between the Caspian Sea, the Don River, and the Sea of Azov. In the time of Herodotus (484–424 B.C.), the Sarmatians roamed from the Tanais (Don) to the Danuvius (Danube). Later they subdued the Scyths of the great plains north of the Black Sea and, by the third century B.C., they had supplanted the Scyths proper on the plains of southern Russia.

Roman geographers called all inhabitants of central and southern Russia between the Vistula River and the Caspian Sea the Sarmatae. By Sarmatia, Tacitus seems to have understood Moldavia and Wallachia, and, perhaps, part of southern Russia. The term Sarmatia is applied by later writers to as much as was known of what now is Russia, including both European and Asiatic territories.

Sauromatae was the form used by the early Greeks; later Greeks and Romans made this Sarmatae. Nostradamus has Gallicized the earlier spelling into Saurome, and he appears to agree with some ethnologists who suppose the Sauromatae to have been the ancestors of the Slavs. Soviet Russia's battalions of death composed of women had their prototypes in the Amazonian warrior maidens of Sarmatia, sung by Greek epic poets. Nostradamus apparently had his eye on Hitler's prewar pose as the champion of civilization against Bolshevist "Sarmatia."

As a province of the Roman Empire, Pannonia was bounded on the north and east by the Danube and on the west by the mountains of Noricum and upper Italy, while on the south it reached a little way across the Save, thus including part of modern Hungary, all Slavonia, and parts of Bosnia, Croatia, Styria, and Lower Austria.

Hence, Pannonia embraced most of the Nazi-coveted territory covering the heart and center of modern Austria-Hungary. The Pannonians were brave and warlike, but cruel and treacherous. Frequent rebellions compelled the Romans to build a large number of fortresses in the province, of which Vindobona, the present Vienna, was the most remarkable. During the decline of the Roman Empire, Pannonia fell into the hands of the Huns and from them it passed successively to the Ostrogoths, Langobards, and Slavs, till, in the ninth century, the Magyars settled on it and kept it until the modern Huns moved in with Adolf Hitler at their head.

Rather than risk their political power and pelf in an election in May, 1936, the French Radical-Socialist Government looked on helplessly while Hitler marched into the Rhineland. Had the French army opposed the German Reichswehr then, Hitler's rise to rule would have been cut short. Thus the politicos avoided war in 1936, but at what a cost!

In giving in supinely to Hitler, Europe's so-called statesmen made war inevitable later. First came the bloodless (for France) German *Anschluss* with Austria (part of Pannonia), then the surrender of part of Czechoslavakia at Munich (1938). Hitler's seizure of the rump Czech state in 1939 made the descent upon Poland (part of Sarmatia) later that year possible through the expropriation of Bohemia's munitions factories, needed in the Second World War which came about because "one could not know what he was to become."

In the tenth quatrain of the Tenth *Centurie*, Nostradamus passes this verdict on Nazi Germany's *Mehrer des Reichs*:

Tasche de meurtre, enormes adultères,
Grand ennemy de tout le genre humain

Que sera pire qu'ayeules, oncles ne peres
En fer, feu, eau sanguin et inhumain.

The blot of murder and enormous adulteries,
The great enemy of all the human race
Who will be worse than his grandsires, uncles, and fathers
In sword, fire, bloodshed, and inhumanity.

Our sixteenth-century French prophet seems here to have the English gift for understatement in his description of the Pannonian paperhanger.

It is not possible to dwell or even to touch upon all Nostradamic prophecies which are wholly or even partially understandable. There are two quatrains that are strangely close to the beliefs of Nazism. The first of these is No. 67 of the Third *Centurie*:

Une nouvelle secte de Philosophes,
Mesprisant mort, or, honneurs et richesses:
Des monts Germains ne seront limitrophes,
A les ensuyvres auront appuy et presses.

A new sect of philosophers,
Scorning death, gold, honors, and riches;
They will not be limited by the German mountains,
They will have the support of henchmen and the press.

Before the advent of Nazism, this had been construed as referring to Nietzsche's credo, to theosophy, or to Rudolf Steiner's anthropos-ophists, but the first half of the quatrain may be applied tentatively to the Nazis, who pretend to scorn death and riches, are without honor, and base their currency on slave labor, not on gold. Certainly Hitlerism has not been "limited by the German mountains" and its author has had "the support of [brown-shirted] henchmen and the press" under the control of Dr. Goebbels.

Quatrain 76 of the Third *Centurie* (76 reverses the digits numbering the preceding stanza, No. 67) may be applied to the rise of the German Nazis, accompanied by Dr. Alfred Rosenberg's pagan cults worshiping the ancient Teuton gods Wotan, Fricka, and the like:

> *En Germanie naistront diverses sectes*
> *S'approchant fort de l'heureux paganisme,*
> *Le coeur captif et petites receptes*
> *Feront retour a payer la vraye disme.*

> *In Germany will arise sundry cults*
> *Strongly resembling carefree paganism,*
> *The captive heart and small receipts*
> *Will cause a return to paying the true tithe.*

The revival of the ancient cult of militaristic force and the attempted substitution of the old Teutonic pagan gods in Nazi Germany is a remarkable proof of the Sphinx of Issachar's prophetic vision. The second half of the prediction—a return to true Christianity—awaits fulfillment. A recent editorial article in the New York *Sun* entitled "Ersatz Mysticism" puts the case pithily:

> It seems that the German people just cannot get along without their little shot at mysticism. Since the mysticism of ordinary religious faith is in bad repute with the Nazi masters of that land, its makers of ersatz religion are having a field day. Among them is a group of persons calling themselves by a German word which is translated as "God believers," but the deity in which they believe is described in these nonsensical sentences: "In the bloodstream of the people is contained the mysterious force

from which new life continually develops. This force that gives life is the Divinity." That seems to mean that deity and race—or at least deity and continuity of the race—are one and the same thing. As for Christianity, here is how the God-believers dismiss that venerable institution:

"Christianity can offer to the believer in God nothing that can give him a greater conviction, a strong force, and a better support. We cannot find that Christianity has helped the German people. On the contrary, our people have been ruined by Christ and the priests. Only a return to our ancient beliefs has made us free again. We have no need of Christianity for the salvation of our people."

The foregoing translation is taken from *Christianity and Crisis* for June 30. That journal is content to publish it without comment. Two famous Frenchmen have, however, supplied most of the basic comment that anybody needs. One was Voltaire, who once said in a letter that if God did not exist, it would be necessary to invent Him. The other was La Rochefoucauld, who said in one of his maxims that hypocrisy is a homage which vice pays to virtue. This ersatz mysticism not only invents a divinity—to replace the God of whom it is purposed to deprive the German believer—but at the same time apologizes for the necessity of inventing him.

That editorial was written by James C. Craig, not by Nostradamus. Nostradamus never warned his beloved France to beware Hitler more clearly than he did in the sixth supplementary quatrain to the Eighth *Centurie:*

Las quel désir ont princes estrangers!
Garde toy bien qu'en ton pays ne vienne

Il y aurait de terribles dangers
En maints contrées, mesme en la Vienne.

That longing which foreign princes have!
Guard thy welfare lest it come to thy country.
There will be terrible dangers
In many countries, just as in Vienna.

In late February, 1938, just two weeks before the German army marched into Vienna, French parliamentary opinion was completely muddled. Perhaps at that moment no French deputy expected that the forcible Austro-German union would happen so soon or so brutally, but most delegates were aware of "that longing" which Germany's uncrowned kaiser had in his heart (if any). One deputy warned the Chautemps Government against the danger of an Austro-German *Zollverein*, ignoring the greater peril of an *Anschluss*. No one, however, had any clear idea how the *Anschluss* could be prevented if Hitler willed it. Austria was Hitler's test of his "One Folk-One Realm" policy.

When the Reich's Chancellor entered Austria on March 12, 1938, the French Government did not budge. In fact, there was no French Government on that day. France's state of political confusion spurred Hitler into his Austrian adventure without further ado. Four days before the *Anschluss,* Premier Camille Chautemps resigned without awaiting a test vote of confidence and under even stranger circumstances than he had resigned less than two months previously.

Parisian wits punned: "M. Chautemps, ayant prevu les temps chauds, a donné sa demission."

Translated: "Mr. Hot Times, having foreseen hot times, has resigned."

Ex-Premier Chautemps heatedly denied this slur, but the fact remains that, but for his amazingly unexpected decision to resign,

France would not have been without any Government on the day that Hitler's armored cars clanked into Austria to end the bloodless revisions of the Versailles Treaty's territorial clauses. Until the formal incorporation of Austria into the Third Reich on March 13, 1938, treaty violations had not passed beyond Germany's borders.

Nor was the Chamberlain Government of Britain blameless in the rape of Austria. Robert Dell commented in The Manchester *Guardian* on March 14, 1938:

> Had the British Government agreed to the French proposal immediately after the Berchtesgaden ultimatum (February 11, 1938) that England and France should tell Hitler they would tolerate no further interference in Austria, he might have been checked without war. The proposal was rejected by Chamberlain, who explained away the Berchtesgaden ultimatum and pretended that there was voluntary agreement between Hitler and Schuschnigg.

The Archbishop of Canterbury told the House of Lords on March 29, 1938, that he welcomed Hitler's "inevitable achievement without any bloodshed whatever." The hundreds of Austrian anti-Nazis beaten to death in German stockades apparently lost none of that life-giving human fluid unmentionable in polite King's English except by princes and prelates.

The Austrian-born house painter daubed the home town with red.

After his words of caution to France, Nostradamus turned to warn his other cherished order, the Holy Roman Church, in quatrain 92 of the Fifth *Centurie*:

Apres le siège tenu dix-sept ans,
Cinq changeront en tel revolu terme:
Puis sera l'un esleu de même temps
Quis des Romains ne sera trop conforme.

After holding the see seventeen years,
Five [years] will change in such a full term:
Then one will be elected simultaneously
Who will not be very suitable to the Romans.

His Holiness Pope Pius XI was elected on February 6, 1922. He died seventeen years and four days later, on February 10, 1939. Half of the five years since his death have brought tremendous changes within the term of his successor and friend, Cardinal Eugenio Pacelli, Papal Secretary of State, who became Pius XII on March 2.

The second half of this stanza is obscure and open to dual interpretation—preterist and futurist. The former sense is the fact that Cardinal Pacelli's election was regarded as a blow in the eye for Benito Mussolini and his sons of the Roman she-wolf. The futurist analysis is that Pius XII's successor, perhaps the predicted French Pope, will be displeasing to the Roman populace. If this is the correct interpretation, the next Pope is to be elected in February or March, 1944.

A six-line Nostradamus prediction, No. 53, well may be cited here in connection with the foregoing quatrain regarding the papacy:

Plusieurs mourront avant que Phenix meure
Jusque six cens septante est sa demeure,
Passé quinze ans, vingt et un, trente neuf,
Le premier est subject à maladie,
Et le second au fer danger de vie,
Au feu à l'eau est subject trente neuf.

A good many will die before the Phoenix is dead
Until six hundred seventy is her residence,
Fifteen, twenty-one, thirty-nine years passed,
The first is subject to illness,

And the second to the sword, danger of life,
To fire and to water is the thirty-ninth subject.

The Phoenix is used in Christian symbolism as an emblem of
the Resurrection. It is said that there never is but one existing at the
same time, which, according to fabulous writers, lives five hundred
years. When her end approaches, she makes a nest in which, fired
by the sun's heat, she is destroyed; out of the ashes arises another
phoenix. Nostradamus appears to say that "a good many will die
before the Holy Roman Church is dead." The figures in the second
line once were interpreted as yielding the year 1970, so the inference
is that the Holy See will remain at Rome until 1970.

In September, 1936, when Pius XI had been Pope fourteen years
and eight months, he was stricken with endocarditis, a heart in-
flammation, which persisted until early in 1937, fifteen years after
his election in 1922. Twenty-one years from the last date would
be 1943, when another Pope may be in "danger of life" from "the
sword," if Nostradamus has been read aright.

"To fire and to water is the thirty-ninth subject" is supposed by
some commentators to relate to the war which broke out on land
and sea in 1939, thirty-ninth year of the twentieth century; but others of numerological bent believe that this portends a conflagration
and inundation at Rome in 1961, thirty-nine years from 1922.

The fortieth quatrain of the Second *Centurie* has been linked
with the preceding two verses:

Un peu apres non point long intervalle
Par mer et terre sera fait grand tumulte,
Beaucoup plus grande sera pugne navalle,
Feux, animaux qui plus feront d'insulte.

A little after a not at all long interval
By sea and land there will break out great tumult,

Much greater will be the naval battle,
Fires and beasts who will bring more than insults.

Pius XII was crowned on March 12, 1939, and the war began
with the German invasion of Poland on September 1, 1939, "a not at
all long interval." Germany's onslaught on land was called officially
"counterattack with pursuit" as armed troops crossed the Polish
frontier. Two days later Great Britain declared war on Nazi Germany and when a U-boat torpedoed the steamship *Athenia*, bound
for Montreal from Glasgow and Liverpool, which sank with the loss
of 112 lives, the Battle of the Atlantic began. This "naval battle" may
become "much greater" if and when it spreads into an ocean much
greater than the Atlantic. The last line of the quatrain is sheer poetic
embroidery as meaningless as grandma's tatting.

Here is a stanza which recalls very clearly Hitler's bullying
meetings with the wretched Schuschnigg, inept Chamberlain (at
Godesberg), tragic President Hacha of Czechoslovakia, and a slew
of toadying Balkan straw bosses, being the fourth supplementary
quatrain of the Eighth *Centurie*:

Beaucoup de gens voudront parlementer,
Aux grands seigneurs qui leur feront la guerre.
On ne voudra en rien les escouter,
Helas! si Dieu n'envoye paix en terre.

Many nations will wish to parley
With the great lords who will war against them.
They will not wish to hear anything from them,
Alas! unless God sends peace to the earth.

During the debates on foreign policy in the French Chamber of
Deputies in February, 1938, Jean Ybarnégaray, parliamentary spokesman for the nationalist Croix de Feu, was cheered when he declaimed:

"There is no dearth of people who will pack the waiting rooms of Ribbentrop, Goebbels, and Goering and who, without any mandate and without any power from the Government, go there, like so many pilgrims, to collect promises and assurances. It is their lookout, but I venture to suggest to them that in so doing they are not serving the interests of France."

When Kurt Schuschnigg, Austria's chancellor, was called to Hitler's eyrie at Berchtesgaden, he was forbidden the consolation of so much as one cigarette and forced to listen to the Nazi *Fuehrer's* thrasonic tirades and low-born table-thumping to the tune of *Deutschland über Alles.* Hitler sneered: "Are you relying on France and England? You are mistaken. When I took over the Rhineland in March, 1936, they didn't budge. Do you think they are going to budge for you?"

The central episode covered by this stanza is the conference of Munich, in September, 1938. The fruitless negotiations which preceded that fateful parley sprouted their persimmons in war. The democracies let Hitler take Czechoslovakia and lost their last chance when Premiers Chamberlain and Daladier agreed to the annexation by Nazi Germany of the Czech Sudetenland which Hitler had demanded. Munich is a landmark in the numbered days of France.

In the following lines, quatrain 47 of the First *Centurie,* the League of Nations obviously is intended:

Du Lac Leman les sermons fascheront,
Des jours seronts reduicts par les sepmaines,
Puis mois, puis an, puis tous defailliront
Les Magistrats damneront les loix vaines.

From Lake Geneva sermons will bore, first by days,
Then brought to weeks, then months, then years;
Then they all will fail.
The magistrates will damn the futile laws.

Is that not the windy talk from the League of Nations, to whose activities Nostradamus has dedicated several verses? He accused the modern Tower of Babel of defeating its own high purposes by fostering misunderstandings among the nations and abetting the martial spirit. The implication here is that the harangues coming from the shores of the Lake of Geneva served to arouse anger and bitterness while days, weeks, months and, finally, years passed in foolhardy jockeying for diplomatic positions; then the ridiculous structure fell apart, with its members denounced because of the inane measures they had adopted.

In quatrain 44 of the Ninth *Centurie*, the Seer of Salon dates the official collapse of the League:

> *Migrés, migrés de Geneve trestous,*
> *Saturne d'or en fer se changera,*
> *Le contre Raypoz exterminera tous,*
> *Avant l'advent le Ciel signes fera.*

> *Flee, flee all ye of Geneva,*
> *The golden Saturnalia will be transmuted to iron;*
> *The counter agent will exterminate all,*
> *Before the advent Heaven will show signs.*

The adherents of the Geneva system of collective insecurity are warned that the golden age of saturnine diplomacy has been superseded by Bismarckian *Blut und Eisen* (blood and iron), streamlined to the times by Marshal Hermann Goering's "cannon, not butter."

Raypoz is the anagram of Zopyra, an Achaemenian nobleman notorious for having engineered the recapture of rebellious Babylon by Darius I of Persia. After a siege of nearly two years, the great city, which the Persian King had recognized as his most important objective, fell in 519 B.C. The Persians thereafter were enabled to attack their opponents individually, just as the Nazis are doing now, and Darius became undisputed master of the empire by 516 B.C.

The story of Zopyra is taken from a romantic legend recounted by Herodotus (Book III, sections 153–160). While Darius was besieging Babylon, Zopyra vowed to himself that he would assure his master's conquest of the revolting city. Having cut off his nose and ears, this early fifth columnist entered the Babylonian capital by pleading the cruelty of the monarch, who, he said, had mutilated him so brutally and ignominiously.

Introducing himself as a deserter, Zopyra, after gaining the confidence of Babylon's defenders, delivered to the Persians the two gates over which he had been made captain of the guard. Zopyra received the satrapy of Babylon for himself and his descendants as recompense for his own loss of face, a reward which his grandson repaid by deserting the Persians for the Athenians.

Nor were Zopyra's the original tactics of terror. Previously there had been a deadly fifth column countermining Babylon in 539 B.C. Babylonia's last king, Nabonidus (555–539 B.C.), was a monarch of fine character, absorbed in intellectual pursuits and religious exercises. The hierarchy of Babylon's tutelar deity, Bel-Marduk (Baal-Merodach), hated the King because of his reform program and religious toleration. These priests sold out to the invader when Babylon was attacked by the great Persian king Cyrus.

The Babylonian army, under the King's son and agent, Belsharutsur, the Belshazzar of the Bible (Daniel, Chapter v, used against the Nazis in the V-for-Victory campaign), made a show of defense, but soon was vanquished by the Persians. The traitorous priests opened Babylon's gates to admit the besiegers, who entered the great city unopposed, indeed, welcomed, by the bulk of the inhabitants as deliverers from worse evils than those they brought. Babylon, once the envy of the world, fell, never to rise again successfully.

Zopyra's is an almost forgotten name, but it serves to recall today's traitorous prototype of the fifth columnist, Major Vidkun

Quisling. Germany's brief campaign in Norway, beginning on April 9, 1940, revealed Hitler's vaunted new "secret weapon," eighteen centuries old. Just why the Berlin High Command disclosed the terrifying tactics of total warfare, particularly the Trojan horse plan, before unleashing the best German armies against the western front is impossible to fathom.

Though Norway was a Nazi victory, it may prove to have been a Pyrrhic one, because it opened the world's eyes to entire herds of wild Trojan horses. Germany's neighbors across the Rhine were unable to sweep out their Augean stables in time, but Britain tried an iron broom soon enough. Winston Churchill turned Hitler's horseplay into a mare's nest.

Geneva's era came to an official and ignominious end on July 26, 1940, when Joseph A. C. Avenol, who had been secretary of the League of Nations since July 1, 1933, announced his resignation, sighing that the realities of the present time made his office necessary no longer.

As to the signs in the heavens before the advent of Hitler's Zopyran tactics, it may be remembered that there was a great deal of interest shown by the American press and citizens in the unusual line-up of five planets in the western sky during late February and early March, 1940. *Life* magazine, in its February 26 issue, showed three pictures of that line-up—Mars, Saturn, Venus, Jupiter, and Mercury in the constellation of Pisces (the Fishes). *Life* also commented that such an alignment is so rare that no astronomer knows when it occurred before or if it ever again will happen.

Other stanzas pertaining to the League of Nations are not so well documented, but quatrain 81 of the Sixth *Centurie* is applicable:

Pleurs, cris et plaincts, hurlements, effrayeurs,
Coeur inhumain, cruel, noir, et transy:
Léman, les Isles, de Gennes les majeurs,
Sang espancher, profaim, à nul mercy.

Tears, cries, and groans, howls, fears,
An inhuman heart, cruel, black, and chilling.
Lake Geneva, the Isles, the greatest of Genoa,
Blood shed, profanely, without mercy.

Obviously, Hitler has "an inhuman heart, cruel, black, and chilling." Reference to the British Isles follows the mention of Geneva, while "the greatest of Genoa" has been taken as a metaphor for Mussolini. Genoa on February 9, 1941, was bombarded heavily by British warships, strengthening the belief that "the Isles" referred to are Britannic. This war has seen much "blood shed, profanely, without mercy."

Here is quatrain 85 of the Fifth *Centurie*, predicting war on land, sea, and in the air because of the failure of the sorry "sanctions" policy of the sorrier League of Nations:

Par les Sueves et lieux circonvoisins,
Seront en guerre pour cause des nuées,
Camp marins locustes et cousins,
Du Léman fautes seront bien desnuées.

Because of the Suevi and their neighboring places,
They will be at war for the sake of vast numbers,
Armies, navies, locusts, and gnats,
The failings of Geneva will be clearly revealed.

Suevi originally was a collective name comprising several Germanic tribes which formed a rude sort of union. It was thus used by Caesar and Tacitus. Drusus, son of Tiberius, in A.D. 19 had settled the Suevi north of the Danube, between the March and Waag rivers. In the fourth century the name was applied to a single tribe, one branch of which settled along the Neckar (Swabia), while another branch broke into Gaul and in 409 crossed the Pyrenees and penetrated into Spain, where they embraced Christianity, conquered Galicia, and formed a kingdom, united with the Visigothic empire in 585. Hitler has revived the name of Swabia for that one of his thirteen satrapies which is in the extreme southwest of Germany proper, embracing parts of Württemberg, Baden, and Bavaria. Nostradamus uses the name Suèves aptly as a French synonym for Germans, since the newly created province is bounded on the west by the Rhine.

The "neighboring places" are the Third Reich's engorged neighbors, in the order of Hitler's 1938–1940 bill of fare—Austria, Czechoslovakia, Poland, Denmark, The Netherlands, Belgium, Luxembourg, and France. One small morsel remains to complete a perfect perimeter around the Teutonic banqueting table: Switzerland, a stony mouthful.

Nostradamus' use of locusts to describe Hitler's panzer divisions of tanks and armored cars is similar to St. John's vision in Revelation, ix, 3–11. *Les cousins* are not kith and kin, but bombing and fighting planes. Though the League of Nations offered a promise of better feeling and security, being planned chiefly as an instrument to prevent war, it served only to hammer home the salty truth that peace requires more than marbled halls of the eight winds.

Perhaps quatrain 55 of the First *Centurie* refers to the land, sea, and aerial battles of the present war:

> *Soubs l'opposite climat Babylonique*
> *Grand sera de sang effusion,*
> *Que terre et mer, air, ciel sera inique*
> *Sectes, faim, regnes, pestes, confusion.*

> *At the time of the struggle against Babel*
> *The bloodshed will be great,*
> *With land and sea, air and sky iniquitous*
> *Sects, hunger, realms, plagues, confusion.*

Babel is the Hebrew name of Babylon (the Greek form of Babel); also the name of the tower which Noah's descendants began to build, soon after the deluge, on the plain of Shinar, but which, in consequence of the confusion of tongues, they did not finish. Sir Henry Rawlinson's investigations at Birs Nimrud showed that the tower of Borsippa was called *E-urimin-an-ki,* "house of the seven divisions of heaven and earth," symbolizing the entire universe and connecting the earth, as it were, with the heavens. It seems not unreasonable for Nostradamus to compare the League of Nations with the Tower of Babel.

Nostradamus characterizes Adolf Hitler, the vegetarian, in the ninth quatrain of the Second *Centurie:*

Neuf ans le regne le maigre en paix tiendra
Puis il cherra en soif si sanguinaire;
Pour luy grand peuple sans foy et loy mourra,
Tué par un beaucoup plus débonnaire.

Nine years the meatless one will keep the realm in peace,
Then he will fall into such a bloody thirst
That a great people will die for him without faith and law,
Slaughtered by a most casual masterstroke.

The last French soldiers of the army of occupation at the Kehl bridgehead of the Rhine were withwrawn on June 28, 1930, to Strasbourg, capital of Alsace; and Baden was entirely freed. The French evacuation of the Rhineland was completed on June 30 of that year.

That same year Hitler began his first real climb to power. In the summer of 1930, Germans still able to think for themselves blenched on hearing the frenzied *Fuehrer's* words: "And when I come into power, many heads will roll under the executioner's ax." As a result of the Reichstag election of May 20, 1928, the Nazis acquired only twelve seats, polling 809,541 popular votes, but the September 14, 1930, election brought them 107 seats, representing 6,406,397 votes.

Nine demoralizing years later, in Poland, in their encircling movements, the German forces in the Warsaw area crossed the Vistula and the San rivers; in the north they spanned the Bug River, south of Ostrow. The Carpathian mountain barrier also was traversed. Gdynia, the Polish naval base and port near Danzig, was surrendered to the German besiegers. The Polish ambassador at London, Count Raczynski, exhorted the British to help the Poles more effectively. The Duke of Windsor was a tea guest at Buckingham Palace—his first appearance there since his abdication. (His expatriated American-born duchess was not in London.) French troops on the western front advanced again into the sector between Hornbach and Saarbruecken.

Hitler is said to have become a vegetarian in his starveling years, when his *kampf* was a struggle to obtain food and shelter. One of his jobs was as a stool pigeon for Bavaria's political police.

The Nazi *Fuehrer's* herbivorous habits are described by G. Ward Price, of Britain's Associated Newspapers in *I Know These Dictators:*[3]

The sobriety of Hitler's private life is well known. He is a vegetarian, teetotaler, and non-smoker. His favorite dishes are *Nudelsuppe,* a soup with little dumplings in it; spinach; apples, either baked or raw; and *Russische Eier,* which are cold hard-boiled eggs with mayonnaise sauce. At tea-time, despite anxiety to avoid putting on weight, he is fond of chocolate éclairs. He drinks neither tea nor coffee, but only mineral water and infusions of camomile or lime-flowers.

Sometimes at the end of a hard day, or when he thinks he

---

3. Henry Holt and Company, New York, 1938, page 15.

may have caught a chill, he swallows a little brandy in milk—but with distaste. He finds the smell of tobacco so unpleasant that no one is allowed to smoke in his presence, even after dinner, which to Germans is a serious deprivation.

Sired by Popeye, whelped by Mrs. Jack Sprat, as it were.

The great people without faith or law are the Germans, who are slaughtering and being slaughtered by Hitler's "most casual masterstroke" which plunged an entire continent into unwanted war.

Abandoning all pretense or rival ideologies, Adolf Hitler (that scion of the Schicklgrubers) and Joseph Dzhugashvili (who prefers to call himself Stalin) negotiated a deal in August, 1939, as Nostradamus foretold in quatrain 95 of the Third *Centurie*:

> *La loy Moricque on verra défaillir*
> *Après une autre beaucoup plus séductive,*
> *Boristhènes premier viendra faillir,*
> *Par dons et langue une plus attractive.*

> *You will see the Moric law default*
> *Before another much more seductive doctrine.*
> *The Dnieper will become the first to fail*
> *Because of the gifts and tongue of a more attractive one.*

Moric is the adjectival form of the surname of Sir Thomas More, recently canonized saintly author of the first share-the-wealth program, *Utopia*, published in Latin in 1516, when Nostradamus was thirteen years old. *Utopia* describes an imaginary insular commonwealth based upon the idea of community of goods.

"The literature of communism," according to Doubleday's *Encyclopedia*, "begins with Plato's *Republic* and is continued in More's

Utopia," while Appleton's *New Practical Encyclopedia* remarks that "Bacon, More and other English theorists wrote treatises which look toward the ultimate establishment of communism."

The "much more seductive doctrine," a revival of Russian land-grabbing imperialism, was hinted at in the German press before Joachim von Ribbentrop, Nazi Foreign Minister, sold Stalin his case of counterfeit champagne. Walter Lippmann commented in the New York *Herald Tribune* that "Stalin did not join the Franco-British alliance because he believed, correctly enough, that Russia would receive the brunt of the attack, and because he feared, not without some justification, that the Western Powers might be tempted to let the war become an anti-Communist crusade." So the sneak seemed to bear more attractive gifts.

Boristhenes was the name which the Greeks gave to the Dnieper, next to the Volga and Danube the greatest and most important river of Europe. It rises in the Smolensk region, at the foot of the Valdai Hills, which are near Moscow. Hence, Boristhenes is a synonym for the Russian capital.

Moscow was the "first to fall"—even before Poland—when, on August 24, 1939, the Communazi pact was signed on the dotted line by Comrade Molotov and Ribbentrop, the former champagne salesman. Stalin looked on calmly in this Kremlin drama enacted "because of the gifts and tongue of a more attractive one."

Henry C. Wolfe put it this way in *The Imperial Soviets:*[4]

> That Stalin does not trust "Ribbi" goes without saying . . . But the point is that no one would trust von Ribbentrop in the slightest. A power politician's rating for truth and trustworthiness is low enough. But "Ribbi's" rating is even lower than average. And that is saying a good deal.

---

4. Doubleday, Doran and Company, Inc., New York, 1940, page 193.

When Stalin and Hitler joined hands, each reserved a dagger behind his back, as Nostradamus implied in the first quatrain of the Fifth *Centurie*:

Avant venuë de ruyne Celtique
Dedans le temple deux parlementeront,
Poignart coeur, d'un monté sur coursier et pique
Sans faire bruit le grand enterreront.

Before the coming of Celtic ruin
Two will come to terms within the shrine,
The heart stabbed, the one mounted on a charger and spiteful
Without making any noise they will bury the great one.

This alliance gave Hitler a free hand to invade, in turn, Poland and France. The Slavic Poles were conquered in three weeks, the Celtic French less than a year later. Hitler's sneaky emissary and Stalin came "to terms within the shrine" of once Holy Russia, Moscow's Kremlin, which comprises an extraordinary aggregation of public buildings, palaces and churches of fantastic form and varied color. The distant aspect of the group, with its curious spires and bulbous cupolas, is impressive, wholly unique, and, withal, quite shrinelike.

Among the Kremlin's cathedrals are the Uspenski (1474), where the czars were crowned, and the Arkhangelski (St. Michael's), the burying place of the czars down to the revolutionary era of Peter the Great. Another shrine is the Chudov monastery (monastery of wonders), which is remarkable for its 320-foot-high bell tower.

It takes little imagination to see "the heart stabbed" as Hitler plunged his Nazi poignard into the budding alliance between Soviet Russia, Europe's heartland, and the Franco-British bloc. Nor does it take extrasensory feeling to see "the one mounted on a charger and spiteful" as Hitler, the dictator, Germany's man on horseback who despises both democracy and communism.

"Without making any noise they will bury the great one" may be interpreted satisfactorily as: Without any fanfare or publicity the Russian comrades will shelve the principles of Marx, stepfather of communism, and Lenin, author of the bolshevist state, who is enshrined in the Kremlin, a mecca for so many Soviet citizens.

Mr. Wolfe provides a footnote to the foregoing two quatrains with his remark in *The Imperial Soviets* that[5]

> if Stalin came to terms with Hitler, he could probably stay out of war if he chose to do so. The ensuing conflict would involve the principal nations in that "other world" which Stalin was resolved to destroy. Furthermore, according to what appears to be the best information available, the Soviet dictator knew that Britain and France could not afford to stand by while Hitler overran Poland. They would have to fight, unless someone would be obliging enough to do their fighting for them.
>
> A Soviet pact with Hitler would undoubtedly spur the Fuehrer to attack Poland immediately. Thus a Nazi-Soviet entente would not only start the war that Stalin was trying to promote; it would likely spare the Soviet from involvement. The war would embroil four of his enemies at one time. For the Bolsheviks were too well informed to share the Hitler-Ribbentrop belief that a Berlin-Moscow deal would scare the British and French into standing by while the Nazis destroyed Poland.

For Comrade Stalin, it was a "much more seductive doctrine" than a Franco-British alliance. In his conclusion, Mr. Wolfe remarks that

> where the Nazis are desperately reckless, the Bolsheviks pursue cautious policies. Their strategy is to force their enemies into

---

5. *Ibid.*, pages 175–176.

risking gambles. Stalin is not influenced by whispering voices; he does not live in a mystic's half world. Hitler is carried away by supernatural myths. He consults astrologers. Stalin, the stark materialist, cold-bloodedly charts his course.

Both would have profited from what Nostradamus had to say. In quatrain 29 of the Fifth *Centurie,* Nostradamus recounts the politico-economic consequences of the Russo-German tie-up:

La liberté ne sera recouvrée,
L'occupera noir, fier, vilain, inique:
Quand la matière du Pont sera ouvrée,
D'Hister, Venise faschée la republique.

Liberty will not be recovered,
A black, fierce, villainous, unjust man will occupy it:
When the goods of the Black Sea will be opened
Into the lower Danube, Venice vexes the republic.

On December 5, 1936, Soviet Russia's citizens adopted a written constitution establishing a two-chambered parliamentary body, with the assembly to be elective on the basis of universal suffrage and a free ballot; freedom of speech and worship and similar liberties fundamental in democracies, but hitherto unknown in Russia, were also established. With the advent of the Communazi compact, all these rights were whisked away.

Ukase after ukase was promulgated by the "black, fierce, villainous man" who brooded in the Kremlin like a double-headed Russian eagle of ill omen. Stalin is of Georgian stock, a swart, brunet people, "black and fierce."

Writing in *Harper's Magazine* on "The Silent Soviet Revolution," Bertram D. Wolfe recounted "a lengthy series of changes during the last two years." He found:

To a degree unknown even in old Russia, these changes introduce fixity and abolish individual will and individual right. They attach the peasant permanently, from birth to death, to his collective farm. They attach the worker permanently, from late childhood to death, to his particular factory and task. No one is to change his position or status except on order of his superiors and as the interests of the state may dictate. . . .

On October 3, 1940, the Soviet system of free, universal education, with stipends for higher education, was summarily abolished—although this, too, had been guaranteed in the Constitution of 1936 and has been a model for the rest of the world. . . . The Red Army itself has undergone a transformation. The authorities have eliminated the last vestiges of democracy, initiative from below, comradely relations between officers and men—all the things which gave the Red Army its specifically "proletarian" or "socialist" coloring. . . .

The remilitarization of the army has in turn reacted upon industry. As "war industries" are increasingly placed under the army, the Soviet Union is increasingly turned into one vast military encampment.

The "New Order" that is thus shaping itself in the Soviet Union has little in common with the socialism that was envisaged by the founders of the socialist movement. But there is much—each day more and more—of old Russia. . . .

It has become a testing ground where mankind can determine whether it is possible to operate industry, to foster science, even to conduct modern warfare, by combining old-fashioned army discipline with a prison regime and universal labor conscription. This "new order" surely can have little attraction for other peoples.

A map published as the frontispiece of Henry C. Wolfe's *The Imperial Soviets* shows how oil, food, and other resources for waging warfare, "the goods of the Black Sea," had been "opened into the lower Danube" while Russia was helping Nazi Germany. The French term for the Black Sea is Le Pont or Le Pont-Euxin, derived from its ancient name, Pontus Euxinus. Oil tankers steamed 550 miles across the sea, from Batum to the mouth of the Danube, while grain shipments sailed ninety miles from Odessa to the Danubian delta ports.

The Danube was known to the Greeks as the *Ister*, while the Romans called the lower reaches of the river *Hister* or *Ister*. Some recent Nostradamian commentators have attempted to read *Hister* as a tolerably plain hint at Hitler, since, in addition to the remote resemblance of the two words, Hitler has been identified with the upper part of the Danubian basin, but these analogies do not appear to be at all conclusive. In any case, the Danube along most of its course was called *Danuvius* or *Danubius* by the Romans. Nostradamus spelled Franco's name quite correctly; would he not have done the same had he cared to name Hitler?

Venice to Nostradamus seems to mean Italy as a whole. During the sixteenth and seventeenth centuries, the Venetian Republic was Italy's most powerful state and almost the sole bulwark against the aggressive power of the Turks. During those two centuries Venice repeatedly was engaged in war both for and against nearly every European power.

In April and May, 1940, when the breakup of the Danubian ice floes permitted barges to start up the river with their cargoes of Russian goods, Fascist Italy's controlled press began demanding soil and spoil from the French Republic, but Mussolini continued his behind-the-scenes horse-trading until June, when the race ended for France. Thus he vexed the republic in its last days.

The Sphinx of Issachar saw the Munich beer-hall explosion, which just missed ending the menace of Adolf Hitler, in quatrain 37 of the Sixth *Centurie*, but the seer failed to say who planted the time bomb:

L'oeuvre ancienne se parachevera,
Du toict cherra sur le grand mal ruyne,
Innocent faict mort on accusera,
Nocent caché, taillis à la bruine.

The ancient task will be terminated,
From the ceiling dire ruin will fall on the great one,
The innocent will be accused of the deadly deed,
The guilty hidden in a thicket in a drizzling rain.

Hitler's "ancient task" was the reconquest of Poland, a self-appointed mission of fire and sword imposed upon themselves by the Teutonic Knights of 1230. A few minutes after Hitler left the Bürgerbräu hall in Munich, where he had addressed old-timers of the Nazi movement, a time bomb exploded in the place, killing eight persons and wounding sixty-three. It was the eve of the sixteenth anniversary of the first Nazi putsch (1923), which failed when the Munich police opened fire on an armed gang led by an Austrian paperhanger named Adolf Hitler and the former World War commander, General Erich Ludendorff.

The shrine of Nazism was almost wrecked by the bomb, which blew down the ceiling. At that time it was believed generally outside Germany that the Gestapo had arranged the bombing outrage to enhance Hitler's popularity and to arouse the dulled German populace to fury against Britain. The next day, the Nazi-controlled newspapers announced that the secret police had succeeded in capturing two dangerous British spies. The instigator of the plot against the *Fuehrer,* the German Government charged, was the British Intelligence Service.

One British agent arrested was Major Sigismund P. Best, described as the chief of the European division of the British Counterespionage Bureau, and the other was Captain Richard H. Stevens, called his closest collaborator. It was reported from Berlin on November 21 that

Georg Elser, thirty-six years old, had confessed after his arrest that he had planted the time bomb in the pillar of the beer hall at the behest of British secret agents who had bribed him.

Thus were "the innocent . . . accused of the deadly deed." Who were "the guilty hidden in a thicket in a drizzling rain"?

The New York Times, on September 3, 1940, published this report:

> The crime was not faked. It was genuine, and the police had nothing to do with it. It had been prepared and carried out by foes of Herr Hitler, apart from all foreign interference or incitation.
>
> In the occurrence, the British and French have deliberately spared Herr Hitler's life. The plotters wanted to be supplied with the electric appliance necessary to time accurately the explosion of the bomb. The French and British could hardly conceal a feeling of horror; they were actually asked to associate with terrorists! They were determined not to have anything to do with them.
>
> The result was that the conjurators had to piece together some kind of clockwork as best they could. They did it rather clumsily and the infernal machine went off six or seven minutes too late. Herr Hitler was safe.

The next quatrain, the twentieth of the Seventh *Centurie,* pictures Italy in the spring of 1940, when Mussolini could not make up his mind which way the *lupo dorato* (translated either as "golden wolf" or "jackal") of Romulus and Remus should jump:

> *Ambassadeurs de la Toscane langue,*
> *Avril et May Alpes et mer passer:*
> *Celuy de veau exposera l'harangue,*
> *Vie Gauloise ne venant effacer.*

Ambassadors of the Tuscan tongue
Pass the Alps and sea in April and May:
A shirker will explain the harangue,
Not wishing to rub out Gallic life.

In the section entitled "The Stooge" of *The Shape of the War to Come*,[6] an anonymous author reported that

> what certainly was clear was the fact that Italy's joining the Allies remained a latent possibility in her moves from September, 1939, to April, 1940. All this time, Hitler was putting pressure on Mussolini to come in with him. . . . But Mussolini was careful to see that his co-operation came just too late to be of any use, and it was not until May that he began to thump his war-drums and play on his *leit-motif*—"We hate the Allies; war against the Allies." Even then he was still stalling.

Perhaps *Il Duce's* explanation of his harangues to the French Government was that he did not wish to destroy his Latin neighbor or cause Gallic blood to be shed. On June 10, Italy declared war on France and Britain, and President Roosevelt made his "hand that held the dagger" speech even as the fine Italian was slipping the stiletto between Marianne's shoulder blades.

What seems to be a particularly shrewd analysis of Franco-British relations is made in quatrain 93 of the First *Centurie*:

Terre Italique pres des monts tremblera,
Lyon et Coq non trop confederez,
En lieu de peur, l'un l'autre s'aidera,
Seul Castulon et Celtes moderez.

---

6. Longmans, Green and Company, New York, 1940, page 49.

The Italian land shall tremble near the mountains,
The Lion and the Cock will not be well allied,
Shall have fear hold them together;
Only Cazorla and the Celts will be moderate.

When Mussolini launched his campaign of intimidation, French Alpine chasseurs could hear the artillerists on the Italian side of the border at target practice and Fascist engineers blasting out mountain roads for the threatened invasion of southern France. That the British Lion and Gallic Cock were not getting along well in their historically unnatural entente already is a widely accepted fact. Obviously, only Germanophobia was holding them together.

With *Castulon,* Nostradamus interjects another of his engaging posers. During Roman times, Castulo was an important city of the Tarroconensian province of Spain and now is called Cazorla. The Sphinx of Issachar here may be trying to tell us that only Spain and the Celtic Irish will remain aloof from the European holocaust.

In the first supplementary quatrain of the Eighth *Centurie,* Nostradamus took note of the Allies' infantile paralysis and suicidal inactivity when the so-called phony war still was in progress during the first eight months:

Seront confus plusieurs de leur attente,
Aux habitants ne sera pardonné,
Qui bien pensaient persévérer l'attente,
Mais grand loisir ne peur sera donné.

Several will be confused by waiting,
It will not be pardoned in the populace
Who expected to persevere in the attempt,
But a great deal of time will not be given to them.

Accounts of Franco-British shortsightedness have been rendered for the 1936–1940 era many times. There appeared to be either an unreadiness or actual inability to see things as they were, not as the democratic politicians and military advisers wished them to be. After war was declared, General Maurice Gustave Gamelin conducted his "sitzkrieg" from behind the ramparts of the Maginot Line, while he let George (VI) do it as far as building up a modern armored force to invade Germany was concerned.

When one of France's own officers, Charles de Gaulle, outlined, then detailed, the shape of the war to come six years before the Nazi panzer divisions screamed into France and outflanked the Maginot wall, General Maxime Weygand succeeded in discrediting the young apostle of the new strategy.

It was during these first eight months that France's tragic lack of national unity grew into a national scandal. The labor unions were divided, and the twenty-four-hour working day was not instituted until May 21, 1940, a month before France capitulated. Four years of utopian socialism had sapped the economic and national vitality.

All winter long the world was guessing what Hitler was going to do. The German fortress troops kept showing propaganda signs across the Rhine while French poilus and British Tommies were bored to death "somewhere in France." Thus, while the Nazis were planning the blitzkrieg, the Allied leaders were "confused by waiting." This was not "pardoned in the populace," which cried that the war was a stumer. The democratic peoples, enemies of Hitlerism, "expected to persevere in the attempt," "but a great deal of time" had not been "given to them."

It had taken more than four years of war and all the resources of the Allies, in fact, of virtually all the world, to defeat the German Kaiserdom. France was defeated within forty days from the start of the Nazi offensive on May 10, 1940, by a Germany fighting alone against Britain, France, The Netherlands, and Belgium. Eight months was not enough time to organize for victory.

The fifth-column infiltration into France, lulling a portion of the nation into an attitude of false security, might be indicated by quatrain 34 of the First *Centurie:*

> *L'oyseau de proye volant à la fenestre,*
> *Avant conflit fait aux François parure.*
> *L'un bon prendra, l'autre ambigue sinistre,*
> *La partie foible tiendra par bonne augure.*

> *The bird of prey, flying to the window*
> *Before the conflict, will make the French unaware.*
> *One part of the people will believe, the other think it sinister;*
> *The minority will consider it a good omen.*

"Fascist Fomentations Threaten France," Chapter XXVII of Mr. Rowan's *Terror in Our Time,* tells how the Roman and German eagles beaked and clawed at France's heart before the outbreak of the Second World War. Mr. Rowan discloses:[7]

Late in 1938 both general staff and secret service officers in France were aware that there must soon be war with Nazi Germany. We who admire France have been inclined to count too much on the instinctive patriotism of Frenchmen in an hour of national peril. The Nazi menace—Hitler's vastly superior war machine and the already organized *offensive* mechanism of espionage, sabotage and propaganda terrorization—was identified by many operatives of the French Secret Service. They understood and feared the untimely impact of destructive "fifth

7. *Op. cit.,* page 282.

column" strategy in the event of a war crisis. Yet influential "fifth columnists"—French Fascists—were allowed to hamper the secret service.

Populaire, a Paris socialistic newspaper, accused the French Government itself of making "possible the insulting audacity of Hitler's agents and, even more, of encouraging them."

"Scratch a political conspirator and you find a potential traitor," Mr. Rowan concludes. "Among the thousands of Cagoulards and their 'friends'—Frenchmen plotting to defeat the Popular Front by force of arms—it now seems certain that there were hundreds at least who took the next step and sold themselves to the German or Italian enemy. Time alone may divulge a documented record of this unparalleled multiplication of Benedict Arnolds."

The eagle also figures in quatrain 81 of the Fifth *Centurie:*

L'oyseau Royal sur la Cité Solaire,
Sept mois devant fera nocturne augure:
Mur d'Orient cherra, tonnerre esclaire,
Sept jours aux portes les ennemis à l'heure.

The royal bird over the solar city,
Will make a nocturnal augury seven months before:
The wall to the east will fall, thunder and lightning
The enemies at the gates in seven days on schedule.

As the lion is represented as the king of beasts, so the eagle is deemed the "royal bird." Paris, "City of Light," of course, is the "solar city." The French capital heard its first air-raid alarm during the day of September 5, 1939, but it was not until the seventh siren signal was sounded on November 13, 1939, that scouting eaglets of the German Luftwaffe flew over Paris by night. This "nocturnal augury" led the French Government, on November 16, 1939, to warn the Parisians to obey the air-raid precautions regarding complete blackouts.

Seven months and one day from the first nocturnal augury of the German eagles, on June 14, 1940, the steel-shod Nazi Juggernaut tooled into the City of Light unopposed by the betrayed armies of the Third French Republic.

The second half of the quatrain is explained by quotations from the World Almanac:

June 5—In France, at 4 A.M., a new battle of the Somme was begun when the Germans attacked Gen. Weygand's rearranged French Army along a 120-mile front from the Channel, at Abbeville, to Laon on the canal connecting the Aisne and Oise rivers. A great number of tanks, infantry and bombing planes was used. The German offensive spread in the three main sectors of Amiens, Peronne and Laon, and strove to drive converging spearheads toward Paris. It was then that the new system of Gen. Weygand was put into action for the first time. *The Maginot theory of fixed fortified positions was dropped* [italics mine] and defenses designed to absorb and break up tank attacks gradually were employed.

The Maginot Line, "the wall to the east" of the battling armies, had fallen completely because it had been outflanked by the *Donner und Blitzen* ("thunder and lightning") tactics of the modern Mongol invaders. Seven days after the battle of the Somme began, according to the almanac:

June 11—Guns of the approaching Germans were heard in Paris, which was befogged by the enemy's smokescreens. Barricades were thrown up in the streets. Waves of diving planes swept over the suburbs. The thoroughfares were clogged with civilians fleeing southward in the wake of the government officials and foreign diplomats. . . . The French provisional capital is at Tours.

The Government had left Paris at the close of the previous day on the advice of the French High Command. Nostradamus put it: "The enemies at the gates in seven days on schedule."

Even the construction of the Maginot Line was foreseen in the eightieth quatrain of the Fourth *Centurie:*

> *Pres du grand fleuve grand fosse terre egeste*
> *En quinze parts l'eau sera divisée:*
> *La cité prinse, feu, sang, cris, conflit meste,*
> *Et la plus part concerne au collisée.*

> *Near a great river a mighty fortress is hollowed out of the earth;*
> *It will divide the stream into fifteen segments:*
> *The conflict puts the captured city to fire, blood, cries*
> *And the greater part concerned is in the collision.*

The great river is interpreted as the Rhine. The Maginot system of fortifications extended 125 miles along the Franco-German frontier, which means the Rhine for most of that distance, from Switzerland to Luxembourg. Trenches "hollowed out of the earth" linked a series of casemates—shellproof vaults with cuspated embrasures through which cannon and machine guns were fired. A glorified trench system of steel and concrete, it was built so that the troops were hidden from enemy view.

Tons of cement and steel for more obstacles, traps, pits, trenches, gun emplacements, and field fortifications of all kinds, as well as concrete casements and blockhouses, were added to the line in 1940. This system of fortresses was divided into fifteen main sectors, any of which was devised to be shut off from the rest by flooding. The "mighty fortress" was avoided by the eternal enemy, who entered France through Belgium.

After the last terrible week of the Battle of France, Paris was occupied (June 14) by German troops. The latter advanced south rapidly after outflanking the Maginot Line. France's position became hopeless, with ten million poor and helpless refugees from Belgium and northern France jamming the roads and cities of central and southern France. It was the largest and most pitiable mass of human beings ever devastated by war.

The last two lines of the foregoing quatrain depict the result of the capture of Paris and the exodus of "the greater part" of its inhabitants "concerned in the collision." The previous paragraph gives a picture of the evacuation scene.

Quatrain 63 of the Second *Centurie* tells how André Maginot would not live to see his extensive system of fortifications circumvented:

> *Gaulois, Ausone bien peu subjuguera,*
> *Pau, Marne et Seine fera Perme l'urie:*
> *Qui le grand mur contre eux dressera,*
> *Du moindre au mur le grand perdra la vie.*

> *Italy will subjugate the French only a very little,*
> *Parma shall pollute the Po, Marne, and Seine:*
> *The great one who shall raise up the wall between them*
> *Shall lose his life from the lowliest at the wall.*

L'Ausonie (Ausonia) is poetic French for Italy. The Ausones were one of Italy's most ancient tribes. From them, southern Italy sometimes is called Ausonia. Italy stabbed France in the back on June 10, 1940, and the Italo-French armistice was signed on June 24. The "irresistible" Fascist legions failed to see much action during the fortnight of war, though they were faced by only four French divisions (sixty thousand troops) defending a formidable mountainous frontier.

Hence, the Italians subjugated "the French only a very little." Nostradamus uses Parma euphemistically for Italy. It requires little imagination to picture vulgar Italian soldiery of the army sent to occupy neighborly France making a latrine of the Marne and Seine rivers, or even to picture the reserves polluting their own Po in the north of Italy.

"Sergeant" Maginot died of typhoid fever in 1932, when he was fifty-five years old. The epicurean French Minister of War contracted his fatal disease from tainted oysters. The most favored locality for oyster beds is one where the currents are not too strong and where the sea bed is shelving and covered by mud and gravel. Oysters also attach themselves to rocks, reefs, and similar objects, where they remain until they are collected by dredging. Thus, their habitat is a wall beneath the sea.

So the veteran of Verdun, six feet and three inches tall, who raised "up the wall between" France and Germany, lost "his life from the lowliest at the wall." What could be lowlier than an oyster at the bottom of the sea?

Nostradamus also recounts, in quatrain 77 of the Second *Centurie*, how the Maginot Line would be broken through on the Saar front between Saint-Avold and Saaralben:

Par arcs, feux, poix et par feu repoussez,
Crys, hurlements sur la minuict ouys:
Dedans sont mis par les ramparts cassez,
Par cunicule les traditeurs fuis.

By bows, fire-irons, pitch and by flame repulsed,
Cries, howlings heard at midnight:

Those within are put broken onto the ramparts,
The traitors flee by subway passages.

By June 16, 1940, the German Army had cut through all except a few miles of the rear of the Maginot Line. Five mechanized divisions with big new flame-throwing tanks, supported by mobile siege guns, were employed with devastating effect against the French armored turrets. "Fire-irons, pitch and by flame," said Nostradamus.

Paul Reynaud, premier just before France fell, had warned his fellow-countrymen in the Chamber of Deputies (February, 1938): "There is not a single expert who will claim that any line of fortifications can resist indefinitely against an indefinite accumulation of tanks and artillery." The German General Staff proved that he was only too right.

The smashing of the Maginot Line was facilitated by Germany's Trojan horse operations within the fortress. There were traitors ready at key points along the sector where the tanks charged. These fifth columnists betrayed redoubts and turrets and saw to it that bridges were not blown up until the Nazi combat cars had roared past. By relaying true information falsely and misquoting official orders at crucial moments, they helped the Germans pierce the lines.

Maginot's chain of forts included an elaborate system of subterranean tunnels through which the traitors fled to safety while the garrison—all that was left of the broken French armies—manned the ramparts for the last stand against the Teutonic hordes. Despite all this confusion, half a million poilus managed to withdraw from the shattered Maginot Line.

There is yet another allusion to *Le Grand Maginot*, the nineteenth quatrain of the Seventh *Centurie:*

Le fort Nicene ne sera combatu,
Vaincu sera par rutilant metal,

Son faict sera un long temps débatu
Aux citadins estrange espouvantal.

The fort of victory will not be engaged,
It will be conquered by shining metal,
This fact will long be debated
Tremendously odd to the citizens.

The adjective Nicene has nothing to do here with the creed summarizing the chief tenets of the Christian faith. It is derived from the Greek noun *nikē* (victory). It is estimated that the original "fort of victory" and its weaker extension along France's northern frontier cost half a billion dollars. This extension was built after France's declaration of war against Germany and was not so formidable or costly as the original line, which took five years to build.

It is the Nostradamic suggestion that after the war it will be realized that it was clinking gold ("shining metal") which arranged that the original Maginot Line should not reach the sea and which developed the faulty disposition and defeat of the French armies. Marshal Pétain ignored the warnings of France's brilliant young General Staff officers that the millions squandered fortifying the national frontier would be expended more profitably by building up a mobile armored force, backed by the Foch doctrine of "the decisive attack."

Furthermore, it was the French General Staff's plan that a quarter of a million fortress troops and garrisoned specialists would be sufficient to man the Maginot Line fully in time of war, backed up by pooled armies of maneuver. The rough-spoken, halting Maginot had put his thick thumb on France's historic military weakness—a chronic inability to be ready to withstand the original brusque attack of the furious and eternal enemy across the Rhine. The "Sergeant" knew his histories of 1870 and 1914.

When the War Minister finally persuaded the Tardieu Government in 1929 to underwrite his project of anti-Teutonic insurance, his selling argument was that his great chain of forts would hold back the enemy while France, working night and day, rearmed to meet whatever new tactics Berlin's Great General Staff pulled out of the changeling *pickelhaube*. Maginot's costly dream proved to be a neophobic nightmare. The old maxim was borne out once again: France had entered the campaign of 1940 adequately prepared—for 1914.

"This fact will long be debated—tremendously odd to the citizens." Tremendously tragic, too.

A fatal break came on May 28, 1940, when King Leopold III of the Belgians, that Old Etonian, fagged out and in a black-and-blue funk, capitulated. The battle of Eton was lost on the playing fields of Waterloo.

Nostradamus relates what the British call "the miracle of Dunkirk" in quatrain 41 of the First *Centurie*:

Siège à Cité et de nuict assaillie,
Peu eschappes non loin de mer conflit,
Femme de joye retour fils defaillie,
Poison es lettres caché dedans le plic.

The besieged city is attacked at night;
Few escape the conflict not far from the sea,
The return of the son in the harlot's defeat,
Poison in the letters hidden within the pleat.

On May 29, 1940, the British Expeditionary Force held only a strip twenty-seven miles long on the Franco-Belgian coast with its besieged center at Dunkirk. Fog for two days and nights helped in holding the invested seaport by rearguard actions against the Nazi onslaught. Most of the troops caught in the Flanders pocket around the coastal base were evacuated in the teeth of the Luftwaffe. The feat was accomplished, as Nostradamus implies, because during the retreating operation fog was a screening factor limiting the effectiveness of the Nazi dive-bombers.

But the British Navy and English civilian yachtsmen were used to operating, if necessary, in pea-soupers almost as dark as night. The cream of the British Regular Army was removed from Dunkirk with minimum loss of life. On June 3 the London Admiralty announced that more than 335,000 men had been rescued after what the new Prime Minister, Winston Churchill, later called "the most colossal defeat in all British history." Thirty thousand Britons were killed, wounded, or missing. All equipment had been left behind, along with 900,000 French and Belgian soldiers either dead, injured, or captured. What a fearful price in lives the Germans paid for their victory the world will not know until all is over. Since Nostradamus said "few escape the conflict not far from the sea," the German losses must have been tremendous. One does not make an omelet without breaking a few eggs, Hitler once remarked without devastating originality.

The defeated harlot must be Nostradamus' cordially hated French Republic, to the Seer of Salon more vile than a Paris streetwalker. "Poison in the letters hidden within the pleat" is the prophet's essay on the Nazi credo indoctrinated by prisoners of war in Germany's stockades before "the return of the son" to his native France.

A stock of Nostradamic parable, the wolf signifying Germany, is employed in quatrain 33 of the Third *Centurie*:

En la cité où le loup entrera,
Bien près de là les ennemys seront:
Copie estrange grand pays gastera,
Aux monts et Alpes les amys passeront.

Into the city which the wolf shall enter,
Close by the enemies shall be:

A foreign force will despoil a great country,
The friends shall pass to the mountains and Alps.

The lycanthropic Teutons converged on Paris in two main thrusts—from the east and the north. When the occupying force entered Paris unopposed, the two invading forces swept on south. Thus, the enemies still were close by when the German tanks, motorized detachments, and plodding infantry paraded along the shuttered Champs Elysées.

In another week it was all over. France was prostrate and there was nothing to do but capitulate. With half her army destroyed and her lands overrun by the German steamroller, the great French Republic had ceased to exist. The bitter truth of the third line is a matter of current history.

On June 15, 1940, the day after the Nazis entered Paris, the retreat of the French troops left in the Maginot Line began. Many of these last-ditch fighters for France cut their way along the Vosges mountains and into Switzerland, where they were interned.

There are two Nostradamic verses alluding to the occupation of Paris:

VI-96

Grande Cité à soldats abandonnée,
One n'y eut mortel tumult si proche,
O qu'elle hideuse calamité s'approche
Fors une offense n'y sera pardonnee.

The great city abandoned to the soldiers
Never had mortal tumult been so near.
Oh, what a hideous calamity approaches,
No one there will be excused for any offense.

In Paris the local police and other French officials exercise an authority restricted by the German army of occupation. The last line tells how drastically the law is interpreted.

II-54

Par gent estrange et de Romains loingtaine,
Leur grand cité apres eau fort troublée:
Fille sans main, trop different domaine,
Prins, chef terreure n'avoit esté riblée.

By the strange nation and distant Romans,
Their great city greatly troubled about water:
The daughter without a hand, a very different estate,
Taken, the principal terror not having been civilized.

To Nostradamus, the Germans always are "the strange nation." Appending the tag-along *Duce* shows that the time is now. The second line may mean that there is or is to be a water scarcity in Paris, or may refer to the Axis machinations to grab what's left of the French Navy. Marianne no longer has a weapon (*main*) if the fleet is lost, while Vichy is a quite different estate for France, to say the least. In regard to the last line, let Bernard Fäy, French biographer, testify:

"In modern times, the real heir of the French Revolution was Adolf Hitler."

As for M. Fäy's usage of the past tense, *Le plus tôt sera le mieux.* The sixth quatrain of the Second *Centurie* is a tale of two cities:

Auprès des portes et dedans deux citez
Seront deux fléaux one n'aperceu un tel,
Faim dedans peste, de fer hors gens boutez,
Crier secours au Grand Dieu immortel.

Close to the gates and inside two cities
Will be two scourges never before so appearing;
Famine, pestilence within, folks booted out by hobnails
Shall implore succor from the great, immortal God.

With a stab into the dark, on the off-chance that Nostradamus is punning with *porte* (gate) and *port* (seaport), the two harassed cities may be named as Nantes and Bordeaux, which were not occupied after the Franco-Prussian War, but today are under Nazi garrisons.

In one of his summarizing sextets, *Prediction* No. 23, Nostradamus exhorts Paris to stand and be delivered of the oppressor:

Quand la grand nef, le prouë et gouvernal
Du franc pays et son esprit vital,
D'escueils et flots par la mer secoüée,
Six cens et sept et dix coeur assiégé
Et des reflus de son corps affligé,
Sa vie estant sur ce mal renouée.

When the great ship, the prow and helm
Of the free country and its vital spirit,
Of reefs and tides shaken off by the sea,
Six hundred and seven and ten heart-besieged
And of the ebb tides of its body afflicted,
Its life being renewed after this evil.

The arms of the City of Paris are a white galley on a red ground and above this are three golden fleurs-de-lis on a blue chief.

Here, in the fourteenth quatrain of the Third *Centurie*, is the octogenarian Marshal Pétain:

Par le rameau du vaillant personnage,
De France infime, par le pere infelice:

Honneurs, riches, travail en son vieil age,
Pour avoir creu conseil d'homme nice.

By the bough of the valiant person,
Of lowest France, by the unhappy father:
Honors, wealth, toil in his old age,
For having believed the counsel of a trickster.

The last line yields yet another Nostradamic trick playing with Hitler's character. Deriving *nice* from the Greek *nikē* gives "man of victory," but pronouncing it *niche* turns it into "man of tricks."

In the following verse, the ninetieth quatrain of the Sixth *Centurie*, the French debacle is described in no very flattering words:

L'honnissement puant abominable,
Apres le faict sera félicité:
Grand excuse pour n'estre favorable,
Qu'à paix Neptune ne sera incité.

The stinking, abominable disgrace
Will be applauded after the deed
The great excuse for not being favorable
Will be that Neptune has not been goaded into peace.

According to the terms of the Franco-German armistice, more than half of France remains under German occupation, including all Channel and Atlantic ports. What was left of the French Army was ordered to lay down its arms and surrender all its stores, equipment, and munitions. All the industries and resources of France were impressed to assist Germany in the war against the thoroughly aroused British Empire. Thus France, willy-nilly, but mostly willy, as far as the Vichy Government was concerned, became part of Hitler's new European order and a German ally against Britain.

Berlin's glib excuse for these harsh terms was that England, the great maritime overlord (Neptune), had not been frightened into suing for peace.

The next stanza, quatrain 33 of the Seventh *Centurie*, hits it on the head:

Par fraude regne, forces expolier,
La classe obsesse, passages à l'espie
Deux faincts amis se viendront t'allier,
Esveiller haine de long temps assouipie.

By fraud a realm and forces are despoiled,
The fleet beset, passages to the spy:
Two feigned friends will come to be allied,
A hatred for a long time lulled is aroused.

Write your own ticket here. Could the realm despoiled by fraud be France, sapped by internal dissension? When Marshal Pétain and his motley crew of defeatists began truckling to Hitler, it became imperative that the British Navy seize or sink as many of the capitulating French warships as possible to prevent a German grab. On July 3, 1940, the Royal Navy forestalled Nazi seizure of many powerful French warships by attacking the squadron off the harbor of Mers-el-Kebir, naval base for Oran. The French warships beset in English and Scottish ports included two battleships, two cruisers, several submarines, eight destroyers, and almost two hundred naval auxiliaries. The rest of the French Navy was bottled up in various ports, British and foreign. "Passages to the spy" describes fifth-column work.

The two feigned friends could be almost any two European countries; they all hate one another but are ever-ready to pretend friendship when it is politic to do so. As a suggestion, it might be recalled that England and France waged a conflict which continued off and on seven hundred years, while that magnum of champagne labeled *Entente Cordiale Gout Français* is the vintage of 1904 and has gone slightly flat (little champagne more than twenty years old is fit to drink).

There are two more quatrains detailing the intrigues revolving around the fate of French sea power:

IX-79

Le chef de classe, par fraude stratageme,
Fera timides sortir de leurs galleres,
Sortis meurtris chef renieux de cresme,
Puis par l'embusche luy rendront les saleres.

The chief of the fleet, by deceit and ruse,
Will make the timid leave their warships;
The chief, denied the picked men, left bruised,
Then they will give him the worst of it by an ambush.

VII-37

Dix envoyez, chef de nef mettre à mort,
D'un adverty, en classe guerre ouverte:
Confusion chef, l'un se picque et mord,
Leryn, Stechades nefs, cap dedans la nerte.

Ten having been sent forth to put the chief of the ship to death
Forewarned by one, strife begins in the fleet:
Confusion master, one stings himself and dies,
The Isles of Lérins and Hyères ships, the captain in the brig.

The Isles of Lérins, much visited by Riviera excursionists, are in front of Cannes. The three Isles of Hyères, known to the Romans as the Stoechades, are off the Provençal coast and not far from Toulon, one of France's chief naval stations.

Premier Daladier made Jean-François Darlan the French Admiral of the Fleet in 1939. François Pietri, a former Minister of Marine, praised the new naval chief as "not only extremely intelligent, but a tireless worker," adding that Admiral Darlan, "while prudent, took any chance when necessary."

Perhaps that is why Free French leaders regard Admiral Darlan as "twice as dangerous" as that true chameleon, Pierre Laval. Last summer immense "Darlan s'est vendu" ("Darlan has sold himself") notices were scrawled in chalk on billboards and factory walls in German-occupied France. Anti-Vichy Frenchmen warn that Admiral Darlan is no friend of the British and that he is a twister of boundless ambition who hopes to step into Marshal Pétain's shoes to lead a revived French nation.

Darlan must dream of the day he will be in Pétain's place. In his mind he already is. A speech he made at Uriage on June 2, 1941, was studded with phrases such as "my fleet," "the policy that I have chosen," and "I have decided."

Americans who have returned from France recently report that Darlan's ambitions have been fired by the Nazi masters of the unhappy Gallic nation. Germans have led him on to envisage a grand career as a leader of the new order in Nazified Europe which, when it suits their purpose, Berlin pictures as a united entity wherein France "will find her real place," with "a great French admiral" winning a great naval victory over Britain, such a victory as only the French fleet, the Nazis whisper, could hope to achieve.

Lest this grapevine report be thought exaggerated, readers well may digest the words of a recent article in *L'Illustration,* probably the most important French periodical. This particular issue portrays Admiral Darlan on the cover, in full-dress uniform, with another photograph on the principal inside page showing him in mufti. Jacques de Lesdain's accompanying article declaims that "the principal thing today is the downfall of the power of the English and the entry of France into the European fatherland."

While Admiral Darlan preens as the putative hero of a great naval battle, reversing the misfortune which befell Napoleon's Admiral Villeneuve at Trafalgar, it must not be forgotten that there are others in the French Navy who put honor higher than ambitious expediency. It is not sufficiently known that the new battleship *Richelieu*, based at Dakar, received an order from Admiral Darlan to return to Brest, but the sailors, fearing that their ship was to be surrendered to the Germans, refused to obey. An attempt to replace them by the crews of three destroyers failed completely. Time may bring a more explicit account of the French Navy's role in the sorry game of power politics.

Nor does the octogenarian Marshal Pétain appear to be destined for any niche except one in the Hall of Infamy, if quatrain 61 of the Fourth *Centurie* has been identified correctly:

> *Le vieux mocqué et privé de sa place*
> *Par l'estranger qui le subornera;*
> *Mains de son fils mangées devant sa face*
> *Les frères à Chartres, Orléans, Rouen trahyra.*

> *The oldster will be mocked and deprived of his place*
> *By the stranger who corrupted him:*
> *The hands of his son eaten before his face*
> *He will betray the brothers to Chartres, Orléans, and Rouen.*

Isn't "the stranger who corrupted him" Hitler? What of the third line? Perhaps the son is the French Army, the republic's mailed fist, which was gnawed to flesh and bone by the monstrous German stegosaurus. Once the poilus adored Pétain because of his protective doctrine: "Fire kills."

Stanton B. Leeds put the father-and-son relation this way in *These Rule France:*[8]

> The army is made up of all its soldiers, and what revivified the French army . . . was *his* conception of war. . . . He stopped mass murder. . . . For this the French were grateful, naturally, and Pétain became a symbol of the policy that spared men. As a symbol he was admired. . . . All the public really knew that the army admired Pétain.
>
> He symbolized the army, but he also stood for the past, and the past foreshadows the future.

Possibly Nostradamus "foreshadows the future," too, in the last line. A habit of the Seer of Salon is to make places appear to be doing things, generally meaning that the peers and prelates who take their titles from these places are doing the actions bespoken. The last French prince to use the Chartres title was the grandson of King Louis-Philippe and second son of Ferdinand, Duke of Orléans. Robert, Duke of Chartres, is known to American history from his service on the staff of the Federal Army in the War Between the States.

Chartres was made a duchy by Francis I and given as an appanage to the Dukes of Orléans. Hence, the title of Duke of Chartres was used by the eldest son of the Duke of Orléans. These titles now belong to Henry, Duke of Guise, formerly the Count of Paris, who is the Orléanist pretender to the French throne. Many think that he will be the conquering king predicted by Nostradamus. He is the grandson of the American Civil War fighter.

The genealogical background accounts for Chartres and Orléans. Rouen was the capital of the Norman duchy. The king of England

---

8. Copyright, 1940; used by special permission of the publishers, The Bobbs-Merrill Company.

was sovereign over the Channel Islands as Duke of Normandy. This seagirt dukedom is the only English territory occupied by the Nazis (June 30, 1940). The inference, therefore, is that "the oldster" will betray "the brothers" (Hitler and Mussolini?) to the Chartres-Orléanist faction and to the English in revenge for the smarting defeat of France's Army and for the seizure of the vestige of William the Conqueror's French possessions.

The transfer of the French Government to Vichy probably is the subject of quatrain 49 of the Third *Centurie:*

> *Regne Gaulois tu seras bien changé,*
> *En lieu estrange est translaté l'empire,*
> *En autres loix et moeurs seras rangé,*
> *Roüen et Chartres te feront bien du pire.*

> *Gallic realm thou shalt be greatly changed,*
> *The empire is transferred into a strange place,*
> *Thou shalt be regimented with other laws and customs,*
> *Rouen and Chartres shall do much the worse for thee.*

The reference to England and the Orléans royalist is repeated in the last line.

Another allusion to Marshal Pétain has been inferred from quatrain 85 of the Tenth *Centurie:*

> *Le vieil tribun au point de la trehemide*
> *Sera pressée captif ne delivrer,*
> *Le vieil non vieil, le parlant timide,*
> *Par legitime à ses amis livrer.*

> *The venerable tribune on the point of palsy*
> *Will be pressed not to hand over the captive,*

The oldster not venerable, speaking timid evil,
To play traitor to his friends lawfully.

Perhaps "the captive" is the French fleet, which came closer to Nazi fingers on August 12, 1941, when Marshal Pétain committed the Vichy regime to full collaboration with Germany a few hours after Admiral Darlan, his vice-premier, had received supreme military powers. The palsied patriarch declared that he had conferred these exceptional powers on his political heir, "the oldster not venerable, speaking timid evil," despite the fact that French opinion "never was always favorable nor always fair" to the Admiral.

When Darlan was placed in charge of general organization of national defense and the distribution and use of the armed forces and obtained supreme inspection rights over the army, navy, and air force, these concentrated powers left his hands freer to dicker with the Nazis for "collaboration." Thus, he may "play traitor to his friends lawfully."

To Ludwell Denny, the Scripps-Howard columnist, "the reason Hitler is hastening the Nazification of France, through promotion of his puppet, Darlan, is clear. Hitler needs the French navy and the North African and West African bases for the battle of the South Atlantic aimed at the strangulation of England which failed in the North Atlantic." But Mr. Denny ponders: "Will Gen. Weygand take Hitler's orders through Darlan, or will the French army in Africa march to such orders if given? And can Admiral Darlan be sure even of his navy?"

Nostradamus seems to have said that he cannot.

Two million French prisoners of war in Nazi concentration camps may be seen in the first quatrain of the Tenth *Centurie:*

L'ennemy, l'ennemy foy promise,
Ne se tiendra, les captifs retenus:

Prins prême mort, et le reste en chemise,
Donnant le reste pour estre secourus.

The enemy, the enemy will not abide by the promise he gave,
The prisoners will be kept back:
The overwhelmed taken dead and the rest in their shirts,
Giving the others to be relieved.

A year after the Franco-German armistice, the Germans had released only fifteen thousand Frenchmen, veterans of both the 1914–1918 and 1939–1940 wars. A few sick and wounded soldiers were freed along with a limited number of fathers to whom a fourth child had been born while they were imprisoned. The old Marshal had relegated fair treatment to his "generous foe" who was going to make Europe such a nice place for everyone!

It is estimated that those "overwhelmed, taken dead" in the Battle of France totaled eighty thousand. Prisoners of war sent back from Germany to France received "Huntziger suits" of blue denim work shirts and pantaloons and fifty francs. If they could not find jobs, they were sent to toil in French labor camps—out of the fire into the frying pan again.

Hitler's refusal to heed his promise of the wholesale release of French prisoners gives Berlin a club to hold over the Vichy Government's head. The Germans insist that the captives cannot be freed until the French have learned to obey Vichy completely.

Mention is made of France's hunger in quatrain 63 of the Fifth *Centurie:*

De vaine emprinse l'honneur induë plainte,
Gallots errants, par latins froid, faim, vagues:
Non loin du Tymbre de sang la terre tainte
Et sur humains seront diverses plagues.

Honor complains unduly of the vain enterprise,
Frenchmen wandering because of Latins, cold and hungry;
Waves not far from the Tiber, the earth bloodstained
And on humans there shall be various plagues.

Most complaints from Vichy take care to mention that India-rubber quality, Honor. Free French forces fight under the motto *Honneur, Patrie.* The former word is missing from Vichy's slogan.

Quatrain 21 of the Fourth *Centurie* may refer to General Charles de Gaulle, leader of the Free French movement:

Le changement sera fort difficile,
Cité, province au change gain sera:
Coeur haut, prudent mis, chassé luy habile
Mer; terre, peuple son estat changera.

The change will be most difficult,
City and province shall gain through change:
A prudent man of high heart chased overseas by the cunning
    one;
People shall change in estate on land.

Some notion of the principles inspiring the Vichy Government may be gleaned from a recent speech by Marshal Pétain envisioning "a hierarchy of families, professions, communes, administrative responsibilities and spiritual families federated to form a nation and animated by one movement, one soul and one idea, with a view to producing a hierarchy of men selected by services rendered to the community, of whom a small number will be councillors, a few will give orders and at the top a chief will rule."

"Goodby to the sovereignty of the people and to the ridiculous system which makes authority depend on the counting of votes," jubilantly wrote Charles Maurras, traditionalist editor of *L'Action Française*, who has spent his lifetime fighting democracy. The young Count of Paris broke with Maurras in 1937, though the Maurras creed is "rule from above."

Just how "city and province shall gain through change" of the Maurras variety remains to be seen. Before the French Revolution, France was divided into provinces. In the older regions the government and laws were more or less uniform. Those added to the kingdom during the four hundred years preceding the Revolution had assemblies levying separate taxes. These newer provinces also enjoyed special privileges denied to the older subdivisions. Provinces and privileges were abolished in 1789. Instead, departments were set up, with elective local governments. Consequently, the rule of France was highly decentralized.

Marshal Pétain definitely ordered on August 20, 1941, the reorganization of France along medieval provincial lines. He instructed his National Council to create virtually autonomous provincial regimes, ruled by governors whose authority and prestige would be incontestable. The new set-up carried out one of the petulant patriarch's favorite ideas of "centralized decentralization"—authoritative local governments subject to the central state authority only for general policies. At the head of each re-created province is to be "a governor, a high personality representing the Chief of State." Provincial councils are to be simply advisory bodies "in no case transformed into political assemblies."

This authentic manifestation of France's latent medievalism was formulated by Lucien Romier, long editor of the Paris *Figaro* and advocate of "the restoration of the ancient peasantry." When Romier returned to France in 1927 after visiting the United States, he wrote that America's greatest lack was a disciplined peasant class. He found that American farmers were much too inclined to become individualistic businessmen, and he called our country too diffuse for political discipline and impermeable to a superior culture. Such were the findings of a French editor whose policy is a mélange of appease-porridge-cold feet and Pied-piping-hot Fascism.

When a coterie of French defeatists capitulated abjectly to the Nazis in the belief that *L'Albion Perfide*, too, was doomed, General de Gaulle escaped to England to rally France's empire to carry on the fight. A few days after the first German break-through at Sedan, General de Gaulle had persuaded Premier Reynaud to continue the war despite the arguments of Weygand, Pétain, and others. The young French general flew to London to tell Prime Minister Churchill that France would see it through. When General de Gaulle returned, General Weygand refused to shake hands with him. When Reynaud lost heart and resigned in Pétain's favor, General de Gaulle flew to London for good.

It may be that quatrain 76 of the Fifth *Centurie* carries on the de Gaullist saga:

En lieu libre tendra son pavillon,
Et ne voudra en citez prendre place:
Aix, Carpen, l'Isle volce, mont Cavaillon
Par tout ces lieux abolira la trasse.

In a free place he will pitch his tent,
And he will not take his place in cities:
Aix, Carpentras, the Volces' island, Mount Cavaillon
Throughout all these places he will abolish the worthless.

General de Gaulle has rallied two-fifths of the French colonial empire to his cause of freedom, but there are few large cities within his territory. Aix was the capital of Provençe; Carpentras and Mount Cavaillon are in the Venaissin, near Avignon; while the Volces were a Gaulish tribe dwelling directly across the Rhone, in the enclave between the Ardeche and Gard—hence, on an island bounded by rivers.

The hundredth quatrain of the Third *Centurie* begins with a clearer allusion to General de Gaulle:

> *Entre Gaulois le dernier honoré,*
> *D'homme ennemy sera victorieux,*
> *Force et terroir en moment exploré,*
> *D'un coup de traict quand mourra l'envieux,*

> *Among Gauls the last honored*
> *Will be victorious over the enemy man;*
> *Force and terrain explored at the moment,*
> *When the envious will die by an arrow shot.*

General de Gaulle may be called fairly the last-honored among the Gauls (no pun intended). The day after the Germans broke through at Sedan, Colonel de Gaulle, commander of the 507th Regiment of combat cars, was made a general to lead a hastily assembled armored brigade. The insane jealousy of the bureaucratic *État-Major* could pin him in a colonelcy no longer. *Le Général* has the seven-league advantage of being the one French officer who knew enough about what was wrong with the army to write two prophetic books about it. Between 1932 and 1936 he wrote *Au Fil de l'Epée* (translated as *The Philosophy of Command*), which called for individualized initiative by commanders instead of the French traditionalist method of fighting only according to previous plan, and *Vers l'Armée de Métier (The Army of the Future)*, which broke completely with preconceived French tactics.

He foresaw (1934) this army of the future moving on caterpillar treads and warned that the Maginot Line was limited in depth, leaving northern France exposed. He predicted France's defeat through concentrating on "the supreme value of the defensive." He discounted France's stridently touted morale—"neither bravery nor skill can any longer achieve anything except as functions of equipment." Marshal Pétain sneered at "such witticisms" and General Weygand was provoked by the tank tactician's "evil remarks."

While France was sitting out the war in January, 1940, Colonel de Gaulle again dared to speak. From his tank command in Lorraine, he sent a seventeen-page report to General Gamelin, Premier Daladier, and twenty other higher-ups warning: "The Maginot Line, however reinforced, can be crossed. The defender who limits himself to resisting in a fixed position with antiquated weapons is doomed."

Germany was the first nation to honor Charles de Gaulle when it stole from his book the tank strategy which won the Battle of France. England and the remaining free nations have paid him homage. France gave him her last grudging honor when he received his general officer's stars on the battlefield.

De Gaullists slip into France at every opportunity to scout out the strength of the German forces of occupation and to map possible terrain for the coming of a liberating army cut to *Le Général's* pattern. Which of the envious ones who betrayed France through jealousy will die in the twinkling of an arrow shot?

Another verse, the ninth quatrain of the Fourth *Centurie*, does not clear up that last point:

Le chef du camp au milieu de la presse,
D'un coup de flesche sera blessé aux cuisses,
Lors que Genève en larmes et en de detresse
Sera trahy par Lozen et Souysses.

The chief of the army in the middle of the throng,
Will be wounded in the thighs by an arrow shot,
When Geneva, in tears and in distress,
Will be betrayed by Lausanne and the Swiss.

Some Nostradamians believe that this quatrain portends a revolution in Switzerland; others think that it signifies a German invasion of Switzerland. It is placed here only because it repeats the "arrow shot" remark of the hundredth quatrain of the Third *Centurie*.

The next, quatrain 71 of the Fifth *Centurie,* calls to mind the tragically bitter humor of grim jests a year ago when Adolf Hitler discovered that the Luftwaffe's wings were not water wings:

> *Par la fureur d'un qui attendra l'eau,*
> *Par la grand rage tout l'exercite esmeu,*
> *Chargé de nobles a dix-sept batteaux,*
> *Au long du Rosne tard messager venu.*

> *By the fury of one who will reach the water,*
> *By the great rage all the maneuver confused,*
> *Burdened with the nobles in seventeen boats,*
> *A messenger comes late along the Rhone.*

Fureur, for Nostradamus, is a fair pun on *Fuehrer*: Anglice, it's Furor. France's Channel and Atlantic coasts passed under German control on June 27, 1940. The Nazi *Fuehrer* showed his rage the following July 19 when he prophesied "that this struggle, if it continues, can end only in the complete annihilation of one of the two adversaries. Churchill may believe it will be Germany. I know it will be Britain." Twenty miles of water had nullified a land power's grand maneuver.

History will have to clear up the second half of the quatrain at a later date, when censorship has been lifted. The French squadron at Alexandria, spiked by agreement with the British Admiralty on July 9, 1940, included one battleship and four cruisers. Some of the eighteen cruisers which France had when she concluded the armistice with Germany, London reported at that time, remained in French hands and "will have to be watched."

A little arithmetic shows that the total of "seventeen boats" is quite a possible number for those beset by the British Navy. That may have been the burden of a secret message sent from the Toulon naval base and relayed "along the Rhone" to Vichy. It must have been too late to do Hitler's projected invasion of England any good.

There are implications of the north African Mediterranean campaigns in quatrain 68 of the Fourth *Centurie*:

> *En l'an bien proche eslongné de Vénus,*
> *Les deux plus grands de l' Asie et d'Affrique:*
> *Du Rin et Hister qu'on dira sont venus,*
> *Cris, pleurs à Malte et costé à Lygustique.*

> *In the year very near the greatest elongation of Venus,*
> *The two greatest powers of Asia and Africa:*
> *It will be said that they have come from the Rhine and Danube,*
> *Cries and tears at Malta and a broadside at Genoa.*

By "greatest elongation" is meant the greatest apparent angular distance from the sun; a planet then usually is situated most favorably for observation. In 1941, Venus will be at greatest elongation, east of the sun at forty-seven degrees, sixteen minutes, at noon on November 23. Mystagogues who interpret the Great Pyramid of Giza prophetically predict that November 21, 1941, will witness a spectacular development of this war. We shall see soon enough if Napoleon's bombastic speech, "forty centuries look down on you," was made almost under the shadow of a pyramidal oracle.

Certainly those who "have come from the Rhine and Danube" have traveled far this year. There are German armies on the march in Russia and Africa and Japanese allies swarming over Asia. Doubtless many Axis air raids upon Malta have evoked "cries and tears" and British battleships bombarded Genoa on February 9, 1941, pouring thundering broadsides into the hapless port.

Lygustique is used for Genoa by poetic license, being derived from the old Roman and modern Italian province of Liguria, whereof Genoa is the capital.

The Hitler-Mussolini alliance described in quatrain 23 of the Fifth *Centurie* includes a clear reference to the fall of Fascist Italy's "great African" empire:

> *Les deux contents seront unis ensemble*
> *Quand la pluspart à Mars sera conjoint:*
> *Le grand d'Affrique en effrayeur et tremble,*
> *Duumvirat par la classe desjoint.*

> *The two satisfied ones will be united together*
> *When the greatest part will be joined to Mars:*
> *The great African is in fear and trembling,*
> *The duumvirate divided by the fleet.*

When Mussolini muscled into the final shakedown of France, he almost seemed to be a big-time gambler betting on a certain winner. Now he looks like an extinct hyaenodon trailing a saber-tooth tiger. Parenthetically, the hyaenodon was not a swift runner or very efficient in the capture of prey. While probably a savage fighter, it doubtless subsisted chiefly as a carrion-feeder and scavenger.

"When the greatest" of the Axis partners was "joined to Mars" against France, Mussolini signed away Italy's birth-right for a mess of ersatz pottage. Soon, the Fascist imperium was "in fear and trembling" when the British Navy began closing the inland Mediterranean by cutting it off from the rest of the world by blockade. Instead of slashing Britain's aorta of empire between Sicily and Tunisia, Mussolini found that the British had blocked him from transporting reinforcements and supplies to Libya.

So was "the duumvirate divided by the fleet."

The next set of stanzas foretells how Yugoslavia and Greece

would fall into the Nazi maw like two ripened clusters of grapes. The first of these, quatrain 26 of the Fifth *Centurie,* covers the events leading to the ousting of Prince-Regent Paul:

> *Le gent Esclave par un heur martial,*
> *Viendra en haut degré tant eslevé:*
> *Changeront Prince, naistre un provincial,*
> *Passer la mer copie aux monts levé.*

> *The Slavonic race, by a martial stroke,*
> *Will become stirred up to such a degree*
> *They will change their Prince, born a provincial,*
> *A force set up in the mountains to pass overseas.*

By using Esclave for Slavonic, Nostradamus has employed a pun to name the south Slavs and tell what fate had in store for them. As a French noun, *esclave* means slave, while as an adjective it signifies slavish. French dictionaries still translate L'Esclavonie as Slavonia, which so recently was enslaved by the Nazis. The Byzantine Greeks gave the name of Esklabinos to the Slavonic peoples of the Balkans. Medieval Latin rendered this as Sclavonia.

Under the Austro-Hungarian Empire, the area between the Drave and the Save rivers, inhabited principally by Serbs, formed part of the semiautonomous province of Croatia-Slavonia. With the reorganization of the semifeudal Hapsburg states after the First World War, Slavonia became Yugoslavia's autonomous province of Syrmia.

Prince Paul, the regent deposed in a *coup d'état* by the Serb generals, can be described correctly as a provincial because his mother was a Russian and he was born at St. Petersburg. As a matter of fact, his birthplace and heredity counted against him in Yugoslavia, since the masses always had refused to accept him as a real Serb.

On the early morning of Palm Sunday, April 6, 1941, the German juggernaut invaded Yugoslavia and Greece. One smashing blow followed another. On the fourth day, Salonika was taken and two days later the Germans had established contact with the sorry Italian lot in Albania, thus isolating the Yugoslav armies from the Greek and British forces to the south. By the ninth day the Greco-British troops began to fall back from one line to another, fighting desperately against German pressure and with their backs to the sea. Greece, and, later, Crete, became two more Dunkirks for those Britishers lucky enough to escape.

Thus the British troops sent up into the Pindus mountains were forced "to pass overseas." This particular quatrain had been considered a brilliant forecast of the Napoleonic campaign into Russia until the retreat from Moscow. Others have attempted to interpret it in connection with the current Russo-German War. Its naturally complete dovetailing with the drive into the Balkans in the spring of 1941 should quash further Procrustean efforts.

Italy's entrance into the war has meant the extension of military activities into the Mediterranean, Africa, and the Balkans. The main Axist strategy is to threaten Britain's proverbial life line—the sea communications between England and the Afro-Indian empire. Lusting for a Roman triumph, Fascist Italy's tinsel Caesar took what future historians may write down as this war's most fateful decision—he invaded Greece, as Nostradamus put it in quatrain 83 of the First *Centurie*:

La gent estrange divisera butins
Saturn et Mars son regard furieux,
Horrible strage aux Toscans et Latins,
Grecs qui seront à frapper curieux.

The strange race will divide the plunder,
Saturn and Mars his raging look,
Horrible strife to the Tuscans and Latins,
Greeks who will be onlookers to be smitten.

Obviously, Italy is the weakest link in the chain Hitler is using to survey the boundaries of Greater Germany. The look on the face of the saturnine, warlike Nazi *Fuehrer* must have been raging indeed when it became clear that Italy's armies invading Greece were in desperate straits. If the Germans—always "the strange race" to Nostradamus—were to obtain any plunder to divide with the Italians, with the usual lion's share destined for the Teutonic beast, Hitler had to go to the rescue of his worthless partner in crime.

It was "horrible strife to the Tuscans and Latins" of *Il Duce's* legions until the full weight of "the strange race" smote the courageous Greeks, who had hoped to be bystanders in the Second World War. The British political object had been to weld Greece, Yugoslavia, and Turkey into an anti-Axis Balkan bloc. The third quatrain of the Third *Centurie* is suggestive of the diplomacy preceding the Greek campaign:

> *Mars et Mercure et l'argent joint ensemble*
> *Vers le midy extrême siccité.*
> *Au fond d'Asie on dit a terre tremblé,*
> *Corinthe, Ephèse lors en perplexité.*

> *Mars and Mercury and silver joined together*
> *Toward the midland extreme drought.*
> *In the depths of Asia they report an earthquake,*
> *Corinth and Ephesus then in perplexity.*

Mars symbolizes war, Mercury represents intrigue, while silver is the traitor's Judas price. It was reported during the spring that Middle Europe's crops were expected to be well under the average because of the dry weather in that midland area. When the British Navy won its smashing victory over an Italian squadron south of Cape Matapan, Foreign Minister Matsuoka of Japan was visiting the Axist capitals. Since Nostradamus frequently uses an earthquake to indicate war, the visiting Nipponese fireman's reports to Tokio, "in the depths of Asia," may be juxtaposed into the third line.

As the result of its defiance of Rome, Corinth was utterly destroyed in 146 B.C. by Mummius, and "the light of all Greece" was extinguished for a century. It was rebuilt by Julius Caesar and soon rose again to be a populous and prosperous city. Its connection with earthquakes makes the Nostradamic use of Corinth as a symbol for all Greece quite likely. The site of Corinth was occupied by a small town, Gortho, laid in ruins by an earthquake in 1858 and New Corinth was almost destroyed by another temblor on April 23, 1928.

Ephesus, ancient city of Asia Minor, was situated on the Cayster, near its mouth. The river falls into the Gulf of Scala Nova, on Asia Minor's western coast. Since it became the chief mart and metropolis of Asia Minor and was the administrative capital of the Roman province of Asia, Nostradamus may be held justified in using Ephesus as a synonym for Ankara (Angora), Turkey's new capital. Toward the end of the thirteenth century, the Turks erected a new city, Ayasalouk, on the site of Ephesus.

Both Greece and Turkey were perplexed when it became evident that, with the Italian chestnuts on fire, the Nazi gorilla was thumping its chest in earnest. The downfall of Greece is the subject of quatrain 31 of the Fifth *Centurie*:

Par terre Attique chef de la Sapience,
Qui de présent est la rose du monde:
Pour ruyné et sa grand préminence,
Sera subite et naufragée des ondes.

Into the Attic land, hub of wisdom,
Which is the rose of the world for the present:
Toward ruin and her great preeminence
Will be subdued and wrecked by the waves.

Athens, capital both of Greece and of the nomarchy of Attica, frequently has been called the "hub of wisdom" and "rose of the world." Greece has been "subdued and wrecked by the waves" of greedy Axis invaders.

Frederick Crane, an American oil export manager who returned from Athens recently, reported that the Germans were sending vast quantities of Greek food to Germany and even were taking over the Greek canning industry, with the result that the Greeks faced a winter of starvation. He also said that three similar-sized flags— Greek, German, and Italian—flew atop the Acropolis, with the white Greek cross on a blue field in the middle. The Greeks would look at the flags, Mr. Crane remarked, and say: "Christ hung between two thieves."

The result of this wholesale looting is told in the ninetieth quatrain of the Fifth *Centurie*:

Dans les Cyclades en Perinthe et Larisse,
Dedans Sparte tout le Pelloponesse;
Si grand famine, peste, par faux connisse,
Neuf mois tiendra et tout le cherronesse.

In the Cyclades, in Perinthus and Larissa,
Within Sparta and all the Peloponnesus;
Such a great famine and plague by false knowledge,
Nine months will grip the entire peninsula.

The Cyclades are an archipelago in the Aegean Sea and Perinthus was an important city in ancient Thrace, while Larissa is the capital city of Thessaly. The purpose of the first two lines is to show how completely pillage and hunger are to cover Greece. "Plague by false knowledge" is an accurate rendition of the Axis propaganda poison. The last line foretells how long this savagery will last. Confirmation of this prophecy was printed in *The New York Times* for July 2, 1941, in a dispatch from Ankara by C. L. Sulzberger, who quoted travelers returning from Greece as saying that "the Greek people face an unprecedented famine ... since there is such a shortage that plague and famine are already beginning to break out." Other details were:

During the war Greece never had more than two weeks' food reserves. Not only has this disappeared long ago, but the rich Macedonian and Thracian wheat lands have been taken from Greece and given to Bulgaria. Ruined communications systems have not been restored, livestock has dwindled. Numerous cases of children dying of hunger have been reported. Women waiting outside the tragically empty stores for their tiny bread rations are frequently seen to faint from weakness. Underfed horses have from time to time dropped dead before their wagons, and dogs and cats lie dead in the streets of Athens.

The lack of bread is the greatest disaster in Greece. Bread is an absolute necessity to the Greek peasant, who has little else but olives, cheese and fish to live on. Today the daily bread ration in Athens, Patras and Salonika is sixty drams—one-tenth the peace-time norm required by the Greek workman.

No fruits are available to the city dwellers. Sugar is almost nonexistent. Virtually all beans and lentils were eaten up by the armies in Albania. Tons of potatoes are rotting in Argos because there is no way of distributing them to Athens.

There are relatively few draft animals, since many horses, mules and donkeys were killed in the war in Albania. This also reduces the acreage of field cultivation.

It is reported that at the Island of Santorin there is nothing to eat but tomatoes and chick peas; at Samos only grapes and olive oil. For more than thirty days there has been no bread in Santorin.

If this famine began in July, it should last until March, 1942. Does this presage an evacuation of Greece by beaten Axists?

In the ninetieth quatrain of the Ninth *Centurie* Nostradamus, with uncanny accuracy, foresaw the incredibly fantastic flight of Rudolf Hess, third ranking Nazi and an official Hitler heir, to Scotland:

Un grand Capitaine de la grand Germanie
Se viendra rendre par simulé secours
Au Roy des Roys ayde de Pannonie,
Que sa revolte fera de sang grand cours.

A great captain of the great Germany
Will come to present himself with feigned rescue
Help of Pannonia for the King of Kings,
So his rebellion will cause great bloodshed.

When Rudolf Hess parachuted onto a Scottish croft on May 11, 1941, he wore the sky-blue uniform of the German Air Force with a captain's shoulder straps and the yellow collar patches of the flying personnel. His descent "upon this blasted heath" evoked this transposition of characters from Scene III, Act I, of *Macbeth*:

Donner und Blitzen. Enter the three Nazis.
    No. 1 NAZI. Where has thou been, sister?
    No. 2 NAZI. Killing swine.
    No. 1 NAZI. Sister, where thou?
    No. 3 NAZI. A sailor's wife (Britannia) had (Italian) chestnuts in her lap, and munched, and munched, and munched: "Give me," quoth I:—"Aroint thee, witch!" the rump-fed ronyon cries. Her husband's (John Bull) to Aleppo (Syria) gone, master o' the Tiger: But in a sieve (parachute) I'll thither sail, and, like a rat without a tail, I'll do, I'll do, and I'll do.

No. 1 Nazi. I'll give thee a wind (Goebbels?).

No. 3 Nazi. Thou art kind.

No. 2 Nazi. And I another (Gayda?).

No. 3 Nazi. I myself have all the other (Nazis); and the very ports they blow, all the quarters that they know i' the shipman's card. I'll drain him dry as hay: sleep shall neither night nor day hang upon his penthouse lid; he shall live a man forbid. Weary sev'n nights, nine times nine, shall he dwindle, peak, and pine: Though his bark cannot be lost, yet it shall be tempest-tossed. . . .

All. The weird sisters, hand in hand, posters of the sea and land, thus do go about, about: Thrice to thine, and thrice to mine, and thrice again to make up nine. Peace!—the charm's wound up.

But the mainspring was broken. Captain Hess, plummeting down too abruptly, injured his ankle. "*Donnerwetter,*" he exclaimed, an expletive Shakespeare put into Macbeth's mouth much more flossily with "So foul and fair a day I have not seen."

All this, it is submitted, is quite as accurate a summation of the Hess incident as any of those which have been concocted by "well-informed sources," "authoritative quarters," and "their sisters, their cousins, and their aunts." However, most explanations admit the possibility that the Hess affair was based upon a "feigned rescue" which offered "help of Pannonia." The usage of Pannonia by poet's privilege for Huns and Germans already has been explained.

George VI, "by the Grace of God, King of Great Britain and Ireland and of the British Dominions Beyond the Seas, Defender of the Faith, Emperor of India" is a bit long for quatrains, so Nostradamus boils it down to a pithy "King of Kings." That the Hess "rebellion will cause great bloodshed" seemed established at least in part when Germany on June 22, 1941, attacked the Communist Russia which the Number 3 Nazi hated so ardently.

Before Hitler invaded the Soviet Union, it was necessary to consolidate himself in Europe, as quatrain 32 of the Tenth *Centurie* shows:

Le grand empire chacun en devoit estre,
Un sur les autres le viendra obtenir:
Mais peu de temps sera son regne et estre,
Deux ans aux naves se pourra soustenir.

Everyone wanted to be in the great empire,
One will come to obtain it over the others:
But there will be little time for his realm and creature,
Two years can he sustain himself by his ships.

Chief among the diplomatic achievements of 1940 was the tying of Japan to the Rome-Berlin kite. Hungary, Rumania, and Slovakia later joined the Axists. The signing up of the three latter puppet states was accompanied by brass-band ballyhoo, ending Hitler's campaign of blackmail and bully-ragging which had started in September and continued into November. The year 1941 saw the abject truckling of Bulgaria and France, while Spain and Sweden definitely have gravitated into the orbit of Axis satellites. Finnish troops are fighting Russians as German quasi allies. It can hardly be said that the other nations overwhelmed by the Nazis "wanted to be in the great empire." The role of the conquered nations depends on their readiness to "cooperate" with their victors in the "new world order" extending from the Arctic to Zanzibar with Hitler's hairy Herrs as sole heirs.

The sense of the third line is that this new order awaits the outcome of the war for consummation. When the Axis powers lose the war, the friable structure will crumble swiftly. With the sinking of the brand-new German superdreadnaught *Bismarck* by the British revengers in the summer of 1941 and the repeated bombing of the battleships *Scharnhorst* and *Gneisenau* and the heavy cruiser

Prinz Eugen in Brest by the Royal Air Force, Hitler's sea power began to ebb to the point of nonexistence, so far as surface warships were concerned. Thus, the time allotted by the last line of the above stanza appeared to be running out.

This thought is carried on in quatrain 33 of the Sixth *Centurie*:

Sa main dernière par alus sanguinaire,
Ne se pourra plus la mer garentir;
Entre deux fleuves craindra main militaire,
Le noir l'ireux le fera repentir.

Her last force in bloody drydock,
No longer could guarantee herself the sea;
Between two rivers she will fear the mailed fist,
The madman will make the black one repent.

Soon after the *Bismarck* was sunk (May 27, 1941), it became known that the *Scharnhorst* and *Gneisenau* had been badly battered in their docks at Brest and the *Prinz Eugen* limped into port after barely eluding the British pursuers. Whether four big warships to replace these have been completed by the Germans remains problematical at best. It is fairly obvious that Germania "no longer could guarantee herself the sea."

In regard to the last half of the quatrain, be it remembered that vast, sprawling Russia spawns many large rivers and that the main reason for Hitler's attack upon the Red Army was his desire to finish off a potential enemy in the east before it became too strong. Doubtless this move had some politico-economic motive, too.

According to Major George Fielding Eliot, writing in the New York *Herald Tribune*:

The Red Army had had more than a year in which to repair the damages and apply the lessons of the Finnish war. It was becoming a dangerous force in European affairs; would be more dangerous with every month that passed.

There was no possibility now of Hitler's moving against Britain with all this power. He would never dare to leave his Russian front unguarded.... Hitler made his choice; he turned east. He made the choice for two-front war in very truth; the two-front war which has ever been the nightmare of German strategists and on occasion the ruin of German hopes.

It may have been the wiser decision; yet it was the decision his enemy (Britain) would have had him make, and it is rarely wise in war to do the thing which your enemy desires. It remains to be seen how this decision will turn out for Hitler.

The Nazi army of the south already has overrun Ukrainia as did the Germans after the notorious annexationist treaty of Brest-Litovsk on March 3, 1918. Should the Russians be unable to maintain a front behind the winter line, Germany still would be forced to maintain an enormous army of occupation to cope with guerrilla warfare. This new turn in the war has given Britain the opportunity to reinforce her military might and, by the help of American mass production, to prepare the eventual offensive on the European continent.

The next verses cited will show more clearly why "the madman" is Stalin, who "will make the black one (Hitler) repent" his *Drang nach Osten*. Black is fascism's doleful color.

Quatrain 76 of the Ninth *Centurie* hints at the result of Hitler's treacherous attack upon his former ally:

Avec le noir Rapax et sanguinaire,
Yssu de peaultre de l'inhumain Néron,
Emmy deux fleuves main gauche militaire,
Sera meurtry par Joyne chaulveron.

With the black and bloody Eagle
Sprung from the pallet of the inhuman Nero,
The military left wing between two rivers
Will be bruised by the young baldpate.

Rapax is a Latin synonym for the eagle. One identification is with the eagle-topped battle standard of Legio XXI (Rapax), a regiment of old renown nicknamed "The Irresistibles." Rapax also signifies the greed and rapacity of the Roman legionaries. The Twenty-First's station was at Vindonissa, now Windisch, east of the point where the Rhine turns to flow north and not far from Munich, Nazism's birthplace, and Braunau, where Hitler was born. The German heraldic eagle is black with red beak and talons.

The Nero-Hitler parallel has been drawn with micrometric precision up to the present. For nine years Nero indulged himself in a tyrannical orgy which has made his name a timeless byword. Absolute power was conferred on Hitler by the Reichstag's enabling act of March 5, 1933. Nine years later will be March 5, 1942.

In July, A.D. 64, two-thirds of Rome was burned down; men whispered that the conflagration had been planned by the Emperor himself. Dion Cassius and Suetonius reported that Nero actually started the burning of Rome, but the Emperor announced that the thing had been done by the obscene sect of Christians, upon whom a frightful persecution was visited. The German Reichstag building in Berlin was destroyed by fire on February 27, 1933. Many believe that Hitler ordered this deed, but Germany's Supreme Court found Marinus van der Lubbe, a young Dutch Communist, guilty, and he was beheaded. The anti-Semitic campaign carried on ruthlessly in Germany has out-Heroded the Neronian persecution of Christians.

The most groundless suspicions and the most unnatural jealousies drove Nero to actions which the cruelest tyrants never have committed except in frenzied passion. He killed all those whom he feared. Anyone who offended him, or whom he distrusted, was murdered with or without recourse to law. In A.D. 65 a conspiracy was formed against him, but it failed. To crush an incipient revolt against him by the radical Nazis, Hitler personally led the blood purge of June–July, 1934.

The principal events of Nero's reign were the long war with the Parthians, the insurrection of the Jews, and the rebellion in Britain under Boadicea. On his return from a journey into Greece, in A.D 68, Nero was overwhelmed by an insurrection in Gaul, Spain, and Rome itself. Galba, one of the provincial generals, led his troops against the Infernal City. When he heard the tramp of the approaching troops, the tyrant fled and killed himself in the house of one of his freedmen a few miles from Rome.

Theatrical to the end, his last words were: "What an artist is lost in me!"

"One day I made up my mind that I would be a painter, an artist," Hitler wrote in *Mein Kampf,* but he later decided that "he was an architect, not a painter." After the fire, Nero planned the rebuilding of Rome on a magnificent scale, especially the construction of the new imperial palace. Hitler has tried his hand at lifting Berlin's architectural face.

When Germany's armies deployed along the vast Russian battlefront, they comprised the extreme left flank in Finland and the Baltic States, the "military left wing" with its armored divisions and war-tried veterans thrusting against Moscow, and a powerful force on the right striking into Bessarabia and the Ukraine. The great battle of the middle sector was between Vitebsk and Smolensk, the former on the Dvina and the latter on the Dnieper rivers.

All reports tend to show that though the Nazi armies have swung through Finland and the Baltic States and struck deeply into the lush Ukraine, they wallowed in a bloodier battle than was expected when they pressed against Moscow. The first seven weeks of fighting cost Germany a million and a half men killed, wounded, or taken prisoner, it was reported both by the Soviet Information Bureau at Moscow and by "well-informed military sources" at Vichy, making this campaign the bloodiest in history.

The Russians also claimed that six thousand Nazi tanks and six thousand Luftwaffe warplanes had been destroyed and that eight thousand German guns had been put out of action. The same figure for German tank losses was mentioned by a foreign military expert at Istanbul, Turkey, who reported that the German Army had suffered at least 700,000 casualties in the battles around Smolensk. The observer at Istanbul told the London *Daily Express*:

> While it is still too early to see clear signs of a catastrophe for Germany, I can state for an absolute fact that Russian resistance has completely upset the German calculations. Months ago, when the German High Command was ordered to assess the possibilities of an invasion of Russia, the German military attachés in Moscow and Ankara estimated that Russian resistance would be broken in three weeks at the most. They stuck to this opinion when they were asked again in June. The Ambassador and other diplomatic officials in Moscow advised against any attempted invasion.
>
> The great advantage the Nazis have is in their seasoned troops and their brilliant staff, but the Russian geography and poor communications will put even this staff to the acid test. The time element is also beginning to take on the shape of a nightmare for the Nazis. The Germans must finish the job before Russia's early winter sets in, or else they will be sunk.

Whatever figures prove to be accurate, it must be admitted that on any of these bases "the military left wing" has been "bruised between two rivers"—Nostradamus did not say vanquished or routed. But who is "the young baldpate"?

"Tough, stone-bald, peasant-born Marshal Semion Konstanti-novich Timoshenko is about as young a marshal as a great nation ever had," *Time* commented in its issue for June 30, 1941. "That is his advantage, for while not all young generals are geniuses, most of history's generals with genius have been younger men. It is many generations since Russia has produced a great general and perhaps one is due."

Marshal Timoshenko commanded the Red Army in the battle between the Dvina and Dnieper; then he was transferred to the southern front to face a supreme test defending the industrialized Donets Basin, which is between the Dnieper and the Don and Volga rivers.

Napoleon, too, wanted to teach his former ally, Russia, a lesson. Levying half a million soldiers for his *Grande Armée*, the Little Corporal (like ex-Corporal Hitler) invaded Russia in May, 1812. The Russians declined gage of battle, withdrawing constantly until halted at Borodino, where the Corsican defeated them, but he lost heavily, withal.

When the remnants of the Grand Army reached Moscow, the city was in flames, and all the French could do was to retire. It was difficult for the retreating invaders to obtain food from the surly Russian peasantry. Russia's greatest strategist, "General Winter," rallied his forces early.

Napoleon tried to follow a route to the west, but his path was blocked by new Russian armies. Snowstorm followed snowstorm, with the French troops starving. At least a third of the Grand Army was captured, but more died from starvation and exposure to the unwonted cold. Of the half million men, Europe's greatest army up to that time, few were left when, a fortnight before Christmas, they crossed the Niemen into Prussia.

That "disturber of the peace of the world" met his real Waterloo at Leipzig less than a year later, on October 19, 1813. Will Hitler "play the Roman fool" in his last act to prove that "he that killeth with the sword must be killed with the sword"?

The next stanza of this cycle, quatrain 21 of the Sixth *Centurie*, is far less coherent, yet it appears to belong properly right here:

> *Quand ceux du pôle arctique unis ensemble,*
> *En Orient grand effrayeur et crainte,*
> *Esleu nouveau soustenu le grand temple,*
> *Rodes, Bizance de sang barbare teinte.*

> *When those of the Arctic Pole united together,*
> *In the Orient great fright and dread,*
> *A new appointee sustaining the great temple,*
> *Rhodes and Byzantium stained with barbarian blood.*

Both the British Empire and Soviet Union, the northerly powers, have possessions within the Arctic Circle. For that matter, the Stars and Stripes was the first flag to be planted at the North Pole (Admiral Peary, April 6, 1909). An Anglo-Russo-American joint drive against Hitlerism was under way by August 15, 1941. At the same time, the largest British convoy to reach Malaya since the European war began landed thousands of Australians at Singapore. A spokesman said that the Far Eastern Army was considered sufficiently numerous and powerful "to make any potential invader think ten times before striking at the British Empire's interests in the Orient."

Pope Pius XII has refused to hallow Hitler's treacherous offensive against Soviet Russia as a crusade against atheistic Communism. However, *Time* noted in the issue for August 4, 1941, that "the Roman Catholic Church is not letting any grass grow between the advancing German troops and the first wave of Catholic missionaries sent out to win the occupied districts of Russia for Catholicism. . . .

"Last week the Vatican reported that the first batch of missionaries had already reached Hungary and Rumania en route to their new posts in the conquered areas of Russia. Other priests soon will follow.

"Catholics do such long-range planning even when facing regimes as anti-religious as Russia's."

On March 2, 1939, the Vatican radio flashed to the world: "The Holy Church has a new Pope." In the long-range Nostradamic view, that still would permit the description of newly elected for Pius XII.

Rhodes already has been stained with the blood of barbarous Italian Fascists through numerous British air raids upon that unfortunate East Mediterranean island. Istanbul (the Greek Byzantium) has not yet become involved in this war, but it is not in an altogether happy position.

A future Russian counterattack against Germany may be the implication in the last two lines of quatrain 94 of the Fifth *Centurie:*

Translatera en la grand Germanie,
Brabant et Flandres, Gand, Bruges et Bologne:
La treve fainte, le grand duc d' Armenie,
Assaillira Vienne et la Cologne.

He shall convey Brabant and Flanders, Ghent, Bruges,
And Boulogne into the Greater Germany:
The truce feigned, the grand duke of Armenia
Will attack Vienna and Cologne.

Though the German Army occupies all the places mentioned in the first half of this stanza, Hitler has not yet actually incorporated Brabant and Belgium and French Flanders within the Greater Germany he is creating, but he appears to have such a decree in mind. Belgium and the French holdings were retained by the Holy Roman Empire after the disastrous Peace of Westphalia (1648).

In his Uriage speech, previously alluded to, Admiral Darlan let the cat's head and forepaws out of the bag with: "It probably will be necessary to cede Alsace and Lorraine. French Flanders probably also will be taken away, but it is less a question of cession than of exchange. Germany will offer us Wallonia [Belgium's French-speaking portion] and the Swiss Romande [also French-speaking]."

That the Communazi compact was a "truce feigned" has been painfully obvious for some little time. "The grand duke of Armenia" may identify Stalin, born in Georgia, which, with Armenia and Azerbaijan, formed Russia's Transcaucasian Federation. The English word "grand duke" or French *"grand due"* was used to translate the title borne by members of the imperial family of Russia before 1918. Stalin's regime is an imperium, too.

Mr. Wolfe concludes his *The Imperial Soviets* with:[9]

> Inasmuch as Germany's "Samson psychosis" may spell doom
> to the Reich and may ultimately destroy the present order in
> western Europe, it serves the Kremlin's ends. It works against
> a negotiated peace. It may make Stalin the eventual victor of
> the "second imperialist war." It threatens either to make a victorious Reich the master of Europe or to incorporate a defeated
> Reich in the expanding Soviet empire. It promises to answer the
> question as to which of the two revolutionary imperialisms will
> gain control of the other.

Nostradamus has indicated that the Red czar will reach Vienna and Cologne, but he failed to say how long he would stay. Furthermore, quatrain 54 of the Fifth *Centurie* indicates that all his battles will not be victories:

> *Du pont Euxine et la grand Tartarie,*
> *Un Roy sera qui viendra voir la Gaule,*
> *Transpercera Alane et l'Armenie,*
> *Et dans Bizance lairra sanglante Gaule.*

9. *Op.cit.*, page 287.

From the Black Sea and great Tartary
A King will come who would see Gaul,
He will pierce through Asia Minor and Armenia,
And in Constantinople he will suffer a bloody lashing.

In medieval Europe, Tartary was the name used vaguely for the country between the Pacific Ocean and the Dnieper River, presumably because much of it was inhabited by the Tartars. Little Tartary, also called Krim Tartary, became the name for part of Russia and Great Tartary for Turkestan and the surrounding district. Both these regions are in the Soviet Union. Russians especially use the name of Tartars to designate certain populations living in Siberia, the Caucasus and in central and eastern Russia.

The Alani (French, Alane) were an ancient warlike tribe of unknown origin who made incursions into the Roman Empire as allies of the Goths and Vandals, invaded Asia Minor in Aurelian's reign, and cooperated with the Vandals in the invasion of Gaul in A.D. 406.

The appropriateness of the fifteenth quatrain of the Eighth *Centurie* is unquestionable:

Vers Aquilon grands efforts par homasse
Presque l'Europe et l'univers vexer,
Les deux eclypses mettra a telle chasse,
Et aux Pannons vie et mort renforcer.

Great efforts by mankind against the Eagle
To vex almost all Europe and the world,
The two failures will bring such a chase,
To intensify life and death to the Huns.

Nostradamus appears to use eclipse here in its original Greek *(ekleipsis)* meaning of "abandonment, forsaking, failure, or cessation."

Two astronomical eclipses would not be a topical guide, since there are two or three eclipses of one or the other variety annually.

There is another prediction of aerial warfare in quatrain 34 of the Sixth *Centurie*:

> *De feu volant la machination,*
> *Viendra troubler au grand chef assiegez:*
> *Dedans sera telle sedition,*
> *Qu'en desespoir seront les profligez.*

> *The operation of flying fire*
> *Will come to unhinge the great besieged chief:*
> *Within shall be such sedition*
> *That the depraved will be in despair.*

Glen Perry, of The New York *Sun's* Washington Bureau, wrote on August 7, 1941:

The R.A.F., already engaged in heavy raids on occupied France and western Germany, is only waiting for the nights to lengthen to get about the real business of repaying the Reich for what was done to British cities last fall and winter. By the middle of September, the raids will be on in earnest.

It is in this aspect of the war that the United States has one of its most important parts to play, since the British airplane factories are for the most part devoted to the manufacture of pursuit planes, while it is in America that the bombers are being produced not only in ever-increasing quantity, but in such quality that the English unhesitatingly call them by far the best the world has ever seen.

The bombing raids of the future, at least those conducted on a large scale and over considerable distances, will be night affairs.

It appears likely that the Germans will never again have the chance to catch up with the progress the democracies are making in the air. The time lost cannot be regained and the ships and pilots lost have given Britain and the United States a great opportunity to overtake the Germans.

As the supply of heavy American bombers increases, the pressure on Germany will become more heavy. The British are confident that the German people cannot take the pounding that the British took last year, and they intend to test that belief this fall and winter.

It may be inferred that the British feel pretty good about their chances. They do; but they are looking to the United States for more and more bombers, because it is not enough to be able to beat off the enemy's attacks. The British are now confident of their ability to beat off the Luftwaffe at any time, but they are planning to carry the war to Germany itself.

Another prophecy implicit in the sixth quatrain of the Ninth *Centurie* foretells an English-speaking army occupying southwestern France:

> *Par la Guyenne infinité d'Anglois*
> *Occuperont par nom d'Anglaquitaine*
> *Du Languedoc Ispalme Bourdelois.*
> *Qu'ils nommeront apres Barboxitaine.*

> *No end of English will occupy Guienne*
> *Under the name of Anglo-Aquitaine*
> *Of Languedoc, the Isle of Palma, the Bordelais*
> *Which they will name after Barboxitaine.*

Guienne was a province of feudal France. At first part of Aquitaine, it obtained a separate existence in the thirteenth century.

Bordeaux was its capital. Aquitaine, the southwesterly division of ancient Gaul, was between the Garonne, the Pyrenees, and the Bay of Biscay. Once an independent Frankish duchy, it was united with the French crown by the marriage of Eleanor of Aquitaine with Louis VII in 1137. Aquitaine was transferred to England by Queen Eleanor's remarriage in 1152 with Henry Plantagenet, subsequently King Henry II. After long conflicts, Aquitaine was recovered by France in 1453. The name became corrupted into Guienne in the thirteenth or fourteenth century.

At its greatest extent, the pre-Revolutionary province of Languedoc covered south-central France, stretching from the Pyrenees almost to the Loire. On the east it was bordered by the Rhone. Its chief town was Toulouse.

Palma is a fortified port and the capital of Spain's Balearic Isles. It has long been a key to naval control of the western Mediterranean. The wine-growing region known as the Bordelais from its shipping center, Bordeaux, stretches almost a hundred miles up the Gironde and its tributaries, the Garonne and the Dordogne.

Nostradamus uses Enobarbe, Barbe d'Airain and Barbe alone, and Agrippine, derived from the name of Nero's parents, to mean a republic. The suffix *oxitaine* is a phonetic rendition of *occitane,* an old French form for *occident* (western). This appears to imply that an army from the western republic (U.S.A.?) will occupy Languedoc, the Balearic Isles, and the Bordeaux region. Quatrain 34 of the Fifth *Centurie,* interpreted at the end of Chapter 5, might be reread with profitable meaning here.

Here, in quatrain 24 of the Twelfth *Centurie,* is another probable allusion to this occasion:

Le grand secours venu de la Guyenne,
S'arrestera tout auprès de Poitiers,
Lyon rendu par Mont-Luel et Vienne,
Et saccahez par tous gens de mestiers.

The great rescue coming from Guienne
Will make fast all around Poitiers,
The Lion arrived at Mount Luel and Vienne,
And must ransack with all the men of trades.

The French city of Poitiers stands on a hill near the confluence of the Clain and Boivre rivers, sixty miles from Tours. Several battles have been fought near Poitiers. In 507 the Visigoths were defeated in the vicinity by the great Frankish king, Clovis. The great battle of October, 732, between the invading host of Muslims and a Christian army under Charles Martel, sometimes is called the Battle of Poitiers. Resulting in the rout of the invaders, it put a definite stop to the advance of the Muslims into western Europe.

On September 19, 1356, during the Anglo-French Hundred Years' War, an English army of eight thousand commanded by Edward, the Black Prince, vanquished twice that number of Frenchmen and captured King John. Though Poitiers is the capital of the department of Vienne, the last word of the third line more probably refers to the ancient French town of Vienne. It certainly does not mean the Austrian capital.

Vienne is in the department of Isère, on the Gère, and is sixteen miles south of Lyons. Pontius Pilate is said to have been banished to this place, and it was the cradle of western Christianity. Mont-Luel is near Trévoux, just north of Lyons.

The quatrain usually has been taken to mean that a great army from southwestern France will be assembled at Poitiers, while another, whose device is the (British?) lion, will form the other flank around Lyons, then both will drive forward toward Germany. French commentators read the meaning of the last word in the last line, *mestiers,* or, in modern French, *métiers,* as mechanics or artisans, trained in using rapid-fire cannon, machine guns, and the motorized weapons of tanks and armored cars. They have missed another coincidence—General de Gaulle's prediction of the tactics used in the coming invasion of Germany are contained in his *Vers l'Armée de Métier* (*The Army of the Future*)!

These armies of liberation will not be fighting alone, if the seventieth quatrain of the Ninth *Centurie* has been interpreted properly:

> *Harnois trenchans dans les flambeaux cachez*
> *Dedans Lyon le jour du Sacrement,*
> *Ceux de Vienne seront trestous hachez*
> *Par les cantons Latins. Mascon ne ment.*

> *Cutting harness hidden in the candlesticks*
> *Within Lyons on the day of Sacrament,*
> *Those of Vienna will be cut to pieces in their midst*
> *By the Latin districts. The Mason does not lie.*

It is rumored that many small arms of the defeated French Army and some reserve equipment spirited away from arsenals have been hidden so well that even the gumshoeing German Gestapo has been unable to find this "cutting harness." This stanza recounts a future uprising at Lyons on the day of Corpus Christi.

This festival of the Roman Catholic Church in honor of the Holy Eucharist first was established by a bull of Urban IV in 1264 and is celebrated on the Thursday after Trinity Sunday. Incidentally, this Pope's far-sighted policy ultimately led to the final overthrow of the Hohenstaufen dynasty, the hereditary enemy of the papacy. Urban did not live to see the accomplishment of his will.

It was not until the fourteenth century that Corpus Christi was observed generally throughout western Europe. Its special feature is the outdoor procession of the Blessed Sacrament. This festival will be observed next on June 4, 1942.

"The Mason does not lie," a saying widespread among members

of the craft, may indicate that French Freemasons will have a hand in the uprising against the German slave drivers. The context requires that *Vienne* here be *Wien*.

Another line French patriots may take against the Nazi oppressors was indicated by a Free Frenchman broadcasting from London in August, 1941. Able-bodied Frenchmen were urged to join Hitler's volunteer battalions against Bolshevism, then, having obtained arms, to desert to freedom or carry out V-column work. Passionately, the strange new voice exhorted: "At present the army of freedom is clenching its fist and the battalions are secretly forming throughout our invaded Europe and Hitler knows this well." The British Broadcasting Corporation estimates that 80 per cent of the people of France hear its programs.

"Once the French people are in movement, the other peoples of the Continent will join them," Louis Dolivet concluded prophetically in his article, "Volcano Under Vichy," in *The Nation* for July 26, 1941. "They will follow France's initiative in launching the fight for freedom, as they did in 1789 and 1848. There can be no stronger appeal to humanity than the appeal to fight for liberty, independence, and democracy."

What a weltering price in German blood the Nazis will pay for their wars is foretold in quatrain 34 of the Eighth *Centurie*:

> *Apres victoire du Lyon au Lyon,*
> *Sus la montagne de Jura secatombe,*
> *Delues et brodes septiesme million,*
> *Lyon, Ulme à Mausol mort et tombe.*

> *After the victory of the Lion at Lyons,*
> *Great slaughter on the Jura Alps.*
> *The seventh million defeated and bloodied,*
> *At Lyons and Ulm, the dead and fallen in a pyre.*

The implication here is that after the victory of the avenging (British?) lion at Lyons, the German Army will retreat into the broad range of pine-clad Jura Mountains, which lie between the Rhine and Rhone valleys, forming the Franco-Swiss frontier. After further slaughter there, the Nazis will withdraw to Ulm, a city of Württemberg, Germany, at the influx of the Blau into the Danube. Ulm is sixty miles southeast of Stuttgart. On October 17, 1805, General Mack, at the head of an Austrian army of 30,000, there capitulated to Napoleon.

The breakup of Germany into several states after the future Peace of Ulm is foreshadowed by quatrain 46 of the Tenth *Centurie*:

> *Vie, fort, mort, de l'or vilaine indigne*
> *Sera de Saxe non nouveau electeur:*
> *De Brunsvic mandra d'amour signe,*
> *Faux le rendant au peuple séducteur.*

> *Life, skill, death, wretched miser of gold*
> *There will be no new Elector of Saxony:*
> *He will send for the token of love from Brunswick,*
> *The false seducer surrendering to the people.*

Taken by itself, this verse is difficult of interpretation, but read it in conjunction with the so-called prophecy of Mainz, current in the early nineteenth century, it becomes more meaningful:

"William, second of his name, will be the last king of Prussia. He will have no other successors, but there will be a king of Poland, a king of Hanover, and a king of Saxony."

Since the eighteenth century, Saxony had fought against the growing aggrandizement of Prussia at the expense of other German states. As an important member of the moribund Holy Roman Empire, it took part in the war against Napoleon and was an ally of Prussia in 1806, but after the defeat of Jena, Saxony entered the Confederation of the Rhine, the elector changing his title to king.

At the Congress of Vienna (1815), Prussia attempted to annex the entire new kingdom because the king had been Napoleon's steadfast ally. At length, the northern half of the kingdom (7,720 square miles) was handed over to the Hohenzollerns. The Saxons obtained religious and civil liberties early in the nineteenth century, and in 1831 a constitution with an elective legislature and a responsible executive was granted. In 1866, the Saxons sided with Austria; their land was overrun by the Prussians; and the stubborn little kingdom was forced into the German Empire in 1871. Saxony became a socialistic stronghold, and the development of the country not only kept pace with northern Germany but in some respects even outstripped it.

The Nostradamic point may hinge on the kinship of the British royal family and Saxony's former ruling house. Wettin is the surname of the princely Saxon family from which the present British king is descended. The Wettins split into several branches, and until 1918 members of it were kings of Saxony and dukes of the four Saxon duchies. From one of these dukes sprang Prince Albert, consort of Queen Victoria and father of Edward VII. On July 17, 1917, King George V proclaimed that henceforth his family should be known as "the House and Family of Windsor."

The territory which formed the Prussian province of Hanover belonged from ancient times to the family of Brunswick-Lüneburg. In 1814 Hanover was erected into a kingdom by the Congress of Vienna. Guelph (more properly Welf) was the name of the family to which the electors of Hanover and, therefore, the sovereigns of Great Britain, from 1714 to 1837, belonged. On the death of William IV of Britain in 1837, the kingdom fell to Ernest Augustus, Duke of Cumberland, since the Salic law, which excludes heirs female, prevented

Queen Victoria from inheriting it. In 1866, Bismarck seized Hanover and incorporated the domains of its king, George V, into Prussia as a province.

Nostradamus implies that the Hanoverian kingdom will be restored through the collapse of Hitlerian autocracy. Imagine Hitler, "the false seducer, surrendering to the people" of Germany! What would they do with him?

Not long ago it was reported that Adolf Hitler had been seized with an epileptic fit, possibly the forerunner to quatrain 36, Third *Centurie*:

> *Ensevely non mort appoletique,*
> *Sera trouvé avoir les mains mangées*
> *Quand la cité damnera l'hérétique,*
> *Qu'avoit leurs loix ce leur sembloit changées.*

> *Buried in an apoplectic stroke, but not dead,*
> *He will be found to have eaten his hands:*
> *When the city will damn the heretic*
> *Who, as it appeared to them, had changed their laws.*

To be taken with a grain of salt, pepper, and piquant sauce to taste.

The Nostradamic sextet epitomizing the Hitlerian epoch is *Prediction* No. 47:

> *Le grand d'Hongrie ira dans la nacelle,*
> *Le nouveau né fera guerre nouvelle*
> *A son voisin qu'il tiendra assiégé,*
> *Et le noireau avec son altesse*
> *Ne souffrira, que par trop on le presse,*
> *Durant trois ans ses gens tiendra rangé.*

The Great Hun will enter the cockpit,
The new-born will make war
Upon his neighbor, whom he will hold besieged,
And the swarthy fellow will not admit of
His highness, when it is pressed too much,
During three years his people will hold steady.

When Hitler's newly born Third Reich made war upon its neighboring Poland, the Nazi *Fuehrer* gloated over the bombing of fleeing Polish soldiers and refugee civilians from the box-like, enclosed cockpit *(nacelle)* of a well-guarded passenger-carrying airplane. After conquering all his neighbors, Hitler held them in states of siege, but the swarthy brooder in the Kremlin refused to bow to the Nazi bully's ultimate demands in June, 1941, and the push to the east began.

The last line indicates that the Nazi Ring's cycle has circled into its *Siegfried* period with *Götterdämmerung* due by September, 1942.

8

"The Seven Heads Are Seven Mountains"

Clairvoyance is a pretended ability to see clearly that which the senses do not perceive. From this faculty, rudimentary at best in our stage of undeveloped mentality, must be derived whatever ability mankind may have in forecasting the future. This author makes no claims to such Sibylline sensibilities. He is self-complacent as a Boswell ("One who plays the part of sedulous admirer to a person; especially one who collects and records sayings of a great man, as James Boswell [1740–1795] did for Dr. Johnson").

Camille Flammarion has cited apparently well-authenticated cases of foretelling of the future. Unhappily, none of these clairsentient souls attempted to pierce the Nostradamic veil. Some Nostradamians advance the Divine Knowledge theory as their prophet's *raison d'être*. They presuppose that God knows all as an eternal present, that He may reveal the future at will, and that Nostradamus was permitted to share the Almighty's knowledge. This author stakes no claim to such interpretative facilities.

Many prophecies dealt with in this chapter are disjointed, yet they appear to relate to the current period of wars and rumors of wars. Since the events described in most cases have not yet transpired, they are impossible to verify. The one salient feature which arises is that Germany soon will attack Fascist Italy, bringing ruin to Mussolini's dictatorship, which will be replaced by a Red terror, in the course of which Rome will be virtually destroyed.

Quatrain 32 of the Seventh *Centurie* ushers in the villain of the piece, even with his triumphant blackguard march on Rome (October 27 and 28, 1922):

Au mont Royal naistra d'une casane,
Qui cave et compte viendra tyranniser,
Dresser copie de la marche Millane,
Favene, Florence d'or et gens epuiser.

From a tavern will spring to the royal mountain
One who will come to tyrannize over vault and value,
To set up a force in the Milanese march,
Faenza and golden Florence to pump dry.

Benito Mussolini was the son of Alessandro Mussolini, socialistic blacksmith and innkeeper of the hamlet Dovia, in Romagna. A "Sunday child," like Goethe, the future *Duce* was born on July 29, 1883. "The sun had entered within the constellation of Leo eight days before," the superstitious ex-corporal of Bersaglieri once wrote in his own fine Italian hand. Rome sometimes is called "The Royal Mountain," from its Capitoline Hill.

Mussolini organized the first Fascio di Combattimento in March, 1919, while he was in Milan editing *Popolo d'Italia*. Though Mussolini started fascism to combat the wave of anarchy sweeping Italy, he had to control all industries to keep them open and to provide jobs for the workers. Factories remained in the owners' hands, but profits were controlled strictly. Fascism took over the entire national economy to provide a living for all Italians. Thus, *Il Duce* tyrannized "over vault and value." Italy's race for a place in the sun only served "to pump dry" even "golden Florence."

Here is the seventieth quatrain of the Eighth *Centurie*, which probably refers to Mussolini:

Il entrera vilain, meschant, infame
Tyrannisant la Mesopotamie
Tous amis faict d'adulterine dame,
Terre horrible noir de phisionomie.

He will go in villainous, wicked, infamous,
Tyrannizing Mesopotamia,
All made friends of the dame born adulterously,
The earth a horrible black of feature.

The familiar Italian "boot," extending some hundreds of miles into the Mediterranean, makes this peninsula a Mesopotamia ("country between the waters"), as it was explained in Chapter 4. The adulterine origin of fascism also was alluded to in that chapter. Compare Revelation, xvii, 5. Black notoriously is the color of Italian fascism.

To hide his graying hair, the senescent *Duce* kept his head shaved, as quatrain 66 of the Fourth *Centurie* suggests:

Soubs couleur feinte de sept testes rasées,
Seront semez divers explorateurs:
Puyts et fontaines de poyson arrousées,
Au fort de Gennes humains dévorateurs.

Under the sham color of seven shaven heads,
There will be sown several explorers:
Wells and fountains sprinkled with poison,
Humans stifled in the fort of Genoa.

By 1927, Mussolini was not only Premier but also Minister of Foreign Affairs, in addition to holding the portfolios of Interior,

War, Marine, Aviation, and Corporations—seven of the nine cabinet posts.

The next four quatrains have tantalizingly close resemblances to the Spanish civil war:

III-86

Un chef d'Ausonne aux Espagnes ira,
Par mer fera arrest dedans Marseille,
Avant sa mort un long temps languira,
Après sa mort on verra grand merveille.

A chief of Italy will go to Spain,
Will make a stop by sea in Marseilles,
Before his death he will languish a long while,
After his death a great marvel will be seen.

The usage of Ausonia as a poetic form for Italy has been explained.

III-68

Peuple sans chef d'Espagne et d'Italie,
Morts profligez dedans la Cherrenosse:
Leur duict trahy par légère folie,
De sang nager partout à la traverse.

People without a chief in Spain and Italy,
Overwhelming dead within the peninsula:
Their leader betrayed by thoughtless folly,
Blood to swim everywhere in this misfortune.

King Victor Emmanuel III of Italy still reigns, but no longer rules. King Alfonso XIII of Spain was driven into exile before the advent of Franco. Both Spain and Italy are peninsulas. *Duict* is a close Old French approximation for the Italian *duce*. That Mussolini had betrayed his country by "thoughtless folly" was obvious soon after he became the Pie-eyed Piper of Munich's rat Number 1.

II-39

Un an devant le conflit Italique,
Germains, Gaulois, Espagnols pour le fort,
Cherra l'escolle maison de republique
Où hors mis peu seront suffoquez morts.

One year before the Italian war,
Germans, French, Spaniards for the fort;
The schoolhouse of the republic shall fall
Where, except a few, they shall be suffocated to death.

On March 18, 1940, Hitler and Mussolini conferred in *Il Duce's* private car, sidetracked in a snowstorm at the railway station on the Italian side of the Brenner Pass, in the Tyrolean Alps. After that chess game, the Roman Caesar was little more than the Nazi *Fuehrer's* rook. Three months later, Italy was at war with France. On March 28, 1939, a year before the Hitler-Mussolini meeting, Madrid, "the schoolhouse of the (Spanish) republic," surrendered to the victorious Franco, who had conquered Spain with the help of German and Italian "volunteers" and without the hindrance of republican France.

III-12

Par la tumeur de Heb. Po, Tag. Tymb. et Rome,
Et par l'estang Leman et Aretin:
Les deux grands chefs et citez de Garonne,
Prins, morts, noyez, partir humain butin.

By the swelling of the Ebro, Po, Tagus, and Tiber, and Rome,
And by Lake Geneva and Aretino:
The two great chiefs and the cities of the Garonne,
Taken, dead, drowned, human spoils to leave.

Geneva's inability to dam the swelling tide of fascism in the Iberian and Italian peninsulas may be the undercurrent of the first two lines. *Aretin* may compare Mussolini to Pietro Aretino, Italian poet and wit (1492–1556), who achieved notoriety as the author of sixteen exceedingly licentious sonnets (*Sonetti Lussuriosi*). Such fame as remains to him he derives from his letters, five comedies, and a tragedy, *Orazio.* Mussolini's rutting and spawning, breeding and bragging is a closed chapter, while the less said of his play-crafting days, the better. Spanish loyalist refugees fled into France and were concentrated in camps along the Garonne Valley.

The seventh quatrain of the Sixth *Centurie* refers to the invasion of Norway:

Norveigre, Dace et l'Isle Britannique,
Par les unis frères seront vexées:
Le chef Romain issu du sang Gallique
Et les copies aux forests repoulsées.

Norway, Denmark, and the British island
Will be vexed by the united brothers:
The Roman chief sprung from Gallic blood
And the forces repulsed into the forests.

The context here requires that Dace not be regarded as Dacia, Latin name for the province now covered by Rumania, but as Denmark. A fifteenth century roll of 1212 coats of arms gives the shield still used by Danish sovereigns as that of the *"Roy de Dace."* Hitler launched his Denmark-Norway campaign after an attempted peace offensive by his united brother, Mussolini, had failed.

The king of Italy ("the Roman chief") is of the House of Savoy, Savoy being a French province where his family originated. Are not the forests those of Germany, into which the invaders will be pushed in due season?

The ninth quatrain of the First *Centurie* has been fulfilled at least in part:

> *De l'Orient viendra le coeur Punique*
> *Fascher Hadrie et les hoirs Romulides,*
> *Accompagné de la classe Libique.*
> *Trembler Mellites et proches Isles vuides.*

> *The Punic heart shall come from the east*
> *To vex Italy and the heirs of Romulus,*
> *Accompanied by the Libyan fleet.*
> *Malta and the adjacent evacuated isles to shake.*

The use of Punique to describe Britain was explained in Chapter 5. Hadrie is a French rendition of the Adriatic region. The Nostradamic simile, making the Roman fascists heirs of the twin who slew his mocking brother, is subtle satire upon today's sons of the lupine bitch.

Though the British Mediterranean fleet withdrew from Malta under the threat of Italian air power, Italy still was "a prisoner in her own sea." The existence of this sea power in Mare Nostrum is a perpetual pistol at *Il Duce's* temples. After cutting Italy's communications with the Fascist army in Libya, the British Navy and fleet air arm has begun to vex *Il Duce's* own ports and has made a devastating attack on warships actually within the naval base at Taranto.

Possibly more such naval attacks are described in quatrain 23 of the Fourth *Centurie*:

La legion dans la marine classe
Calcine, Magne, souphre et poix bruslera,
Le long repos de l'asseurée place,
Port Selim, Hercle feu les consumera.

The legion in the marine fleet burns greatly,
Sulphur and pitch shall scorch,
The long rest of the assured place,
Port Selim, the Herculean fire shall consume them.

Selinus, a Greek colony in the southwestern corner of Sicily, near the modern Castelvetrano, was destroyed by the seagoing Carthaginians twenty-three centuries ago. That, indeed, has been a long rest. Punic maritime power has a way of bobbing up in the most unexpected places.

Apparently the French will stand aside and cheer while the British knock Italy clean out of the war, if that is what quatrain 52 of the Third *Centurie* means:

En la Campagne sera si longue pluye,
Et en la Pouille si grand siccité;
Coq verra l'Aigle, l'aisle mal acomplic,
Par Lyon misc sera en extrémité.

In Campania there will be such a long rain,
And in Apulia such a great drought;
The cock will see the eagle, the wing poorly completed,
By the lion pushed into extremity.

The Gallic gamecock, or simply the cock, is one of France's national emblems. This bird was the national ensign of Gaul, being derived from *gallus,* a cock. The Gallic cock decorated tricolors during the French Revolution. The eagle here is the Roman standard-symbol which became the device of Fascist Italy. That Mussolini's air force ("wing") had been "poorly completed" was evident when the British lion began pushing the feckless Fascists around all over their "Roman lake."

The feelings of the unhappy Italian people toward their overbearing ally are reflected in the twentieth quatrain of the Sixth *Centurie:*

L'union faincte sera peu de durée
Des uns changez reformez la pluspart:
Dans les vaisseaux sera gent endurée,
Lors aura Rome un nouveau Liepart.

The false unity will not last long,
Some changed, but the most reformed:
A nation will endure with the ships,
Then Rome will have a new Leopard.

That Britain's Royal Navy is durable was proved when Mussolini was made a prisoner in his own sea. When a lion, instead of being side-faced, looks out of a shield full-faced, he straightway becomes heraldically "a leopard"—not the spotted feline of that name, but merely a lion who looks at one. The leopard sometimes ramps, like a lion, but his characteristic attitude is walking with catlike tread, full-faced, and it then is enough to call him "a leopard." The old blazon of the arms of the king of England was "gules three leopards of gold." Herewith the armorial roll of Caerlaverock (1300) describes the arms of King Edward I, "The Hammerer of the Scots":

"Three leopards of fine gold set on red; current, fierce, haughty and cruel; to signify that like them the King is dreadful to his enemies, for his bite is slight to none who brave his anger; and yet towards such as seek his friendship or submit to his power his kindness is soon rekindled."

If a future Pope is a British subject, "then Rome will have a new leopard." The only Englishman to become Pope, Adrian IV (1154–1159), was elected at approximately the time three leopards first stood in the royal arms of England. Nicholas Breakspear was a lowly Anglo-Saxon thrall born at Abbot's Langley, near the ancient city of St. Albans.

Adrian was fifth in that prophecy attributed to the Irish saint, Malachi, concerning every Pope from the twelfth century into the present and beyond. His brief description is *De rure albo*. He was the son of a servant in the great Abbey of St. Albans and the future pontiff himself once occupied a menial billet in the lord abbot's kitchen.

Malachi's prophecy reckons Pope Pius XII as *Pastor Angelicus* ("Angelic Shepherd"). He is to be followed by *Pastor et Nauta* ("Shepherd and Sailor"). Don't forget that the English are a nation of sailors, though Napoleon tried to belittle them as shopkeepers!

The optimistic reader, disheartened by the prowess of the Fascist states, might derive some comfort from quatrain 63 of the Third *Centurie*:

> *Romain pouvoir sera tout à bas*
> *Son grand voisin imiter les vestiges:*
> *Occultes haines civiles et debas*
> *Retarderont aux buffons leurs folies.*

> *Roman power shall be quite put down,*
> *His great neighbor shall follow his steps:*
> *Secret and civil hatreds and quarrels*
> *Will delay the follies of the buffoons somewhat.*

Could this not mean Fascist Italy? Hitler began as a smudgy carbon copy of the determined Napoleonic personality who was bossing the Machiavellian empire south of the German border. Today, contemptuous Nazis refer jeeringly to *Il Duce* as *"Gauleiter von Wälschland"* ("District Leader of Italy"). The last half of this quatrain encloses self-evident truth.

Count Carlo Sforza, former Italian diplomat, reports that the Nazis have too strong a hold on Italy to permit a public uprising now, but he believes that the Italian Navy and part of the Army might undertake a passive strike in the war against Britain, since they "dislike fighting on the side of the Germans."

"It is vain to hope for an internal revolution in Italy," he says. "The Italians know that the true master, Hitler, would march at once on Milan, on Venice, on Trieste—that he would march on Rome. Italy has become a German protectorate, thanks to the stupidity or treason of the Fascists. . . ."

The Count insists that Italians understand that "as long as Fascism remains in power, there are only two alternatives for Italy—either defeat by England or to become a Nazi province."

Mussolini, according to Count Sforza, has "begun to feel that he must rely on Nazi force" to keep down the Italians' "general dissatisfaction."

Because of Mussolini's policies, he comments, Libya is occupied by Germans, the Italian police are completely in the hands of the Gestapo, the Germans control essential Italian industries, and Italian foreign emissaries are under German control.

The sixteenth quatrain of the Sixth *Centurie* is another stanza replete with half-truths:

Ce que ravy sera du jeune Milue
Par les Normans de France et Picardie:
Les noirs du temple du lieu Negrisilve
Feront aulberge et feu de Lombardie.

That which will be ravished from the young center
By the Normans of France and Picardy:
The blacks of the temple of the Black Forest place
Will make a public house and fireplace of Lombardy.

Nazi looters have ransacked and ravished the north of France much as the Viking sea rovers harried the Merovingian province of Neustria before it became the Normandy and Picardy of those fierce Norse invaders.

General Quitanilla, former Bolivian envoy in Rome who was decorated by Hitler with the grand cross of the Order of the Black Eagle, recently arrived from Europe and gave an interview to *El Dia* of Montevideo, Uruguay, which confirms the last half of the above stanza. This interview, published in *El Dia* on May 4, 1941, created a sensation and was reprinted by many newspapers in South America. Since General Quitanilla was known widely for his pro-Axis sympathies, his opinion about the conditions under which Italy is living now is unusually significant. Here are his words:

I spent many years in Germany and Italy, and never hid my admiration for the German army and German and Italian civilizations. This, however, which has taken place in those countries during recent years fills me with a deep abomination. German and Italian armies are so uncontrolled in their lust for robbery and oppression that they are unworthy to be called soldiers.

I am almost frightened by the indescribable poverty which I saw in Europe. I was deeply moved by the suffering through which the people of occupied countries are passing. I visited all the occupied countries and Germany. I lived in Berlin for a longer time. The men who are ruling in Germany are dominated by a lust for power, but the masses of the German people are living in poverty and in the iron grasp of terror, under the Gestapo whip.

I was living in Rome when the war started. There was a

distinct dislike among Italians for this war, and what almost amounted to hate for the Germans. However, the growing unrest and revolutionary state of mind in the majority of the Italian population did not escape the attention of the Germans. Panzer divisions suddenly appeared on the Italian frontier, and gradually entered the country. The Germans are now the real occupants of Italy, and the Italians hate them much more than before.

Numerous street fights occur when a more temperamental Italian spits into the face of a German soldier when they meet on the streets. Every Italian knows that two outstanding Italian generals, loved by the army and respected by the people, but removed by Mussolini, are kept under arrest, and guarded by German soldiers. The most popular saying in Italy is, "Mussolini is the only friend of Hitler in Italy."

In quatrain 38 of the Sixth *Centurie* a hope which has been expressed often and fervently in the columns of the democratic press is seen as fulfilled:

Aux profligez de paix les ennemies,
Apres avoir l'Italie supperée:
Noir sanguinaire, rouge sera commis,
Feu, sang verser, eau de sang colorée.

The enemies of peace to be overwhelmed,
After having overrun Italy:
The bloody black will be exposed to blood,
Fire and blood spilled, water colored with blood.

This seems to portend that the blackshirt regime will come to a bloody end, with communism triumphant in its stead.

Some details of this revolutionary struggle appear in quatrain 22 of the Fifth *Centurie*:

Avant qu'à Rome grand ait rendu l'ame,
Effrayeur grande à l'armée estrangere:
Par escadrons l'embusche pres de Parme,
Puis les deux rouges ensemble feront chere.

Before a great one has yielded his soul at Rome,
There is great terror to the foreign army
From squadrons ambushed near Parma,
Then the two reds will fare well together.

Nostradamus is unlikely to dignify Mussolini as Benito the Great. The first line is far more probably a reference to the Pope of that troubled time.

Tribulation for the Church may be indicated in quatrain 43 of the Fifth *Centurie:*

La grande ruyne des sacrez ne s'eslongne,
Provence, Naples, Sicile, Seez et Ponce:
En Germanie, au Rin et à Cologne,
Vexez à mort par tous ceux de Magonce.

The great ruin of the sacred is not far away,
Provence, Naples, Sicily, Seez, and the Pontine Isles:
In Germany, to the Rhine and to Cologne,
Provoked to death by all those of Mainz.

Seez is a town near St. Maurice, in Savoy. The last half of the quatrain may hint at a revival of Catholicism in Germany. St. Boniface, the "Apostle of Germany," who was born Winfrid, at Crediton, in Devonshire, England, made Mainz his see city as archbishop and primate of all Germany in 745. Refer to the fortieth quatrain of the Sixth *Centurie* in Chapter 6.

Smarting under the ill-concealed contempt of his German

associates, the Italian strawman sought tawdry victories in north Africa and Greece with the result chronicled in quatrain 77 of the Sixth *Centurie*:

> *Par la victoire de deceu fraudulente,*
> *Deux classes une, la revolte Germaine,*
> *Le chef meurtry et son fils dans la tente,*
> *Florence, Imole pourchassez dans Romaine.*

> *By the fraudulent victory of the frustrated one,*
> *Two fleets one, the German revolt,*
> *The chief and his son bruised in the tent,*
> *Florence and Imola pursued into Romagna.*

Mussolini's frustrated cry has been that "Italy must not be a prisoner in her own sea." He was baying at the moon, like the ancient Roman. All his great "victories" have been frauds. The second line portends Britain's gaining control of another navy—perhaps what is left of the French and Italian warships—and the oft-predicted German revolt.

"The chief" may be Mussolini and "his son" actually Count Galeazzo Ciano, his son-in-law and heir presumptive. Imola is not far from Dovia, in Romagna, where the *Duce* was born.

Mutiny in the Italian Army may be the thought which quatrain 68 of the Sixth *Centurie* intends to convey:

> *Lors que soldats fureur séditieuse,*
> *Contre leur chef feront de nuit et fer luire,*
> *Ennemy d'Albe soit par main furieuse,*
> *Lors vexer Rome et principaux seduire.*

> *When the soldiers' seditious fury*
> *Against their chief will make the sword gleam by night,*

The enemy of Alba is to be by the furious hand,
Then to vex Rome and to delude the principals.

Alba here probably means Alba Longa, a very ancient city of Latium, Italy, established by Ascanius, son of Aeneas, several centuries before Rome's foundation. Its remains have been discovered near Lake Albano, sixteen miles southeast of the Eternal City. It was regarded as the mother city of Rome.

In quatrain 65 of the Tenth *Centurie*, Nostradamus warns:

O vaste Rome ta ruine s'approche
Non de tes murs de ton sang et substance:
L'aspre par lettres fera si horrible coche,
Fer pointu mis à tous jusqu'au manche.

Oh, great Rome, thy ruin approaches,
Not of thy walls, or of thy blood and substance:
Biting words will provoke such a horrible score
With the pointed stiletto thrust in clear up to
   the haft.

It smacks of communistic manifestoes and printed broadsides calling the Romans to their last civil war.

In the coming invasion of Italy, "the disaster of Perugia" will bulk large, quatrain 72 of the Eighth *Centurie* presupposes:

Champ Perusin ô l'énorme deffaite
Et le conflit tout auprès de Ravenne
Passage sacre lors qu'on fera la feste,
Vainqueur vaincu cheval manger l'avenne.

Oh, an enormous defeat on the Perugian battlefield!
And all the conflict around Ravenna.

Then by the sacred way they will bring the merrymaking,
The horses of the conquerors and conquered to eat oats.

The Via Sacra, or Sacred Way, was one of the most important streets of ancient Rome and probably derived its name from the many sacred monuments along it or in the vicinity. Beginning at the Capitoline Hill, it went past the Basilica Julia and the temple of Castor and Pollux, crossed the Forum, ran along the north of the temple of Julius Caesar, passed the temple of Antoninus and Faustina and the basilica of Constantine on the other side and the arch of Titus at the southeastern end of the Forum, and thence it went to the Colosseum.

Perugia also is referred to in quatrain 36 of the Sixth *Centurie*:

Ne bien ne mal par bataille terrestre,
Ne parviendra aux confins de Perouse,
Rebeller Pise, Florence voir mal estre,
Roy nuict blessé sur mulet à noire housse.

Neither good nor evil by the earthly battle
Will reach the borders of Perugia.
Pisa to rebel, Florence to be in poor straits,
The king wounded at night on a mule with a black saddlecloth.

Quatrain 78 of the Tenth *Centurie* is bitterly sarcastic:

Subite joye en subite tristesse,
Sera à Rome aux graces embrassées.
Dueil, cris, pleurs, larm, sang excellent liesse:
Contraires bandes surprinses et troussées.

Sudden joy into sudden sorrow
Will be at Rome to the embraced graces.

Mourning cries, weeping, tears and blood, delightful jollity:
Opposing troops surprised and tied up.

The twentieth quatrain of the Tenth *Centurie* forbodes a whole-sale slaughter of Fascist partisans:

Tous les amis qu'auront tenu party,
Pour rude en lettres mis mort et saccagé,
Biens publiez par fixe grand néanty,
Que Romain peuple ne fut tant outragé.

All the friends who had held the party,
For harshness to letters put to death and ransacked,
Wealth proclaimed by a fixed great nothingness,
Which did not bother the Roman people much.

The thirtieth quatrain of the Seventh *Centurie* refers to Fossano, which was identified in Chapter 6 under quatrain 96 of the Third *Centurie*:

Le sac s'approche, feu, grand sang espandu,
Po, grands fleuves, aux bouviers l'entreprinse:
De Gennes, Nice, apres long attendu,
Foussan, Turin, à Savillan la prinse.

The sack approaches, fire, great bloodshed,
The Po, great rivers, the enterprise to the drovers:
Of Genoa, Nice, after long waiting,
Fossano, Turin, the prize to Savillano.

Death and revenge are the cheerful topics of quatrain 21 of the Fifth *Centurie*:

Par le trépas du Monarque Latin
Ceux qu'il aura par regne secourus:
Le feu luyra, divisé le butin,
La mort publique aux hardis incourus.

By the death of the Latin Monarch
Those whom he will have rescued by the reign:
The fire will appear, the plunder divided,
Public execution for the bold fellow travelers.

Clerical cassocks appear to be meant in the first line of quatrain 33 of the Tenth *Centurie*:

La faction cruelle à robe longue
Viendra cacher souz les pointus poignards,
Saisir Florence le duc et lieu diphlongue,
Sa descouverte par immeurs et flangnards.

The faction cruel to the long robe
Will come to conceal sharp daggers,
To seize Florence, the duke and the twice-burnt place,
Her detection by convicts and loafers.

The sixtieth quatrain of the Tenth *Centurie* foreshadows war at the advent of a new year:

Je pleure Nisse, Mannego, Pise, Gennes,
Savone, Sienne, Capue, Modene, Malte:
Le dessus sang et glaive par estrennes,
Feu, trembler terre, eau, malheureuse nolte.

I weep over Nice, Monaco, Pisa, and Genoa,
Savona, Siena, Capua, Modena, and Malta:

Blood above and a sword for a new year's gift,
Fire, earthquake, and water, unhappy ill will.

There are suggestions of Muslim involvement in the coming conflict in the next two quatrains:

IX–28

Voille Symacle pour Massiliolique,
Dans Venise port marcher aux Pannons:
Partir du goulfre et Synus Illyrique,
Vast à Socille, Lygurs coups de canons.

The infidel sails for Marseilles
In Venice harbor to march on the Huns:
To leave from the gulf and the Illyrian Bay,
Wasting in Sicily, gunshots to the Ligurians.

Symacle is believed to refer to Aurelius Symaclus, orator, states-man, and prefect of Rome in 384. A zealous pagan, he persuaded Gratian and Valentinian II to maintain the pagan gods. The analogy between Pannons and Huns has been drawn. The Genoese Liguri-ans already have been bombarded by the British fleet.

V–47

Le grand Arabe marchera bien avant,
Trahy sera par les Bisantinois,
L'antique Rodes luy viendra au devant,
Et plus grand mal par austre Pannonois.

The great Arab will march well forward,
He will be betrayed by the Byzantines,

Ancient Rhodes will fall before him,
And the greatest evil by another Hun.

Apparently the Arabs are to plunge into the later phase of the war. Byzantium was Constantinople's Greek name. *Austre Pannonois* also may punningly indicate an "Austrian Hun," possibly Hitler.

Quatrain 35 of the Fourth *Centurie* is obscure, but perhaps pertinent:

Le feu estaint les vierges trahiront,
La plus grand part de la bande nouvelle;
Foudre à fer, lance les seuls Roys garderont,
Etrusque et Corse de nuit gorge allumelle.

The virgins will betray the extinct fires,
The greatest part of the new band;
An iron thunderbolt and lance will guard the only kings,
Tuscany and Corsica gutted with flames by night.

The seventh quatrain of the Eighth *Centurie* is equally mystifying:

Verceil, Milan donra intelligence,
Dedans Tycin sera faicte la paye.
Courir par Seine eau, sang, feu par Florence,
Unique cheoir d'hault en bas faisant maye.

Vercelli and Milan will give understanding,
Within Ticino the wage will be paid.
Water and blood to flow in the Seine, fire in Florence,
Extraordinary power from above making a nice mess here below.

Verceil is the French rendition of the name of a north Italian town, Vercelli, in Roman times Vercellae, an important stronghold of the Transpadane district. Ticino is Switzerland's most Italian canton.

The last line in quatrain 95 of the Ninth *Centurie* may foretell what fate has in store for Benito Mussolini:

Le nouveau faict conduira l'exercite,
Proche apamé jusqu'aupres du rivage,
Tendant secours de Milanoise eslite,
Duc yeux privé à Milan fer de cage.

The new principle will guide the maneuver,
Approaching openhanded up to and all around the
    bankside,
Bringing rescue to Milan's elite,
The duke, deprived of his eyes, caged in iron at Milan.

"The new principle" may point to a refined fifth-column stratagem. The French *duc* literally is the English "duke" and easily becomes the Italian *duce* ("leader") if imaginative semantics are brought into play. "Deprived of his eyes" may mean that Mussolini's Ovra (Opera volontoria repressione anti-Fascista), supplanted by Hitler's Gestapo, no longer can protect *Il Duce*.

Fascism's Fat Boy would look even more like a chimpanzee inside an iron cage.

Milan also figures in quatrain 31 of the Sixth *Centurie*:

Roy trouvera ce qu'il désiroit tant,
Quand le Prelat sera reprins à tort:
Responce au Duc le rendra mal content,
Qui dans Milan mettra plusieurs à mort.

The king will find that which he wished for so much
When the prelate again will be taken wrongly:

The reply to the duke will give him little satisfaction,
Who in Milan will put many to death.

The sixth quatrain of the Seventh *Centurie* is a clearer prediction of the contemporary German occupation of all Italy:

Naples, Palerme, et toute la Cecile,
Par main barbare sera inhabitée,
Corsique, Salerne et de Sardeigne l'Isle,
Faim, peste, guerre, fin des maux intentée.

Naples, Palermo, and all Sicily
Will be made uninhabited by the barbarian hand:
Corsica, Salerno, and the island of Sardinia,
Hunger, plague, war, the finish of evils begins.

"The finish of evils" cannot begin too soon to knit up the raveled sleave of care.

9

"He That Hath the Key"

When the fascist dictatorship of Italy, destroyed by the coming invasion, plunges the peninsula into civil war, there will be a grievous schism in the Roman Catholic Church and the Pope will leave the Vatican—that is, if the interpretations of several contemporary French commentators on the Nostradamic quatrains have been drawn up accurately. In any event, that summary is the one generally accepted for this chapter, based on eighteen prophetic quatrains.

There appears to be no scientific way of dating these coming events, which already seem to have cast a few dim shadows on the pages of future history. Mankind, however, should be prepared for tremendous changes when the original grave of St. Peter, Prince of the Apostles, is found in the church on the Vatican Hill named for that disciple to whom Our Lord said: "Thou art Peter, and upon this rock I will build my church; and the gates of hell shall not prevail against it." There is both fact and comfort in Matthew xvi, 18.

Dispatches from Vatican City in the autumn of 1940 related that a search was under way for the tomb of the first Bishop of Rome. The renewed excavations were undertaken at the express orders of Pope Pius XII. The first result of this archeological operation was the unearthing of a piece of wall about a yard long which had been part of Nero's Circus, where early Christian martyrs were done to death to disport cruel Caesar. This strip of wall was identified by a stone bearing the seal of the Emperor who fiddled while the Infernal City burned. After eight months' excavating under the great basilica, searching the debris of centuries for archeological relics, workmen found:

1. The sculptured side of a pagan sarcophagus, broken in a hundred pieces.
2. Fragments of the mosaic floor of the first church built on the site and consecrated in the year 326.
3. The floor and entrance to the sacristy of this former church.
4. Pillars of the old basilica.
5. Two cellars in which, during the time of Michelangelo, lime was slaked for construction work on the new basilica, together with unslaked lime of the sixteenth century.
6. Charcoal inscriptions and designs made by workmen nearly four hundred years ago.
7. The skeleton of a worker of that period who was buried where he died in an accident.

The present church of St. Peter's is the second built over the tomb of the Apostle, beside the site of Nero's Circus, at the foot of the Vatican Hill. When part of the original edifice started to give way, Pope Nicholas V decided to rebuild it in 1452, but little work was done until the foundation stone of the new basilica was laid in 1506. As the former church was demolished, the debris was dumped in the basement and it is this wreckage that the workmen are clearing out, four centuries later.

In these excavations, bones other than those of the Prince of the Apostles will be found, the seventh quatrain of the Fifth *Centurie* proclaims:

Du Triumvir seront trouvez les os,
Cerchant profond tresor enigmatique:
Ceux d'alentour ne seront en repos,
De concaver marbre et plomb metalique.

The bones of the Triumvir will be found
In seeking an enigmatical buried treasure:
Those round about will have no rest
From digging into marble and metallic lead.

In ancient Rome, the triumvirs, or tresviri, were members of a commission of three men charged with some specific duty such as repairing temples, coining money, or founding colonies. In addition to being given to certain permanent boards, the name was applied to various extraordinary commissions appointed to perform some special public duty. The coalition of Caesar, Pompey, and Crassus in 60 B.C. often, though improperly, is called the First Triumvirate. Those who constituted it bore no official title and exercised only usurped powers.

The most noted triumvirate was that of Octavian, Mark Antony, and Lepidus, which, in 43 B.C., was charged with the duty of "restoring the republic." Theirs was known as the Second Triumvirate to distinguish it from its private and unofficial predecessor. Legally recognized by the Senate, the three magistrates bore the name of *Tresviri reipublicae constituendae* (triumvirs for arranging public affairs).

"Those round about" already may be restless in their moldering graves with the replicated blows of maul and mattock "digging into marble and metallic lead."

If Mussolini still is doing business at the old stand, according to quatrain 66 of the Eighth *Centurie*, that idle creature, being mechanical, would be well advised to get hence home when the saint's grave is excavated:

Quand l'escriture D.M. trouvée,
Et cave antique à lampe descouverte,
Loy, Roy et Prince Ulpian esprouvée,
Pavillon ruyne et Duc sous la couverte.

When the inscription D.M. is found,
And the ancient vault discovered by lamplight,
Law, king, and Prince Ulpian are put on trial,
The royal banner ruined and the duke under the
table.

The initials D.M. apparently refer to the motto *Deus in Me* as applied to St. Peter. Prince Ulpian was Domitius Ulpianus, who held appointments under Septimus Severus, Caracalla, and Elagabalus, who banished him. After the assassination of Elagabalus, Ulpian became pretorian prefect under Emperor Alexander Severus, in A.D. 222. The severity he displayed toward the Pretorian Guards resulted in his assassination by them in 228. Commentators believe that Nostradamus has taken Ulpian as a prototype for Mussolini.

A Nostradamic clue is concealed within quatrain 66 of the Sixth *Centurie* with the same obvious simplicity that Poe's "purloined letter" was hidden:

Au fondement de la nouvelle secte,
Seront les os du grand Romain trouvez,
Sepulchre en marbre apparoistra ouverte,
Terre trembler en Avril, mal-enfoüez.

At the foundation of the new sect,
The bones of the great Roman will be found,
Poorly hidden; the sepulcher of marble will appear open.
An earthquake in April.

By writing this quatrain's number as VI–66, we may obtain a glimmering of its significance. It becomes the mystical number of the beast, 666, spoken of in the book of Revelation:

"Let him that hath understanding count the number of the beast: for it is the number of a man; and his number is six hundred three-score and six (xiii, 18)." The beast here is equivalent to the Antichrist who for a time will gain dominion over the entire world but in the end will be overthrown by the angels of God (Revelation, xiv, 14ff.; xv, 1ff.).

This Apocalyptic number is supposed to represent the sum of the numerical values of some proper name, written in Hebrew or Greek letters, and attempts have been made to identify the beast with various characters in past and present history.

A possible reference to the predicted future great king of France is contained in quatrain 84 of the Ninth *Centurie*:

Roy exposé parfaira l'hecatombe,
Après avoir trouvé son origine,
Torrent ouvrir de marbre et plomb la tombe
D'un grand Romain d'enseigne Melusine.

The revealed king will end the massed slaughter
After having discovered his origin;
A torrent to open the tomb of marble and lead
Of a great Roman of melusine ensign.

The melusine, a mermaid with two tails disposed on either side, though not unknown in British heraldry, is a more frequent German emblem. Dorceto, a Phoenician goddess, was represented by the head and body of a woman, terminating below in a fish. With certain variations, the mermaid is found in the legendary lore of many nations. The sirens, nereids, and water nymphs of poetry all are forms of the same creature.

The fifteenth quatrain of the Sixth *Centurie* appears to link Spain and Germany with the effects of the tomb's discovery:

Dessous la tombe sera trouvé le prince
Qu'aura le prix par dessus Nuremberg:
L'Espagnol Roy en Capricorne mince,
Fainct et trahy par le grand Vitemberg.

Under the tomb will be found the prince
Who will have the prize over Nuremberg:
The Spanish king puny in Capricorn,
Denounced and betrayed by the great Wittenberg.

Nuremberg, meeting place of the Nazi party jam sessions, and Wittenberg, the German city where Martin Luther expounded the doctrines which Nostradamus, as a loyal Catholic, regarded as utter heresy, are believed by commentators to depict symbolically Hitler and his henchmen. It should be added, in passing, that Nostradamus uses the monarchical language of his era, and that "Spanish king" might equally well mean "Spanish dictator."

Capricorn is the tenth sign of the zodiac, which the sun enters at the winter solstice, approximately December 21. Capricorn also is a constellation which may be seen in the south during autumn. Also called the Goatfish, from being represented with the fore part of a goat and the tail of a fish, it is a small constellation which may be found by drawing a straight line from Vega through Altair. The line will pass through Omega Capricorni, one knee of the kneeling goat.

Since Nostradamus regarded himself as an astronomer rather than an astrologer, and the melusine, not unlike a chimerical goat-fish, is mentioned in the preceding quatrain, it well may be that the season for the described Hispano-German troubles is autumnal rather than the Yuletide. At the same time, as quatrain 65 of the Third *Centurie* suggests, another Pope will be chosen:

Quand le sepulchre du grand Romain trouvé
Le jour apres sera esleu pontife:
Du senat gueres il ne sera prouvé,
Empoisonné son sang au sacré scyphe.

When the sepulcher of the great Roman is found,
The day afterward a pontiff will be elected:
He scarcely will have been approved by the senate
When his blood will be poisoned by the sacred chalice.

"The Cardinals are those Prelates who form the Senate of the Church," according to the Rev. John A. Nainfa, S.S., professor of church history and liturgy at St. Mary's Seminary, Baltimore. Poisoning of "the sacred chalice" was a gentle practice known to a Roman Senate even more ancient than that of the Holy Roman Church.

The fifth quatrain of the Eighth *Centurie* is the last of this series:

Apparoistra temple luisant orné,
La lampe et cierge à Borne et à Breteuil.
Pour la Lucerne le canton destourné,
Quand on verra le grand Coq au cercueil.

The gleaming temple will appear adorned,
The lamp and candle to Borne and Breteuil.
The canton led astray for Lucerne,
When the great cock will be seen at the grave.

St. Peter is always holding the keys of Heaven, but often there is with him also a cock—a reminder of the denial (Matthew xxvi, 69–75; Mark xiv, 66–72; and Luke xxii, 34–61). In symbolical art, the rooster frequently is introduced into paintings of the Passion of Christ, while among the early Christians it was the token of vigilance;

and it was carved on tombs as an emblem of the resurrection, metaphorically signifying the coming of light after the night of death or announcing the general awakening of the resurrection.

There is a touch of the Apocalyptic to quatrain 56 of the Second *Centurie*:

> *Que peste et glaive n'a peu s'en definer,*
> *Mort dans le puys sommet du ciel frappé,*
> *L'abbé mourra quand verra ruyner*
> *Ceux du naufrage, l'escueil voulant grapper.*

> *What plague and sword has little determined,*
> *The summit of heaven smites the dead in the hereafter,*
> *The priest will die when he will see ruin*
> *To those shipwrecked, the breakers willing to grapple.*

Quatrain 75 of the Fifth *Centurie* may depict the enthronement of a Pope:

> *Montera haut sur le bien plus à dextre,*
> *Demourra assis sur la pierre carrée:*
> *Vers le midy posé à sa senestre,*
> *Baston tortu en main, bouche serrée.*

> *He will ascend high on the estate more to the right,*
> *He will remain seated on the square stone:*
> *Toward the midland established on his right,*
> *The crooked staff in the hand, the mouth*
> > *closed.*

This stanza is held to refer to the papacy because of the straight pun of *pierre* (stone or rock) and *Pierre* (Peter). The *baston tortu* (crooked staff) of the last line throws doubt on any analogy with a

Pope. The so-called crozier, more properly a pastoral staff (*baculus pastoralis*), is a symbol of a mere bishop, not of a metropolitan or of the Supreme Pontiff. Early monuments testify that up to the tenth century the Bishop of Rome made use of the crozier employed by his compeers. How this custom ceased is unknown, but it soon was forgotten and legendary and symbolic explanations were advanced to explain the Pope's lack of a pastoral staff. One of the most frequent reasons suggested is that the curved top of a crozier is a sign of limited jurisdiction, hence unsuited to the Supreme Pontiff, who claims universal jurisdiction.

Another familiar explanation was made by Pope Innocent III: "The Roman Pontiff does not use the pastoral staff because St. Peter the Apostle sent his staff to Eucharius, the first Bishop of Trèves (Trier), whom he appointed with Valerius and Maternus to preach the Gospel to the German race. He was succeeded in his bishopric by Maternus, who was raised from the dead by the staff of St. Peter. The staff is, down to the present day, preserved with great veneration by the church of Trèves."

St. Peter must have sacrificed his pastoral staff more than once, since several other cathedral chapters claim to have the real, Simon-pure staff of life.

More likely is the identification of quatrain 25 of the First *Centurie* with a future Pope:

Perdu, trouvé, caché de si long siècle,
Sera pasteur demy Dieu honoré,
Ains que la Lune acheve son grand cycle,
Par autres vieux sera deshonoré.

Lost, found, hidden so long a time,
The pastor will be honored as a demigod,
Even as the moon finishes its great cycle,
He will be disgraced by the other old men.

St. Malachi's *Pastor et Nauta,* previously referred to, is to be followed by the 108th in the Irish prophet's series, labeled *Flos Florum* ("Flower of Flowers"). That putative French Pope's successor is predicted under the style of *De Medietate Lunae* ("Of the Half Moon"). The above stanza may appertain to him.

The fortieth quatrain of the Fourth *Centurie* is reminiscent of Llewelyn Powys's *Rats in the Sacristy:*

> *Les forteresses des assiegez ferrez*
> *Par poudre à feu profondes en abysmes:*
> *Les prodateurs seront tous vifs serrez,*
> *Onc aux Sacristes n'advint si piteux scisme.*

> *The fortresses of the besieged stoned*
> *By fiery powder into the deepest abyss:*
> *All the traitors will be squeezed alive,*
> *Never to the Sacristies had come such a pitiful schism.*

Pastor et Nauta could be the prisoner of the fifteenth quatrain of the Fifth *Centurie:*

> *En navigant captif prins grand pontife;*
> *Grands apprestez saillir les clercs tumultuez:*
> *Second esleu absent son bien debife,*
> *Son favory bastard à mort tué.*

> *The great pontiff taken captive while sailing;*
> *The riotous clercs to project great preparations;*
> *The second elected absent, his advantage put to naught,*
> *His bastard favorite put to death.*

At the same time, the subject of the twelfth quatrain of the Tenth *Centurie* may be the above "second elected absent":

Esleu en Pape, d'esleu sera mocqué
Subit soudain prompt et timide,
Par trop bon doux à mourir provoqué,
Crainte estreinte la nuit de sa mort guide.

Elected as Pope, he will be mocked by the elect,
Unexpected, sudden, prompt and timid,
By too much good nature provoked to die,
Night guides the deadly embrace of his death.

Nostradamus predicts in quatrain 98 of the Eighth *Centurie* that the blood of clerics will flow like water:

Des gens d'Eglise sang sera espanché,
Comme l'eau en si grande abondance
Et d'un long temps ne sera restanché
Vae Vae au clerc, ruine et doléance.

The blood of the Church people will be spilled
Like water in such great abundance
And will not be stanched for a long time.
Woe, woe, to the clergy, ruin and grief.

Quatrain 48 of the Sixth *Centurie* probably involves papal politics:

La saincteté trop faincte et seductive,
Accompagnée d'une langue diserte:
La cité vieille et Parme trop hastive,
Florence et Sienne rendront plus desertes.

The holiness, very feigned and seductive,
Accompanied by a fluent tongue:

The old city and Parma too forward,
Florence and Siena will make themselves more dutiful.

Death presses close to Rome in quatrain 93 of the Second *Centurie*:

Bien pres du Tymbre presse la Lybitine,
Un peu devant grande inondation:
Le chef du nef prins, mis à sentine,
Chasteau, palais en conflagration.

Very close to the Tiber presses Libitina,
A little before the great flood:
The chief of the nave taken, cast into the sink,
Castle and palace in conflagration.

In classical mythology, the Roman goddess Libitina is identified especially with the dead. An undertaker was called *libitinarius*.

A translation of the papacy, by no means so improbable an event as it would have seemed a few years ago, is hinted at in two quatrains, both significantly numbered ninety-nine:

IX–99

Vent Aquilon fera partir le siège,
Par mur jetter cendres, platras, chaux et poussière:
Par pluye apres qui feur fera bien piège,
Dernier secours encontre leur frontière.

The North Wind will cause the see to depart,
To throw out ashes, rubbish, lime, and dust from the wall:
By the downpour thereafter which will make them well snared,
The last rescue is against their border.

VIII–99

Par la puissance des trois Roys temporels,
En autre lieu sera mis le saint Siège;
Où la substance de l'esprit corporal,
Sera remis et receu pour vray siège.

By the power of three temporal kings
The Holy See will be moved elsewhere;
Where the substance of the material spirit
Will be deposited and received for the true seat.

Though some of the quatrains cited in this chapter are obscure, to say the least, the Sphinx of Issachar's meaning in the last two stanzas is only too clear.

10

"The Other Is Not Yet Come"

Of particular interest today are the prophecies of Nostradamus regarding the future of France, his own country. Briefly, the Seer of Salon foretold the coming of a great Prince, named Henry, who would reestablish France's legitimist monarchy and free his people from their German fetters.

With Nostradamus holding out some hope for their future, Frenchmen are widely discussing the four terse lines of quatrain 88 of the Second *Centurie*:

> *Le circuit du grand fait ruyneux,*
> *Au nom septiesme le cinquiesme sera:*
> *D'un tiers plus grand l'estrange belliqueux*
> *Mouton, Lutèce, Aix ne garantira.*

> *The circle of the great deed of ruins*
> *Will be by the fifth of the seventh in name:*
> *Of the third and greatest, the strange, bellicose*
> *Ram at Lutetia, Aix shall not guarantee.*

This prediction may seem vague, but to French mystagogues of royalist persuasion it can mean only one thing. "The great deed of ruins," they sigh, was the supplanting of the monarchies by republics.

The meaning of the second line was brought home to Frenchmen a year ago when the Duke of Guise, pretender to France's nonexistent throne as John III, died.

The quiet old shadow-king has left a son—Henry, seventh Count of Paris. Should he come to wear the crown of France, he would be the fifth Henry actually to rule his nation, though the Count of Chambord regarded himself as "Henry V."

A certain Frank, called Robert the Strong, became Count of Paris in the ninth century, and the Franks chose one, and then another, of his descendants as their Duke. Robert died in 866 and his son, Odo, second Count of Paris, was Duke of the Franks until 887. His brother, Robert II, third Count of Paris, was Duke of the Franks in 922 and 923. Robert's son, Hugh the Great, fourth Count of Paris, became Duke of France and Burgundy on his father's death.

The Frankish throne being vacant by the death of Louis V, the last Carlovingian king, in 987, the great Hugh's son, Hugh Capet, fifth Count of Paris, assumed the royal power, with the consent of many barons, to begin the feudal kingdom of France.

Hugh Capet ruled with moderation, selected Paris, his county seat, as the capital of France, and is said to have been the ancestor of forty French kings. The next Capetian to bear the family's ancient title was Louis Philippe Albert d'Orléans, sixth Count of Paris, born in 1838 the son of Ferdinand, Duke of Orléans, and grandson of Louis Philippe, King of the French. This prince and his younger brother, the Duke of Chartres, accompanied their uncle, the Prince of Joinville, to the United States in August, 1861, and were attached to the personal staff of General McClellan. They remained with the Federal Army several months, serving with bravery and efficiency, especially in the battle of Gaines's Mill.

In 1873 the Count of Paris acknowledged the Count of Chambord as the head of the royal house of France, but, after the latter's death in 1883, the Count of Paris united in his person the claims of both branches of the Bourbons and was accepted by most legitimists as Philip VII. Forced to leave France in 1886 by the expulsion act, the sixth Count of Paris died in England in 1894.

The Count's heir was his son, Louis Philippe Robert, who bore the higher-sounding title of Duke of Orléans, with French royalists hailing him as Philip VIII. He died at Palermo on March 28, 1926, whereafter his cousin, John, Duke of Guise, became head of the House of Orléans. Guise was the son of the Duke of Chartres. As titular King John III, the heir to the Bourbon claims bestowed the most ancient Capetian title in 1929 upon his eldest son, Henry, who thus became "the seventh in name" as the seventh royal Count of Paris and may become Henry V in fact if he realizes the Orléans family motto—"All that is national is ours"—and his father's pledge: "The heir of forty kings who, for a thousand years, have made France."

The obscure third line may mean either that this future Bourbon monarch will become the successor "of the third and greatest" French Republic or the conqueror "of the third and greatest" German Reich. *Double entente* would admit both meanings.

England and Germany, according to those astrologers Nostradamus repudiates, are ruled by "the strange, bellicose" sign of Aries, or the Ram. Among the ancient Romans, *aries* also was the name of the battering-ram, a machine with an iron head used to batter down the walls of besieged towns or forts. Nostradamus is not far-fetching when he calls the Nazi armored divisions which battered through the French armies "the strange, bellicose Ram at Lutetia." Lutetia was the name for Paris in Roman times until the fourth century.

Aix, which "shall not guarantee," presumably is Aix-la-Chapelle, also known as Aachen, the city of Rhenish Prussia on the frontier of Belgium, forty-four miles west-south-west of Cologne. Charlemagne raised the place, of which he was very fond, to a position of importance as his favorite residence and the capital of his empire. The successors of Charlemagne and the emperors of Germany were crowned there from the ninth century until 1531.

It well may be that Nostradamus is seeking to suggest that France is to regain territory on the left or west bank of the Rhine. By treaties with Prussia and Austria before 1800, France had obtained an indefinite right to these lands. By the Peace of Luneville (1801), France gained a clear title to all territories west of the Rhine. This included ancient Aix-la-Chapelle.

While his father lived, the handsome, headstrong young Count of Paris was powerless to push the family's royal claims. He lived like a country squire at his manor in ancient Belgic Gaul and in all things was an obedient son and heir, but those who know the new pretender report that he is restless for power and that he hopes to unite stricken France under the ancient monarchy, restoring the disgraced Bourbon-Orléans line which Louis Philippe led into exile after the Revolution of 1848.

Henri Robert Ferdinand Marie Louis Philippe d'Albret-Nevers-Preuilly-Montoire-Bourbon-Dampierre-Carpet was born in the chateau of Nouvion-en-Thierâche on July 5, 1908. While he had been reared in France, he was forced to follow his father into exile. He married his cousin, Isabelle, Princess of Orléans-Braganza, at Palermo on April 8, 1931. Born in 1911, the Countess was a descendant of the Brazilian Emperor, Dom Pedro II. They have eight children, several of whom are boys.

The French are a superstitious race: they believe in portents and prophecies. They are praying for a strong leader. Deep down in their hearts, many Frenchmen are royalists and might forget all their enervating antagonisms if they had a king of competence for whom to fight. Of all the likely aspirants for this herculean stable cleaning, the one who wears the blue, white, and red livery of the House of Orléans stands out.

Henry, Count of Paris, is romantic enough to stir the imaginative French people. He has demonstrated that he has statesmanlike character. He is well educated and he has the flair for leadership which the nation demands. For instance, though his family has been forbidden to enter France or serve in the army, when this war broke out the Count volunteered for the Foreign Legion under the assumed name of "Robert le Fort" (that Robert the Strong who was the first Count of Paris) and helped to defend his homeland. Such bravery endears itself to the romantic French mind.

It may be no accident that the seventh Count of Paris is named Henry and that he fits the Nostradamic forecasts. "Wait and see," say Frenchmen. "Nostradamus is never wrong."

The Seer of Salon calls Henry V "the real savior of France." This scion of a long line of French sovereigns will lead his countrymen to victory, crushing the enemy—internal and external—to reestablish law, order, and religion. Nostradamus predicts a brilliant career for the last Capetian king. While he is victoriously fighting the Germans, the Italians and those of the East will attack the south of France, but Henry V will succeed in blocking this incursion, also. Battles will rage at sea and on the shore along the southern coasts of France and in the Mediterranean.

About this time a new Pope will be elected, presumably a French pontiff who may be a descendant of the miraculously spared son of Louis XVI, but surely is the French King's kinsman. Henry V will reestablish this new Pope on the pontifical throne after having given him refuge at Avignon, the new capital of France.

Henry V's victory over the Middle East will not be sufficient to bring them into complete submission. A great campaign against Islam, the last and mightiest of the crusades, will be undertaken under the successor of St. Louis, who will capture Constantinople and Jerusalem.

The triumph of western Europe is short lived. Toward the close of King Henry's reign, the East once again will rise against the enfeebled Occident and invade Europe. The French monarchy will not outlast Henry V and, with the King's death, will come Europe's last peaceful years.

Apparently these are to be the last years of the twentieth century. Afterward will come a great cataclysm in which Nostradamus seems to tell a different story each time he returns to his Apocalyptic theme. Sometimes his version is a Biblical one, while at other times he presages a cosmoplastic chaos. These prognostications also can be interpreted as the end of the Christian era, caused by the invasion of western Europe by an aroused East.

Nostradamus is not the first prophet to preach the end of the world and give dates for Daniel's "time, times, and an half." Should Nostradamus be right, there will be no one left to give him credit for his unerring accuracy.

Meanwhile, the nature of all prophecies is such that they are much easier to read backward, when recorded history can be applied to check all facts predicted. Trying to unravel a Nostradamic web of the future is an uncertain, speculative, and generally thankless task.

For example, the next four quatrains mention "the Cock." Orléanists persistently identify this barnyard strutter as a symbol of the Bourbon pretenders, but it may just as well be applied to the French army or to the Gallic nation as a whole. The gamecock's connection with the House of Orléans results from Louis Philippe's action in 1830 restoring the glorious tricolor to the army and topping the flagstaffs with the defiant rooster. The motto emblazoned on the regimental standards was *"Honneur et Patrie,"* which also is used by General de Gaulle's Free Frenchmen.

Arthur Maury, in *Emblèmes et Drapeaux de la France* (Paris, 1904), traces the history of the fighting cock back to the ancient Celts of Gallia (Gaul) and shows that this symbol has remained essentially French since then, being used by all regimes up to the time his book was published. Marshal Pétain's Government does not employ Chanticleer as a device; Reynard the Fox would be more suitable to his vicious regime.

The vulpine story, according to the *Reinaert* of J. F. Willems, a

Flemish poet, written in the first half of the thirteenth century, is as follows:

At the court of the (British) Lion, king of beasts, all the animals came and paid him homage except Reynard the Fox, whom many animals accused of murderous deeds. Reynard was summoned to the court, tried, and condemned to death by the Lion, but when about to be hanged he begged to be allowed to make public confession of his evil deeds. During his confession, he charged that the (German) Wolf and (Russian) Bear had conspired to kill the Lion and make the Bear king in his place. Reynard also hinted that he knew where immense treasures were hidden.

The Lion thereupon pardoned him and caused the Wolf and the Bear to be seized; but, when he was asked to tell where the hidden treasures were, Reynard declared that he was under oath to go to Rome on a pilgrimage and must hasten away. So he was allowed to go. After more misdeeds, including the killing of his companions on the journey to Rome, the Lion became convinced of the Fox's treachery and decreed him to be an outlaw.

As was noted in the preceding chapter, the cock is the emblem of Peter, who denied his Lord, so it may be Nostradamic symbolism with some future and general application to a coming complete and voluntary renunciation of the Christian faith, in favor of either another religion or none.

The cock also has been used as a symbol of Red revolution. In the German peasants' war, which began in 1525, Florian von Geyer, leader of the celebrated Black Company, composed this fighting chant for his embattled farmers:

Als Adam grub und Eva spann,
  Kyrie eleison,
Wer war dann der Edelmann?
  Kyrie eleison.

Spiess voran, drauf und dran!
Setzt aufs Klosterdach den roten Hahn!

When Adam delved and Eve span,
Lord, have mercy,
Who was then the nobleman?
Lord, have mercy.
Level pikes, up and over!
Set the red cock on cloister roof.

To put the red cock on the roof of a monastery or nunnery meant, here, to set it on fire. The peasantry were rebelling against the clerical land-grabbers.

Whatever it may symbolize, the cock is introduced in the fourth quatrain of the Eighth *Centurie*:

Dedans Monech le Coq sera receu,
Le Cardinal de France apparoistra
Par Légation Romain sera deceu,
Foiblesse à l'Aigle et force au Coq naistra.

Within Monaco the cock will be received,
The Cardinal of France will appear
He will be deceived by the Roman delegation,
Weakness will be born to the eagle and force to the cock.

The eagle is or has been the symbol of the Hittites, Persians, Egypt's Ptolemies, ancient Rome, Greek Byzantium, Charlemagne, the Holy Roman Empire, Austria-Hungary, the German Empire, Czarist Russia, the United States of America, the two French empires, Italy's House of Savoy, the Mexican Republic, Fascist Italy, and Nazi Germany.

The sixth quatrain of the Eighth *Centurie* may indicate these hurrying years of our own changing world:

Clarté fulgure à Lyon apparente
Luysant, print Malte, subit sera estrainte,
Sardon, Mauris traitera décevante,
Genève à Londres à Coq trahison fainte.

Vivid light apparent at Lyons
Shining, Malta taken, suddenly he will be embraced,
Sardon and the Maures will deal deceitfully,
Geneva feigns treason to London and to the Cock.

The Sardones were a Basque or Celtiberian tribe of Aquitaine in Roman times who occupied Pyrenean slopes in the neighborhood of Comminges. The Maures is the name for the coast of the French department of Var between Cannes and Hyères. "Hills and pine trees and the sea," wrote Allan Updegraff in *Whatever We Do*, "on the tip of that southernmost French peninsula below Toulon, disdained by continental expresses on their way to Cannes, Nice, Monte Carlo."

Astrologers report that the first line of the fourteenth quatrain of the Fifth *Centurie* dates that quatrain as January 19, 1943:

Saturne et Mars en Leo Espagne captive,
Par Libique chef au conflit attrapé:
Proche de Malte, Heredde prinse vive,
Et Romain sceptre sera par Coq frappé.

Saturn and Mars in Leo, Spain captured
By the Libyan chief, entrapped in the conflict:
Near Malta, Herod taken alive
And the Roman scepter will be struck by the cock.

That the coming great French leader will restore the church to Rome is implicit in quatrain 28 of the Sixth *Centurie*:

> *Le Grand Celtique entrera dedans Rome*
> *Menant amas d'exilez et bannis:*
> *Le grand pasteur mettra à mort tout homme*
> *Qui pour le Coq estoit aux Alpes unis.*

> *The Great Celt will enter Rome*
> *Leading an army of the exiled and banished:*
> *The great pastor will put to death all men*
> *Who united in the Alps for the sake of the cock.*

The last half of the stanza would appear to bear out the view that the cock, in some cases, at least, symbolizes a great apostasy to be avenged.

Stargazers read quatrain 86 of the Fourth *Centurie* as portending a coronation in June, 1944:

> *L'an que Saturne en eau sera conjoinct*
> *Avecques Sol, le Roy fort et puissant,*
> *A Reims et Aix sera reçeu et oinct,*
> *Apres conquestes meurtrira innocens.*

> *The year that Saturn will be conjoined in Aquarius*
> *With the sun, the king is strong and powerful;*
> *He will be received and anointed at Reims and Aix-la-Chapelle.*
> *After conquests he will bruise the guiltless.*

Bruising the innocent does not sound like what the world had been led to expect from the great Henry, so it may be that Nostradamus has succeeded in so obscuring himself that he is sullying his own hero.

The sixth quatrain of the Fifth *Centurie* has been taken to mean the pontifical benison for Henry V:

> *Au Roy l'augure sur le chef la main mettre*
> *Viendra prier pour la paix Italique:*
> *A la main gauche viendra changer de sceptre,*
> *De Roy viendra Empereur pacifique.*

> *The augur to the king to put the hand on the head*
> *He will come to pray for Italian peace:*
> *He will come to change the scepter to the left hand,*
> *He will become from king the peaceable emperor.*

The kings of France are represented on their state seals as holding in the right hand a lance or sword, the instrument of war, while in the left hand they hold a scepter or royal orb surmounted by a cross, as a symbol of peace and dominion.

The fifteenth quatrain of the Seventh *Centurie* presages the translation of the papacy to Avignon:

> *Devant cité de l'Insubre contrée,*
> *Sept ans sera le Siège devant mis:*
> *Le très-grand Roy y fera son entrée,*
> *Cité puis libre hors de ses ennemis.*

> *Opposite the city of the Insubrian country,*
> *The See will be placed for seven years as before:*
> *The very great king will bring it his freedom of access,*
> *The city then free, out of reach of his enemies.*

The Insubres were the largest tribe of Transpadane Gaul, according to Polybius (Book II, 17), and occupied the north Italian upland between Milan and the lakes. Avignon is slightly southwest of the Insubrian country. The Popes lived at Avignon for ten times seven years in the fourteenth century.

The third quatrain of the Sixth *Centurie* depicts the new king as restoring peace and order to broken France:

> *Fleuve qu'esprouve le nouveau nay Celtique,*
> *Sera en grande de l'Empire discorde:*
> *Le jeune prince par gent Ecclesiastique,*
> *Offera le sceptre coronal de concorde.*

> *The river which tries the new Celtic birth,*
> *There will be discord among the Empire's great:*
> *The young prince will furnish the crowning scepter*
> *Of concord through the ecclesiastical people.*

But the tenth quatrain of the Fourth *Centurie* implies that the course of restoration is not altogether smooth:

> *Le jeune Prince accusé faussement,*
> *Mettra en trouble le camp et en querelle:*
> *Meurtry le chef pour le soustenement,*
> *Sceptre appaiser puis guerir escrouëlles.*

> *The young prince, falsely accused,*
> *Will put the army into trouble and quarrel:*
> *The chief bruised for keeping it up,*
> *The scepter to appease, then to heal, the king's evil.*

Though the tenth quatrain of the Seventh *Centurie* is obscure, it may be part of Henry V's epic:

> *Par le grand prince limitrophe du Mans,*
> *Preux et vaillant chef de grand exercite:*

Par mer et terre de Gallois et Normans,
Caspre passer Barcelonne pillé isle.

By the great prince from neighboring Le Mans
Proved and valiant head of a great host
Of French and Normans by sea and land,
The Isle of Capri pillaged to pass Barcelona.

In the seventeenth quatrain of the Seventh *Centurie*, Nostradamus characterizes the king who has not yet come:

Le Prince rare en pitié et clémence,
Après avoir la paix aux siens baillé,
Viendra changer par mort grand cognoissance,
Par grand repos le regne travaillé.

The prince rare in compassion and mercy,
After having given peace to his people,
He will come to change great understanding by death,
The realm toils in great security.

Quatrain 73 of the Seventh *Centurie* may presage Henry V's enthronement:

Renfort de sièges manubis et maniples
Changes le sacre et passe sur le prosne,
Prins et captifs n'arreste les prez triples,
Plus par fonds mis, eslevé, mis au trosne.

Plunder and troops reinforce the seats
The sacred changed and to pass on the sermon,
Taken and captives not stopping the triple prize,
More sent from below, raised, put on the throne.

Stanley's address to England's future Henry VII:

Lo, here, this long-usurped royalty,
From the dead temples of this bloody wretch
Have I plucked it off, to grace thy brows withal

is recalled in quatrain 23 of the Seventh *Centurie*:

Le Royal sceptre sera contrainct de prendre
Ce que ses predecesseurs avaient engagé:
Puis que l'aneau on fera mal entendre,
Lors qu'on viendra le palais saccager.

He will be compelled to take the royal scepter
By those who had pledged his predecessors:
Since they will misunderstand the ring
When they will come to ransack the palace.

Rings also figure in quatrain 21 of the Tenth *Centurie*:

Par le despit du Roy soustenant moindre,
Sera meurdry luy présentant les bagues,
Le père au fils voulant noblesse poindre
Fait comme à Perse jadis firent les Magues.

By the spite of the king, sustaining the least,
He will be murdered presenting the rings,
The father wishing to implant nobility in the sons
Did as the Magi would have done in the Persia of old.

From the Magi, Persian kings had to receive instructions in the art
of reigning and in worship before they could ascend the throne. From
among the most illustrious Magi, the king selected six wise men as

counselors who, together with the monarch, constituted the celebrated council of seven. The heir to the throne was admitted to meetings of the council only for merit and not by divine right. For many centuries the philosophy of the Magi formed the basis of the polity of the Persian monarchy, and without Magian advice the king determined no important act of state.

Quatrain 44 of the Tenth *Centurie* requires interpretation:

> *Par lors qu'un Roy sera contre les siens,*
> *Natif de Bloys subjuguera Ligures:*
> *Mammel, Cordube et les Dalmatiens,*
> *Des sept puis l'ombre à Roy estrennes et lémures.*

> *By then, when a king will be against his own people,*
> *The native of Blois will subjugate the Ligurians:*
> *Memel, Cordova, and the Dalmatians,*
> *Then the shadows of the seven handsels and ghosts to the king.*

Pertinax (André Geraud), writing in *The New York Times* of August 24, 1941, said:

It is impossible to foretell whether the "Free France" of today will prove to be the nucleus of the redeemed France of tomorrow. Gen. de Gaulle is committed, under the "organic declaration," to lay down whatever public authority he holds and comply with the will of the representatives of the nation as soon as it is possible for them to express themselves freely and normally. . . .

Schemers try to induce Gen. de Gaulle to frame plans of his own and even to exert himself for the restoration of the constitutional monarchy. Emissaries of the Count of Paris, heir to the French throne, are said to have visited London. Gen. de Gaulle has created a material and moral rallying point for all Frenchmen who refuse to despair of their country.

Thus the groundwork may be laid for the fusion of Free France and Royal France. If that takes place, then "a king will be against his own people" if he and *le Général* lead a crusade to deliver France from venal Vichy.

Blois, ancient crenelated seat of the Capetian monarchy, is a synonym for the French royal family. The Ligurians are the inhabitants of the Italian Riviera and Genoa. Memel is a town, seaport, and territory of the Baltic. It was given to Lithuania in February, 1923, but was occupied by Hitlerized Germany in March, 1939. Cordova is a province and city of Spain. The Dalmatians are south Slavs dwelling along the Adriatic littoral. Handsels are gifts or tokens of good will distributed at the beginning of a new enterprise to bring good luck.

Presumably "second and third" and first in the initial line of quatrain 28 of the Tenth *Centurie* refer to the three French Republics:

Second et tiers qui font prime musique
Sera par Roy en honneur sublimée,
Pour grasse et maigre presque à demi eticque
Rapport de Venus faux rendra deprimée.

Second and third, which blent the first music,
Will be sublimated in honor by the king,
Almost half-emaciated for fat and lean
The false report of Venus will restore the deprived.

Venus generally is used by Nostradamus as a symbol of scandal and disorder. That France has been "half-emaciated for fat and lean" goes without saying.

Time may clarify the perplexing details of quatrain 97 of the Eleventh *Centurie*:

Par Ville-franche, Mascon en desarroy:
Dans les fagots seront soldats cachez.

Changer de temps en prime pour le Roy.
Par de Chalons et Moulins tous hachez.

By Villefranche, Mâcon in disorder,
Soldiers will be hidden in the faggots.
To change the weather into spring for the king.
All cut to pieces by Chalons and Moulins.

Recalling the opening lines of Shakespeare's *Richard III:*

Now is the winter of our discontent
Made glorious summer by this sun of York.

Perhaps the "flower of the French" will bloom in the spring, too, tra-la!

Quatrain 52 of the Eighth *Centurie* ties together the removal of France's capital to Avignon, the defeat of the Germans at Poitiers, and the twilight of the Teutonic eagles on the banks of the Rhine:

Le Roy de Bloys dans Avignon regner,
D'Amboise et semer viendra le long de Lyndre
Ongle à Poitiers, sainctes aisles ruyner
Devant Boni.

The king of Blois to reign in Avignon,
Of Amboise and to sow he will come the length of the Indre
The talon at Poitiers, to ruin the holy eagles
Before Bonn.

Changes in the prelature are foreshadowed by quatrain 77 of the Fifth *Centurie:*

Tous les degrez d'honneur Ecclesiastique,
Seront changez en dial quirinal:

En Martial quirinal flaminique,
Un Roy de France le rendra vulcanal.

All the degrees of ecclesiastical honor
Will be changed in the Quirinal schedule:
In martial Quirinal spirit,
A king of France will restore the flame.

Quirinal is derived from the Latin Mons Quirinalis, now Monte Quirinale, one of the seven hills of Rome. The Italian royal palace is there; hence, Quirinal refers to the Italian monarchical government, as contrasted with the Vatican. Nostradamus implies that a French king will restore to the papacy whatever has been usurped by the House of Savoy and Fascist Italy.

"Chyren," the Nostradamic anagram designating the first Bourbon king, Henry IV, explained in Chapter 6, is used for the last Bourbon, Henry V, in quatrain 34 of the Fourth *Centurie*:

Le grand mené captif d'estrange terre,
D'or enchaîné au Roy Chyren offert:
Qui dans Ausone; Milan perdra la guerre,
Et tout son ost mis à feu et à fer.

The great one taken captive in a strange land,
Offered in golden chains to King Henry,
Who is in Italy; Milan shall lose the war
And all his host put to fire and steel.

Nostradamus typifies Islam as "Selim" or "Selin," as in quatrain 79 of the Second *Centurie*:

La barbe crespe et noire par engin,
Subjuguera la gent cruelle et fière:

Un grand Chyren ostera du longin
Tous les captifs par Selin bannière.

Crisp Blackbeard will subjugate
The cruel and fierce race by an engine:
A great Henry will strip to the loins
All the captives under Selim's banner.

The Seer of Salon obviously uses as a symbol Selim I Yavuz ("The Inflexible"), Sultan of Turkey (1465–1521), who usurped the throne, deposing and killing his father, with all his brothers and nephews, in 1512. In a war with Persia in 1514 he conquered Mesopotamia, Kurdistan, and Armenia, after defeating Shah Ismail with immense slaughter. After he vanquished Syria in 1516, the title "Servant of the Two Cities" (Mecca and Medina), hitherto reserved to the caliphs, was added to Selim's name in the official prayer. Leading his triumphant army against the Mamelukes, whom he utterly defeated in 1517, he annexed Egypt, wresting the title of caliph from the last of the Abbasides. Thus the Sultan of Turkey, bloodthirsty and cruel beyond expression, became head of the Islamic world.

Henry V's benign rule is to be quite a contrast with that of Gladstone's "unspeakable Turk," quatrain 97 of the First *Centurie* indicates:

Ce que fer, flamme, n'a sceu parachever,
La douce langue au conseil viendra faire,
Par repos, songe, le Roy fera resuer,
Plus l'ennemy en feu, sang militaire.

That which fire and sword has not sealed to perfection,
The gentle tongue will come to bring by good counsel,
By quiet and contemplation the king will fulfill his dream,
The enemy more in fire and martial blood.

In quatrain 77 of the Fourth *Centurie*, Nostradamus foreshadows an amicable unification of Europe:

Selin monarque, l'Italie pacifique,
Regnes unis par Roy Chrestien du monde:
Mourant voudra coucher en terre Belgique
Apres pyrates avoir chassé de l'onde.

Selim monarch, Italy pacified,
Realms united by the Christian king of the world:
Dying, he will wish to lie in Belgic soil
After having driven the pirates from the deep.

Nostradamus has Henry V taking the title of the Muslim leader whom he had conquered just as Napoleon's marshals, when made dukes and princes of the imperial court, commemorated their exploits on the field of battle by annexing the names of their victories.

The seventh quatrain of the Second *Centurie* has been interpreted as foretelling the birth of Antichrist:

Entre plusieurs aux isles deportées,
L'un estre nay à deux dents en la gorge;
Mourront de faim, les arbres esbroutées,
Pour eux neuf Roy nouvel edict leur forge.

Among the many deported to the islands,
One is to be born with two teeth in the mouth;
They shall die of starvation, the trees uprooted,
For them the new king makes up a new decree.

France's best-known penal settlement is the so-called Devil's Island group of small, rocky, torrid islets off French Guiana, in South

America. Nothing has been heard from there lately about newborn babies with unusually precocious milk teeth.

Quatrain 84 of the Fifth *Centurie* stigmatizes Antichrist's parentage:

> *Naistra du goulphre et cité immesurée,*
> *Nay de parens obscure et ténébreux*
> *Quand la puissance du grand Roy revérée,*
> *Voudra destruire par Rouen et Evreux.*

> *He will be born of the pit and measureless city,*
> *Born of obscure and foul parents:*
> *When the power of the great king is venerated,*
> *He will wish to destroy about Rouen and Evreux.*

Rouen and Evreux are in Normandy.

The seventeenth quatrain of the Third *Centurie* refers to Rome:

> *Mont Aventin brusler nuict sera veu,*
> *Le ciel obscur tout à coup en Flandres:*
> *Quand le Monarque chassera son neveu,*
> *Les gens d'Eglise commettront les esclandres.*

> *The Aventine Hill will be seen to burn by night,*
> *The sky dark suddenly in Flanders:*
> *When the king will expel his nephew,*
> *The people of the Church will commit slanders.*

The Aventine Hill (Latin, Mons Aventinus) was one of ancient Rome's seven hills, inhabited chiefly by plebeians.

There is nothing clear about the twelfth quatrain of the Second *Centurie*:

Yeux clos ouverts d'antique fantaisie
L'habit des seuls seront mis à néant:
La Grand Monarque chastiera leur frénaisie,
Ravir des temples le thrésor par devant.

The closed eyes opened to ancient fancy
The attire of the celibates will be put to naught:
The Great Monarch will punish their madness,
To ravish the temples in the presence of the treasure.

A suggestion of France's "war guilt" trials at Riom is contained in quatrain 35 of the Sixth *Centurie*:

Près de Rion et proche à blanche laine,
Aries, Taurus, Cancer, Leo, la Viergo:
Mars, Jupiter, Le Sol ardra grand plaine
Bloys et citez lettres cachez au cierge.

Near Riom and next to white wool,
Aries, Taurus, Cancer, Leo, the Virgin:
Mars, Jupiter, the Sun will scorch a great plain
Blois and writs of summons sealed with the wax taper.

An astrologer might make short shrift of this; the author reneges. There is an oblique reference to racial supremacy myths in the eightieth quatrain of the Fifth *Centurie*:

Logmion grande Bizance approchera,
Chassée sera la barbarique ligue,
Des deux loix l'une etinique laschera,
Barbare et franche en perpetuelle brigue.

Ogmius will approach great Byzantium,
The barbarous league will be driven out,

Of the two laws, the ethnic one will yield,
Barbarous and free in perpetual intrigue.

Nostradamus appears to refer to Henry V as the Gaulish Hercules, Ogmius. This heroic label is appended again in quatrain 42 of the Sixth *Centurie:*

A l'Ogmyon sera laissé le regne,
Du Grand Selin qui plus fera de faict,
Par les Itales estendra son enseigne,
Sera régi par prudent contrefaict.

To Ogmius will be left the realm
Of the Great Selim, no more doing deeds:
He will extend his flag over the Italians,
Who will be ruled by a wise cripple.

Anglophobes hold that quatrain 27 of the Sixth *Centurie* forebodes Britain's loss of her empire:

Dedans les Isles de cinq fleuves à un,
Par le croissant du grand Chyren Selin:
Par les bruines de l'air, fureur de l'un,
Six échappés cachés, fardeaux de lin.

Within the Isles from five rivers to one,
By the crescent of the great Henry Selim:
By the drizzle from the air, fury of the one,
Six escape hidden, burdens of flax.

According to that anti-British reading, the five rivers are the Nile, Niger, Ganges, Euphrates, and Thames. Only the Thames would be left to England. It should be noted well that the first four rivers run through portions of the empire on which the sun never sets. There still would be dominions aplenty: Canada, Australia, New Zealand, South Africa, Newfoundland (temporarily out of dominion status), and Ireland, about whose future not even Nostradamus dared prophesy. The Seer of Salon had no desire to mess up an otherwise perfect record. Perhaps those dominions are the six which "escape hidden." As for the "burdens of flax," where does linen's raw material grow better than in Ireland and what dominion has been a greater burden?

There is no interpretation for quatrain 71 of the Twelfth *Centurie*:

Fleuves, rivières de mal seront obstacles,
La vieille flamme d'ire non appaisée
Courir en France, cecy comme d'oracles:
Maisons, manoirs, palais, secte rasée.

Streams and rivers of evil will be in the way,
The ancient flame of wrath is not appeased
To flow into France, this as in the oracles:
Houses, manors, palaces, and the sect demolished.

Were it not for the last two lines, quatrain 85 of the Third *Centurie* might be taken for the fall of Paris in 1940:

La Cité prise par tromperie et fraude,
Par le moyen d'un beau jeune attrapé,
L'assaut donné. Raubine près de l'Aude,
Luy et tous morts pour avoir bien trompé.

The city taken by deception and fraud
By means of a brand-new trap,
The assault given. Looting near the Aude,
He and the rest dead for having been betrayed.

The Aude is a river of Languedoc which flows into the Gulf of the Lion near Narbonne. Carcassonne is the capital of the Department of the Aude.

The fourth quatrain of the Seventh *Centurie* is a poser:

> *Le Duc de Langres assiégé dedans Dôle,*
> *Accompagné d'Autun et Lyonnois:*
> *Genève, Augsbourg joint ceux de Mirandole,*
> *Passer les monts contre les Anconnois.*

> *The Duke of Langres beset inside Dole,*
> *Accompanied by Autun and the Lyonnais:*
> *Geneva and Augsburg joined those of Mirandole*
> *To pass the mountains against the Anconians.*

The Bishop of Langres was one of the six historic ecclesiastical peers of France, holding a duke's rank. Autun is a city of the Department of Saône-et-Loire, on the river Arroux. Augsburg is in Bavaria, while Ancona is a seaport of central Italy on the Adriatic. Which genealogy and geography bring truth no nearer.

Quatrain 79 of the Fifth *Centurie* may praise Henry V:

> *Par sacrée pompe viendra baisser les aisles,*
> *Par la venuë du grand Législateur:*
> *Humble haussera, vexera les rebelles,*
> *Naistra sur terre aucun aemulateur.*

> *By sacred pomp he will come to lower the wings,*
> *By the coming of the great legislator:*
> *He will raise up the humble, vex the rebels,*
> *No other rival will be born on earth.*

The newly launched royal ship of state may be the topic of quatrain 93 of the Tenth *Centurie*:

La barque neuve recevera les voyages,
Là et aupres transfèreront l'empire:
Beaucaire, Arles retiendront les hostages,
Près deux colonnes trouvées de porphire.

The new bark will take voyages,
Hither and yon they will transfer the empire:
Beaucaire and Arles will retain the hostages,
Near by two columns of porphyry are found.

Quatrain 96 of the Second *Centurie* hints at the aftermath of the Anglo-Russian occupation of Persia in August, 1941:

Flambeau ardent au ciel sera veu,
Pres de la fin et principe du Rosne,
Famine, glaive, tard le secours pourveu,
La Perse tourne envahir Macédoine.

The burning firebrand will be seen in the sky,
Near the issue and outset of the Rhone,
Famine and sword provide the rescue late,
The Persian turns to invade Macedonia.

The first line of quatrain 46 of the Third *Centurie* suggests that even Nostradamus himself wasn't quite certain what he was trying to say:

Le Ciel (de Plancus la Cité) nous présagc
Par clairs insignes et par estoilles fixes,
Que de son change subit s'approche l'aage,
Ne pour son bien ne pour les malefices.

The sky (the city of Plancus) we conjecture
By clear signals and by fixed stars,

That by its sudden change it approaches the age,
Neither for its welfare nor for its spells.

Lyons, the ancient Lugdunum, on the hill of Fourvières (Forum vetus), was colonized in 54 B.C. by Munatius Plancus.

Time alone will tell whether "Mesopotamia" in quatrain 99 of the Third *Centurie* is the McCoy or the customary synonym for Italy:

Aux champs herbeux d'Alein et du Varneigue,
Du mont Lebron proche de la Durance
Camp des deux parts conflit sera si aigre,
Mesopotamie defaillira en la France.

On the grassy plains of Alleins and of Vernegues,
Of Mont Luberon near the Durance
The army of two parts, the conflict will be so bitter,
Mesopotamia will fail in France.

The scene of this action is near Salon, home town of Nostradamus in Provence.

Quatrain 59 of the Twelfth *Centurie* could be applied with conviction to France at this very time:

L'accord et pache sera du tout rompuë:
Les amitiez polluës par discorde.
L'haine envieillie, toute foy corrompuë,
Et l'esperance. Marseille sans concorde.

Good understanding and peace will be altogether shattered:
Friendships polluted by discord.
The age-old hatred corrupting all faith,
And hope. Marseilles without harmony.

But quatrain 88 of the Sixth *Centurie* veers more to the future:

Un regne grand demourra desolé,
Aupres del Hebrose feront assemblées:
Monts Pyrénées le rendront consolé,
Lorsque dans May seront terres tremblées.

A great reign will give up, brokenhearted,
Around the Ebro they will make assemblies:
The Pyrenees Mountains will be restored to console him,
And then in May there will be earthquakes.

However, it is reminiscent of "il n'y a plus de Pyrénées" ("The Pyrenees have ceased to exist"), said to have been addressed by Louis XIV of France to his grandson, Philip V, about to ascend the Spanish throne. This is just another Nostradamic wording seeming to inscribe past, present, and future in a vicious circle.

There are labyrinthine qualities also in quatrain 97 of the Eighth *Centurie*:

Aux fins du Var changer le Pompotans,
Pres du rivage les trois beaux enfans naistre,
Ruyne au peuple par aage competans
Regne au pays changer et plus voir croistre.

At the end of Var the all-potent to change,
Near the beach the three beautiful children to be born,
Ruin to the people by the competent age
To change the country's regime and see it grow greater.

Because Nostradamus called England Le Pempotam in the hundredth quatrain of the Tenth *Centurie* (see Chapter 5), Anglophobes wash their hands with invisible soap over the last word of the first line in the above stanza. They gleefully interpret it as foreboding the closing of the British Doomsday Book. Var is a department of southern France between Marseilles and Cannes.

Possibly the tenth quatrain of the Ninth *Centurie* portrays the celebrated Bear That Walks Like a Man:

> *Moyne moynesse d'enfant mort exposé,*
> *Mourir par ourse et ravy par verrier.*
> *Par Fois et Pamyes le camp sera posé*
> *Contre Tholose carcas dresser forrier.*

> Monk and nun lay out the dead babe in state,
> Put to death by the bear and transported onto stained glass.
> About Foix and Pamiers the camp will be pitched
> The quartermaster to set up the frame against Toulouse.

The fifth quatrain of the Sixth *Centurie* is somewhat suggestive of France's current tribulations:

> *Si grand famine par onde pestifère,*
> *Par pluye longue le long du pôle arctique:*
> *Samarobryn cent lieux de l'hémisphere,*
> *Vivront sans loy, exempt de politique.*

> Such a great famine through the plague-ridden wave,
> By a long downpour the length of the arctic pole:
> Amiens and a hundred places of the hemisphere,
> Will live without law, free from politics.

Anciently, Amiens was Samarobrivo.

The last French crusade against the Muslims may be the theme of quatrain 91 of the Eighth *Centurie:*

Parmi les champs de Rodanes entrées
Où les croisez seront presque unis,
Les deux brassières en pisces rencontrées,
Et un grand nombre par deluge punis.

Entered among the fields of the Rhone
Where the crusaders will be nearly united,
The two braces met with in the fish,
And a great number punished by the deluge.

Quatrain 41 of the Seventh *Centurie* may symbolize the rehabilitation of France's royal household upon its own soil:

Les os des pieds et des mains enserrez,
Par bruit maison longtemps inhabitée,
Seront par songes concavant deterrez,
Maison salubre et sans bruit habitée.

The bones of the feet and hands shut in,
The house a long time uninhabited because of clamor,
The house healthy and lived in without noise,
They will be brought to light by warning dreams.

Sacrilege in the south of France is implied in quatrain 72 of the Ninth *Centurie*:

Encor seront les saints temples pollus,
Et expillez par Senat Tholosain,
Saturne deux trois siecles revollus,
Dans Avril, May, gens de nouveau levain.

The holy temples will be polluted again
And looted by the Toulousan Senate,

A Saturnalia twice accomplished in three centuries,
In April and May the germ of people anew.

Apparently Paris, no matter how many times hell is let loose in it during the wrath to come, somehow will pull through evil occupations because of its storied vital spirit, the eighth quatrain of the First *Centurie* promises:

Combien de fois prinse Cité solaire
Seras, changeant les loi barbares et vaines
Ton mal s'approche, plus sera tributaire,
Le grand Hadrie recouvrira tes vaines.

How many times will the solar city be taken,
Changing the barbarous and vain laws;
Thy evil days approach, more will be tributary,
The great Hadrian will cover over thy vanities.

The name Hadrian (or Adrian) has been borne by six Popes, only two of whom were unimportant.

There is a touch of the Apocalyptic to quatrain 46 of the First *Centurie:*

Tout apres d'Aux, de Lectore et Mirande
Grand feu du ciel en trois nuicts tombera,
Cause adviendra bien stupende et mirande,
Bien peu apres la terre tremblera.

Close by Auch, Lectoure, and Mirande
A great fire shall drop from the sky for three nights,
A stupendous and miraculous case shall happen,
Very soon thereafter the earth shall quake.

Auch, Lectoure, and Mirande are in Gascony.

Quatrain 71 of the First *Centurie* is compact, cryptic, and absolutely unintelligible:

La Tour Marine trois fois prinse et reprinse
Par Espagnols, Barbares, Ligurins,
Marseille et Aix, Arles par ceux de Pise
Vast, feu, fer, pille, Avignon des Thurins.

The marine tower three times captured and recaptured
By Spaniards, Barbarians, Ligurians,
Marseilles and Aix, Arles by those of Pisa
Devastation, fire, iron, pillage, Avignon of the Turinese.

The Aix mentioned here presumably is the one in Provence.

A devastating civil war may be the subject of quatrain 72 of the First *Centurie*:

Du tout Marseille des habitans changee
Course et pour fuitte jusques pres de Lyon.
Narbon, Tholoze par Bordeaux outragee,
Tuez, captifs, presque d'un million.

All Marseilles shall be changed of its inhabitants,
An incursion and put to flight up to Lyons.
Narbonne, Toulouse ravaged by Bordeaux,
Slain, captives, nearly a million.

In quatrain 74 of the Second *Centurie* what appears to be a mass migration transpires:

De Sens, d'Autun viendront jusques au Rosne,
Pour passer outre vers les monts Pyrénnées;

La gent sortir de la marque d'Anconne,
Par terre et mer suivra à grands trainnées.

From Sens and Autun they will come up to the Rhone,
To pass beyond to the Pyrenees mountains:
The people will sally from the mark of Ancona,
Following by land and sea in great trains.

It has been suggested that "the great celibate" in quatrain 29 of the Tenth *Centurie* is a Pope:

De Pol Mansol dans caverne caprine
Caché et prins extraict hors par la barbe,
Captif mené comme beste mastine
Par Begourdans amenée près de Tarbe.

Hidden by the great celibate in the caprine cavern and taken,
Drawn out by the beard,
The captive led as a stupid cur
By the conveying Bigorrans, near to Tarbes.

Among the attractions of the isle of Capri, in the Bay of Naples, are the famous grottoes, or sea caverns, the best known being the Blue Grotto. This probably is "the caprine cavern" referred to above. The old county of Bigorre is part of the present French Department of the Hautes-Pyrénées. Tarbes is its chief town.

The six-lined *Prediction* No. 38 is an adventure into mysticism seeming to epitomize the era of France's last Bourbon monarch:

Par eau et par feu et par grand maladie,
Le pourvoyeur a l'hazard de sa vie
Sçavra combien vaut le quintal de bois,
Six cens et quinze, ou le dix-neuviesme,

On gravera d'un grand Prince cinquiesme
L'immortel nom sur le pied de la Croix.

By water and by fire and by great illness,
The purveyor of his life at hazard
He will know well how to value a hundredweight of wood,
Six hundred and fifteen, or the nineteenth,
The immortal name on the foot of the Cross
Will be engraved by a fifth great Prince.

And as his flickering light burns out, he may repeat the saying attributed to another Bourbon, Louis XV:

"Après nous le déluge" ("After us the deluge").

11

"That Old Serpent"

As Europe's warring armies move toward warmer climates to continue fighting throughout the winter, it becomes more apparent that the possible battlefield for 1941–1942 extends over a vast region approximately coinciding with the empire of Alexander the Great during its widest expanse. The Macedonian conqueror ruled lands reaching from the Danube in the northwest to the Libyan desert on the southwest and the Caspian Sea, Persian Gulf, and Indus River on the east.

The British and Russians are involved against the Germans in war to the knife for the control of this strategic territory. The Nazi base of operations is the already subjugated Balkans, while Britain holds Egypt, Palestine, Transjordania, Syria, and Irak. Russians have occupied Iran from the north while the English have entered from the south. This buffer state occupies the central position between two other Muslim nations—Turkey and Afghanistan—where Anglo-Russian diplomacy already is at close grips with Nazi intrigue.

East of this key battleground lies the Indian Empire; northward are the Soviet Caucasus oilfields, Turkestan, and the Black and Caspian seas; westward is the Libyan desert, where the Axist threat persists, though in diminished force.

The possibility of a German drive through south Russia and the Caucasus into Persia is being envisioned by the British and Soviet general staffs, but the Turkish position is the principal headache. Turkey is a quasi ally of Britain but has signed a treaty with Germany, yet it is the traditional friend of Russia. Thus Turkey is unable to choose a roost.

That Islam's status in the Second World War is worrying England was made obvious recently when the *New Statesman and Nation,* leading liberal weekly in London, joined in strong criticism of the political direction of the war in the Near East. It said that the British Government had followed the policy of "appeasing the wrong people."

"The Foreign Office has preferred to conciliate only the reactionaries—the fifth column among the Arab magnates of Palestine and Irak, our enemies in Vichy and our open foes in Spain," the editorial continued. "Even today . . . that arch-conspirator, the Grand Mufti of Jerusalem, is still at large." He took sanctuary at Rome, of all places!

The chief duty of the Mufti (Arabian, expounder) is to explain Muslim religion and law. The one who takes his title from Jerusalem maintains that he has the right to proclaim a *jihad* ("Holy War") against the enemies of Islam. So the British-German game of pull devil–pull baker in the Eastern world kneads the yeast which may raise the dough for the last crusade.

Anglo-Russian collaboration in the Near East may have unpleasant repercussions upon Muslim morale, Quincy Howe, a radio commentator not easily stampeded by spot news developments, remarked on the same day that British and Soviet troops marched into Persia. "Remember," Mr. Howe said, "that no religion has such followers as the followers of Mohammed. Remember, too, that the Russians have become identified for many years with opposition to all religion. The Anglo-Soviet occupation of Iran may have no immediate effect on the Middle East, but it does give Hitler a propaganda appeal that he can hardly fail to take up at once."

How soon Islam's final struggle with Christendom will begin is any explorer's guess; Nostradamus sees it forthcoming, in the sixtieth quatrain of the Ninth *Centurie:*

> *Conflict Barbar en la Cornere noire,*
> *Sang espandu trembler la Dalmatie:*
> *Grand Ismaël mettra son promontoire,*
> *Ranes trembler, secours Lusitanie.*

> *A barbarous conflict under the black flag,*
> *Bloodshed to shake Dalmatia:*
> *Great Ishmael will put out from its headland,*
> *Frogs to quaver, Portugal help.*

The first line suggests the piratical Jolly Roger flown by the Mediterranean corsairs of the Barbary states of north Africa from the end of the fifteenth to the close of the eighteenth century. Dalmatia is the Adriatic littoral of Yugoslavia.

The Bedouin tribes of northern Arabia, occupying the region between the peninsula of Sinai and the Persian Gulf, are said to descend from Ishmael, son of Abraham and Hagar, Sarah's Egyptian handmaid. The Arabian Bedouins possess many Ishmaelitic traditions.

The quavering frogs, it is intimated, are the French (see Chapter 6). Some commentators suggest that "Portugal help" may mean that the greatest Portuguese colony, Brazil, will become South America's leading power and aid the motherland in repelling a Muslim invasion.

That the contemporary events in Persia have a bearing on the future is the suggestion of quatrain 27 of the Fifth *Centurie:*

> *Par feu et armes non loing de la marnegro,*
> *Viendra de Perse occuper Trebisonde:*
> *Trembler Pharos Methelin, Solalegro,*
> *De sang Arabe d'Hadrie couvert onde.*

By fire and arms not far from the Black Sea,
He will come from Persia to occupy Trebizond:
The Methelin beacon to tremble, the sun lively,
The Adriatic wave covered with Arab blood.

Trebizond is in Turkey, on the Black Sea, 570 miles east of Constantinople. Pharos was the ancient name of a small island off Alexandria, Egypt, famous for its lighthouse, which was numbered among the seven wonders of the world and gave the name pharos to all structures of a similar kind.

Persecution of the Christian Church is implied in quatrain 73 of the Fifth *Centurie:*

Persécutée de Dieu sera l'Eglise,
Et les saints temples seront expoliez:
L'enfant la mère mettra nud en chemise,
Seront Arabes aux Polons ralliéz.

The Church will be persecuted by God,
And the holy temples will be seized:
The mother will put the child naked into the shirt,
There will be Arabs rallied against the Poles.

It seems to be Poland's fate to be the target of recurrent attacks against the Christian faith. This phenomenon is happening now, too, *New Europe* for May, 1941, learned:

All reports arriving from Poland confirm that the persecution is not limited to the Catholic clergy and to Catholic religious life. Its object is any religion. The fury of the German attitude towards any religious symbols is a proof that German racist materialism, based upon hatred, is fighting the most profound spiritual elements of civilization in Poland. The Germans are, however, fully aware of the role of the Catholic Church in Poland. They know that the destruction of Catholicism in Poland will lead to the destruction of national life, to the erasure of Poland from the map of Europe. This is why their hatred turns first of all against the Roman Catholic clergy and its influence, and against the Catholic Church, Catholic social organizations, and Catholic education. This is why one must not consider only material destruction, however heavy. Greater importance must be attached to the systematic extermination of priests and to the systematic destruction of Catholic influence upon social life.

That Italy, too, is to feel the blows of a resurgent Islam is the sense of quatrain 58 of the Fourth *Centurie:*

Soleil ardant dans le gosier couler,
De sang humain arrouser terre Etrusque:
Chef seille d'eau, mener son fils filer,
Captive dame conduite en terre Turque.

The glowing sun to go down into the gullet,
To soak the Tuscan land in human blood:
The chief to guide, his son to draw the bucket of water,
The captive lady led into the Turkish land.

That cavalry and fifth columnists will fight in the last crusade is the intimation in the seventh quatrain of the Seventh *Centurie:*

Sur le combat des grands chevaux légers,
On criera le grand croissant confond.
De nuict tuer, monts habits de bergers,
Abismes rouges dans le fossé profond.

Upon the combat of the great light horsemen
They will shout to confuse the great crescent.

To kill by night, attire of shepherds shown,
Red depths in the deep ditch.

Quatrain 42 of the Ninth *Centurie* gives a preview of occidental sea power winning yet another victory:

De Barcelonne, de Gennes et Venise,
De la Secille peste Monet unis,
Contre Barbare classe prendront la vise,
Barbar poulsé bien loing jusqu'à Thunis.

Money unites the plague from Barcelona,
From Genoa, from Venice, and from Sicily;
They will take aim against the barbarian fleet,
The barbarian repulsed from a long way off clear up to Tunis.

Before the time of the events depicted in quatrain 31 of the Tenth *Centurie*, Germany again will have become a Christian nation:

Le sainct empire viendra en Germanie,
Ismaëlites trouveront lieux ouverts,
Anes voudront aussi la Carmanie,
Les soutenans de terre tous couverts.

The holy empire will come in Germany,
Ishmaelites will find the places opened,
Blockheads will want Carmania also,
The supporters of the earth all covered.

Carmania was an ancient province of Asia on the Persian Gulf.

It may be that the first line in the eleventh quatrain of the Fifth *Centurie* foretells a new cult of sun worshipers:

Mer par solaires seure ne passera,
Ceux de Venus tiendront toute l'Affrique:
Leur regne plus Saturne n'occupera,
Et changera la part Asiatique.

The sea could not be passed by the solarists,
Those of Venus will hold all Africa:
Saturn no longer shall occupy their realm,
And the Asiatic part shall change.

Venus implies disorder while Saturn usually represents the golden age.

The two abbreviated words in the last line of quatrain 25 of the Fifth *Centurie* inspired the title of this chapter as given twice in the book of Revelation (xxi, 9; xx, 2):

Le prince Arabe, Mars, Sol, Venus, Lyon,
Regne d'Eglise par mer succombera.
Devers la Perse bien près d'un million,
Bizance, Egypte ver. serp. invadera.

The Arab prince, Mars, Sun, Venus, Lion,
The reign of the Church will fall by the sea.
Toward Persia nearly a million,
The true serpent will invade Constantinople and Egypt.

Ver. serp. is the abbreviation for *verus serpens* ("true serpent").

The eightieth quatrain of the Sixth *Centurie* delineates the greatest extent of the Muslim conquest:

De Fez le regne parviendra à ceux d'Europe,
Feu leur cité, et lame tranchera:
Le grand d'Asie terre et mer à grand troupe,
Que bleux, pères, croix à mort déchassera.

The reign of Fez will be installed over Europe,
Fire to their city and slashing blade:
The great lord of Asia, with a great host by land and sea,
Will pursue recruits, fathers, and the Cross unto the death.

The second line portends broadsword, saber, and cutlass vanquished by scimitar, yataghan, and creese. Chapter 4 interpreted the place of Fez in future history as foretold in the letter to Henry II.

A semblance of a date for the last crusade may be elicited from quatrain 54 of the Sixth *Centurie*:

Au poinct du jour au second chant du Coq
Ceux de Thunis, de Fez et de Bugie;
Par les Arabes captif le Roy Maroq,
L'an mil six cens et sept de Liturgie.

At daybreak at the second cockcrow
Those of Tunis, of Fez, and of Bougie;
The Moroccan king the captive of the Arabs,
The year 1607 of the liturgy.

There may be some connection here in referring to *Coq* pointing to a link with the preceding chapter on Henry V. Bougie or Bugiah is a seaport of Algeria. During the first three Christian centuries, there were no liturgies in the strict sense of the word. There was a sort of fluid rite, based upon accounts of the Last Supper, which later crystallized into four great liturgies, from which all others are derived. One of these subdivisions is the Gallican rite, which, by a logical assumption, would be the one to which Nostradamus referred. Liturgists suggest that the Gallican rite radiated from Milan as a center all over northwestern Europe and Spain and that it was originated in the northern Italian metropolis by Auxentius, its Cappadocian-born bishop (355–374). Adding 355 to 1607 gives 1962; adding 1607 and 374 gives 1981.

Quatrain 96 of the Tenth *Centurie* yields a complicated anagram:

Religion du nom des mers vaincra,
Contre la secte fils Adaluncatif,
Secte obstinée deplorée craindra,
Des deux blessez par Aleph et Aleph.

Religion will win in the name of the seas,
Against the sect of the sons of the caliphate,
The obstinate, deplored sect will be afraid
Of the two wounded by Aleppo and Aleppo.

The first line suggests that sea power will assure Christianity's continued influence upon history. *Adaluncatif* separates into *an du califat*.

Quatrain 96 of the Eighth *Centurie* may depict the conversion of Islam to Judaism:

La Synagogue stérile sans nul fruit
Sera receuë entre les infidèles
De Babylon la fille du poursuit,
Misère et triste lui trenchera les aisles.

The sterile synagogue without any fruit
Will be received among the infidels.
The daughter of Babylon of the pursued one
Miserably and sadly she will clip her wings.

Prediction No. 27, six cryptic lines, summarizes the last crusade:

Celeste feu du costé d'Occident
Et du Midy, courir jusques au Levant
Vers demy morts sans point trouver racine.

Troisiesme aage, à Mars le Belliqueux,
Des Escarboucles on verra briller feux,
Aag Escarboucle, et à la fin famine.

Celestial fire over the coast of the Occident
And over the Midland, to run up to the Levant,
About half dead without finding even vegetables.
The third age to Mars the Warlike,
One will see fires to sparkle like rubies,
The carbuncle age, and at the end famine.

Escarboucle may be translated either as a ruby or as a malignant boil on the body politic. Here, both meanings are apparent.

12

"His Wrath Is Come"

Interpreting the Revelation of St. John the Divine always has involved insuperable difficulties. The strange, fantastic imagery of the Apocalypse continually has appealed to successive Christian scholars, all of whom hold the utmost diversity of opinions as to the prophecies' meanings.

The book of Revelation has been explained differently by almost every writer who has ventured to interpret it, and it has provided all sorts of sects and fanatics with quotations to support their creeds or pretensions. The modern interpreters are divided into three schools—historical, futurist, and preterist.

The historical school holds that the forecast embraces the entire history of the Christian Church and its foes from the time of writing in the first century to the end of the world. The futurists throw the whole prophecy, except the first three chapters, forward into a time not yet reached by the Church—a period of no very long duration, which is immediately to precede Christ's second coming. Believers in that Messianic millennium are known as chiliasts.

Both these views are improbable, in the opinion of other Biblical scholars, who decry such beliefs as in conflict with St. John's own statement that he was foretelling things which were "shortly to come to pass." Certainly the ancient tendency of prophecy would not project such predictions so far into the future.

Preterists, therefore, hold that all or nearly all the prophecy already has been fulfilled and that it refers chiefly to the triumph of Christianity over Judaism and paganism. If St. John was speaking of the events of his own day, he was referring to the serious persecutions which were threatening the infant Church.

The conflict between Christianity and Caesar worship was at its height, so the Apocalypse may have been written to comfort and encourage the suffering Christians during Domitian's reign. Revelation held out to the Church the promise, which was the main article in the Apocalyptic faith, of the intervention of God, who would destroy His enemies and grant His people salvation.

Twenty-eight Nostradamic quatrains bear at least spotty resemblances to certain passages and phrases in the book of Revelation. Perhaps the reader would obtain a greater fullness of appreciation for these stanzas by reading the last book of the Bible and comparing the Apocalyptic imageries:

I–91

Les Dieux feront aux humains apparences,
Ce qu'ils seront authcurs de grand conflit.
Avant ciel veu serain, espée et lance
Que vers main gauche sera plus grand afflict.

The gods will make appearances in human form
To those who are the authors of the great conflict.
Before heaven will be seen sword and lance
Which will be the greatest affliction to the left hand.

I–29

Quand le poisson terrestre et aquatique
Par forte vague au gravier sera mis,

Sa forme estrange, suave et horrifique,
Par mer aux murs bien tost les ennemis.

When the amphibian fish
Shall be tossed onto the gravel by a powerful wave,
Its strange form, charming yet horrible,
Soon the enemies by sea to the walls.

II–18

Nouvelle et pluye subite, impetueuse,
Empeschera subit deux exercices,
Pierre ciel, feux faire la mer pierreuse
La mort de sept terre et marin subites.

A new and sudden, violent rain
All at once will obstruct two maneuvers,
A meteorite, fires make the sea gritty,
The unexpected death of seven by land and sea.

II–31

En campagne Cassilin fera tant
Qu'on ne verra que d'eau les champs couverts
Devant, apres, la pluye de long temps
Hors mis les arbres rien l'on verra de vert.

In the campaign Cassilis will do so much
That they will see only water covering the fields.
Before and after, rain for a long while,
So that nothing green could be seen except trees.

III–13

Par foudre en l'arche or et argent fondu.
Des deux captifs l'un l'autre mangera
De la cité le plus grand estendu,
Quand submergée la classe nagera.

Gold and silver are melted by lightning in the ark.
Of the two captives one will eat the other.
The great one of the city lain dead,
When the submersible fleet will swim.

IV–29

Le Sol caché ecclipsé par Mercure,
Ne sera mis que pour le ciel second:
De Vulcan Hermes sera faite pasture,
Sol sera veu pur rutilant et blond.

The sun hidden, eclipsed by Mercury,
It will be put only for a second in the sky:
Hermes will be made the pasture of Vulcan,
Sol will be seen pure, bright red and golden.

The next transit of Mercury will be on November 14, 1953. This is in no sense an eclipse, however.

V–32

Ou tout bon est tout bien Soleil et Lune,
Est abondant sa ruyne s'approche,

Du ciel s'advance vaner ta fortune,
En mesme estat que la septiesme roche.

Sun and moon, where all good is all well,
It is abundant her ruin approaches,
From heaven it advances to garner thy fortune,
In the same state as the seventh rock.

VIII–16

Au lieu que Hiéron fait sa nef fabriquer
Si grand déluge sera et si subite,
Qu'on n'aura lieu ne terres s'ataquer,
L'onde monter Fesulan Olympique.

In the place that Hiero built his ship
There will be such a great deluge, so suddenly,
That they will have no place or lands to fall upon,
The surge to ascend Olympic Fiesole.

Fiesole, a city of Italy in Tuscany, stands on an eminence over-looking the valley of the Arno, three miles northeast of Florence. It was one of the twelve Etruscan cities and is enclosed by crumbling cyclopean walls.

I–62

La grande perte las! que feront les lettres
Avant le cycle de l'Aton a parfaict,
Feu, grand déluge, plus par ignares sceptres
Que de long siecle ne se verra refaict.

Alas! the great trash which letters will convey
Before the cycle of Aton has been completed,
Fire, a great deluge, more by ignorant scepters
Than one will see repaired in a long time.

Amenhotep IV, an Egyptian pharaoh of the XVIIIth dynasty, began his reign about 1375 B.C. Thrusting aside all the multitudinous deities of Egypt, the so-called heretic priest-king devoted himself to the monotheistic cult of the visible sun disk. To give this magnified sun god a new identity, unembarrassed by shibboleths and strait-jacketed conceptions, the hitherto rare word *aton*, an ancient name for the physical sun, was employed to designate the great deity.

Amenhotep adopted the name Ikhnaton or Akhenaton and also changed his capital. His one-man religious reformation was backed by force and was opposed by various interests, the chief of which was that of the priesthood of endowed temples. Despite its splendor and attendant naturalistic art, the innovation was short lived, scarcely surviving its creator.

From the hymns to the sun, Atonism appears to have been the worship of the solar energy and to have been a scientific idea apart from the usual type of Egyptian religion. This attempted religious reformation has great historic interest partly because it shows that the idea of essential monotheism underlying a superficial plurality of gods was current in Egypt and even attained official recognition at just about the time of the Egyptian captivity of the Children of Israel. It is aside from the purpose of this book to inquire to what extent "the cycle of Aton" may have influenced the primitive tribal unitarianism of the Israelites. In *The Stream of History*, Geoffrey Parsons sums up:[10]

---

10. Charles Scribner's Sons, New York, 1928, page 165.

A strange young idealist was this pharaoh. His greatness lay in his religious faith. He was the first believer in one god that the world has seen, and he tried his best to convert his people to his lofty faith. But he was far in advance of his time, and he failed and his empire collapsed with him. For he was utterly lacking in practical ability.

V–24

Le regne et loy sous Venus eslevé,
Saturne aura sur Jupiter empire:
La loy et regne par le Soleil levé,
Par Saturnins endurera le pire.

The realm and law upraised under Venus,
Saturn will have ruled above Jupiter:
The law and realm raised by the Sun,
Will endure the worst under the dull wits.

IV–71

En lieu d'espouses les filles trucidées,
Meurtre à grand faute ne sera superstite:
Dedans ses puys vestules inondées,
L'espouse estainte par hauste d'Aconite.

Daughters massacred in place of wives,
Murder will not be pointed to as a great fault,
Within its wells vestal virgins drowned,
The bride extinguished by the upper ten of monkshood.

II-35

Dans deux logis de nuict le feu prendra,
Plusieurs dedans estouff ez et rostis,
Près de deux fleuves pour seur il adviendra
Sol, l'arc et Caper, tous seront amortis.

The fire will take hold of two night lodgings,
Most of those within suffocated and roasted,
Near two rivers he will come unto them
Sun, the bow and goat, all will be paid off.

V-41

Nay sous les umbres et journées nocturne
Sera en regne et bonté souveraine,
Fera renaître son sang de l'antique urne,
Renouvelant siecle d'or pour l'airain.

Born under the shadows and nocturnal revolutions
Will be in the realm and supreme goodness,
His blood will be reborn from the ancient urn,
Renewing the golden age from the brazen.

V-53

Le loy de Sol, et Venus contendans,
Appropriant l'esprit de prophetie:
Ne l'un ne l'autre ne seront entendans
Par Sol tiendra la loy du grand Messie.

The law of the sun and Venus contending,
Appropriating the spirit of prophecy:
Neither one nor the other will be understood;
The law of the great Messiah will be held by the Sun.

I–48

Vingt ans du regne de la Lune passés
Sept mil ans autre tiendra sa Monarchie,
Quand le soleil prendra ses jours lassés,
Lors accomplit et mine ma prophétie.

Twenty years of the reign of the moon passed
Seven thousand years the other will hold her
    monarchy,
When the sun will assume its weary days,
Then it is accomplished and look well to my
    prophecy.

III–21

Au Crustamin par mer Hadriatique,
Apparoistra un horrible poisson,
De face humaine et la fin aquatique,
Qui se prendra dehors de l'hameçon.

At Crustumerium by the Adriatic Sea
Will appear a horrible fish,
Of human face and aquatic end
Which will be caught without a hook.

V–62

Sur les rochers sang on verra plouvoir,
Sol, Orient, Saturne Occidental,
Pres d'Orgon guerre, à Rome grand mal voir,
Nefs parfondrées et prins le Tridental.

They will see blood pour down onto the rocks,
The Sun in the east, Saturn in the west;
Near Orgon, war, at Rome great evil is seen,
Ships foundering and the Trentino taken.

X–71

La terre et l'air geleront si grand eau
Lorsqu'on viendra le Jeudy venerer:
Ce qui sera jamais ne fut si beau,
Des quatre parts le viendront honorer.

Earth and air will freeze so much water
When Thursday will come to be venerated;
He who never will have been much good,
They will come to honor from the four corners.

X–99

La fin le loup, le lyon, boeuf et l'asne,
Timide dama seront avec mastins.
Plus ne cherra à eux la doulce manne,
Plus vigilance et custode aux mastins.

The end the wolf, the lion, ox, and ass,
The timid stag will be with the mastiffs.
No longer the sweet manna will fall to them,
More vigilance and the warden of the mornings.

I-69

La grand montagne ronde de sept estades,
Après paix, guerre, faim, inondation,
Roulera loing, abysmant grand contrades,
Mesmes antigues, et grand fondation.

The great round mountain of seven stages,
After peace, war, famine, and flood,
Will roll a long way, lost in great deeds,
The same ancient things and a great foundation.

Does the first line mean this great round world with its seven
continents and seven seas?

X–75

Tant attendu ne reviendra jamais
Dedans l'Europe, en Asie apparoistra
Un de la ligue yssue du grand Hermés,
Et sur tous Roys des Orients croistra.

He who was so much awaited never will return
Within Europe; One of the sect, issued from the great Hermes,
Will appear in Asia and will increase his power
Over all the kings of the Orient.

Isn't Nostradamus admonishing Europe that the Messiah, "He who was so much awaited, never will return?"

I–67

La grand famine que je sens approcher,
Souvent tourner, puis estre universelle,
Si grande et longue qu'on viendra arracher
Du bois racine et l'enfant de mamelle.

The great famine which I feel approaching,
Often turning about, then becoming universal,
So great and long that one shall pluck
The root from the tree and the babe from the breast.

II–27

Le divin verbe sera du ciel frappé,
Qui ne pourra procéder plus avant,
Du reserant le secret estoupé
Qu'on marchera par dessus et devant.

The divine word will be stricken from heaven,
Who no more could proceed forward,
In revealing the stowed secret
Which one will march overhead and in the foreground.

IV–67

L'an que Saturne et Mars esgaux combust,
L'air fort seiché, longue trajection:

Par feux secrets, d'ardeur grand lieu adust
Peu pluye, vent, chaud, guerres, incursions.

The year when Saturn and Mars are obscured equally,
The air very dry, a long trajectory:
By secret flames, a great place burnt by fire,
Rain scarce, wind, heat, wars, raids.

I–84

Lune obscurcie aux profondes ténèbres,
Son frère passe de couleur ferrugine:
Le grand caché longtemps sous les ténèbres
Tiendra le fer dans la playe sanguine.

The moon obscured in profound darkness,
Its brother passed into rust color:
The great one hidden a long time under the shadows
Will hold the weapon in the bloody wound.

X–72

L'an mil neuf cent nonante neuf sept mois
Du ciel viendra un grand Roy d'effrayeur
Ressusciter le grand Roy d'Angoulmois,
Avant apres Mars regner par bonheur.

The year 1999 and seven months
A great King of fear will come from Heaven
To revive the great King of Angoumois,
Before and after wars to reign in happiness.

In other words, this is July, 1999, according to Dr. de Fontbrune, who explains that the Angoumois were conquered by the Visigoths and later threatened by Attila and his Huns. Several Nostradamians interpret this quatrain as dating a coming invasion of France.

X–74

Au revolu du grand nombre septiesme
Apparoistra au temps jeux d'Hécatombe,
Non esloigné du grand aage Milliesme
Que les entrés sortiront de leur tombe.

In the revolving of the great seventh number
He will appear in the working times of the mass slaughter,
Not far from the great Millenary age
When the buried will leave their tomb.

X–73

Le temps présent avecques le passé
Sera jugé par le grand Jovialiste,
Le monde tard par luy sera lassé,
Et desloyal par le clergé juriste.

The times present with those past
Will be judged by the great Jehovah,
The late world will be lashed by him,
And the disloyal by the legal clergy.

There is one date upon which Nostradamus and followers of the so-called prophecy of the Great Pyramid of Giza virtually agree—the Sphinx of Issachar appears to have believed that the millennium would begin about 1999, while the pyramidologists place it at approximately 2001.

> *If this which he avouches does appear,*
> *There is nor flying hence nor tarrying here.*
> *I 'gin to be a-weary of the sun,*
> *And wish the estate o' the world were now undone.—*
> *Ring the alarum-bell! Blow, wind! come, wrack!*
> *At least we'll die with harness on our back.*

13

"Two Wings of a Great Eagle"

In A.D. 1776, thirteen American colonies renounced British suzerainty. One hundred and sixty-five years later, forty-eight United States offered all-out aid to the mother country in her hour of need through H.R. 1776, the lease-lend bill, a declaration of interdependence. Was this identical numbering just a coincidence, a deliberate Rooseveltian twist to the psychological "white war" of nerves, or are students of prophecies correct in regarding this upturning 1776 as evidence that the hand of Divine Providence is modeling an Anglo-American joint destiny?

In dissecting the Third New Deal's war policy, it may be beneficial to take the testimony of the socialist who became a saint, Sir Thomas More. In a mental exploration of his brave new world, Sir Thomas did not think to mention exactly in what part of the Western Hemisphere Utopia was situated.

The world's first socialistic broadside, published in Latin in 1516 and translated into English in 1551, sixteen years after its author yielded up his life for his steadfast religious faith on Henry VIII's chopping block, took care to point out that in Utopia war was regarded as criminal folly, an absurd official expedient for composing international relations. The second book of *De Optimo Reipublicae Statu, deque Nova Insula Utopia*, however, contains a segment showing that there were causes for which the peace-loving folk of this new world would fight. Of warfare, Sir Thomas recounted:

War or battle as a thing very beastly, and yet to no kind of beasts in so much use as to man, they do detest and abhor. And contrary to the custom almost of all other nations, they count nothing so much against glory, as glory gotten in war.

Thus, those Utopians of the nowhere felt very much the same as do these Americans of the here when war is involved. Yet, they kept their powder dry, just as we have had to resort to military conscription, to fight both their own and their friends' battles:

And therefore though they do daily practice and exercise themselves in the discipline of war, and not only the men, but also the women upon certain appointed days, lest they should be to seek in the feat of arms, if need should require, yet they never go to battle, but either in the defence of their own country, or to drive out of their friend's land the enemies that have invaded it, or by their power to deliver from the yoke of bondage of tyranny some people, that be therewith oppressed.

Sir Thomas stressed that the Utopians combined compassion with good strategy in waging war against an aggressor nation:

Which thing they do of mere pity and compassion. Howbeit they send help to their friends; not ever in their defence, but sometimes also to requite and revenge injuries before to them done. But this they do not unless their counsel and advice in the matter be asked, whiles it is yet new and fresh.

After recounting an imaginary war which the Utopians prosecuted successfully on a friend's behalf, the book remarks:

For the Utopians fought not this war for themselves. . . . So eagerly the Utopians prosecute the injuries done to their friends, yea, in money matters; and not their own likewise. . . . Not because they set less store by their own citizens, than by their friends; but that they take the loss of their friends' money more heavily than the loss of their own.

Because that their friends' merchantmen, forasmuch as that they lose is their own private goods, sustain great damage by the loss. But their own citizens lose nothing but of the common goods, and of that which was at home plentiful and almost superfluous, else had it not been set forth. Therefore no man feeleth the loss. And for this cause they think it too cruel an act, to revenge that loss with the death of many, the incommodity of the which loss no man feeleth neither in his life, nor yet in his living.

One neat Utopian trick, a fifth column in reverse, was to "promise great rewards to him that will kill their enemies' prince," because

They be not only sorry, but also ashamed to achieve the victory with bloodshed, counting it great folly to buy precious wares too dear . . . they in this behalf think themselves much praiseworthy, as who like wise men by this means despatch great wars without any battle or skirmish.

Yea they count it also a deed of pity and mercy, because that by the death of a few offenders the lives of a great number of innocents, as well of their own men as also of their enemies, be ransomed and saved, which in fighting should have been slain. For they do no less pity the base and common sort of their enemies' people than they do their own; knowing that they be driven and enforced to war against their own wills by the furious madness of their princes and heads. If by none of these means the matter go forward as they would have it, then they produce occasions of debate and dissension to be spread among their enemies.

If this way prevail not, then they raise up the people that be next neighbors and borderers to their enemies. . . . And as for money they give them abundance. But of their own citizens they send to them few or none. . . . But their gold and silver, because they keep it all for this only purpose, they lay it out frankly and freely; as who should live even as wealthily, if they had bestowed it every penny.

Yet, after they had won their friend's war, the Utopians took nothing for themselves from the vanquished:

For none of themselves taketh any portion of the prey. But when the battle is finished and ended, they put their friends to never a penny cost of all the charges that they were at, but lay it upon their necks that be conquered. Them they burden with the whole charge of their expenses.

Shades of Versailles and *Mein Kampf!*

Nor did the Utopians wait for the Hitlers of their day to attack them. Sir Thomas concludes his commentary on warfare with:

If any prince stir up war against them, intending to invade their land, they meet him incontinent out of their own borders with great power and strength. For they never lightly make war in their own country. Nor they be never brought into so extreme necessity as to take help out of foreign lands into their own island.

Briefly, it is the object of the lease-lend program, H.R. 1776, to extend every possible aid to Britain, to lend money, munitions, guns, airplanes, ships, and food to the erstwhile motherland. A later point is the use of the United States Navy to convoy the ships carrying the tools needed to save Britain from destruction and to expunge Hitlerism. In the light of Nostradamic prophecy, it may be that the ultimate object of H.R. 1776 is the federation of the so-called Anglo-Saxon comity of nations into one great commonwealth.

An announcement on August 14, 1941, disclosed the first steps in this direction; quatrain 89 of the Second *Centurie* indicates:

Un jour seront amis les deux grands maistres,
Leur grand pouvoir se verra augmenté:
La terre neusve sera en ses hauts estres,
Au sanguinaire le nombre racompté.

One day the two great masters shall be friends,
Their great power shall be increased:
The New World will be at its highest existence,
The number is reckoned up to the bloody one.

Somewhere on the war-infested waters of the Atlantic Ocean, President Roosevelt and Prime Minister Winston Churchill met and agreed on a joint eight-point declaration of their war aims, renouncing all territorial aggrandizement and agreeing to resist all territorial changes not according with the freely expressed wishes of those people concerned. The statement of "the two great masters" was released simultaneously in London, Ottawa, and Washington:

The President of the United States of America and the Prime Minister, Mr. Churchill, representing His Majesty's Government in the United Kingdom, being met together, deem it right to make known certain common principles in the national policies of their respective countries on which they base their hopes for a better future for the world.

FIRST, their countries seek no aggrandizement, territorial or other.

SECOND, they desire to see no territorial changes that do not accord with the freely expressed wishes of the peoples concerned.

THIRD, they respect the right of all peoples to choose the form of government under which they will live; and they wish to see sovereign rights and self-government restored to those who have been forcibly deprived of them.

FOURTH, they will endeavor, with due respect for their existing obligations, to further the enjoyment by all States, great or small, victor or vanquished, of access, on equal terms, to the trade and to the raw materials of the world which are needed for their economic prosperity.

FIFTH, they desire to bring about the fullest collaboration between all nations in the economic field with the object of securing, for all, improved labor standards, economic advancement and social security.

SIXTH, after the final destruction of the Nazi tyranny, they hope to see established a peace which will afford to all nations the means of dwelling in safety within their own boundaries, and which will afford assurance that all the men in all the lands may live out their lives in freedom from fear and want.

SEVENTH, such a peace should enable all men to traverse the high seas and oceans without hindrance.

EIGHTH, they believe that all the nations of the world, for realistic as well as spiritual reasons must come to the abandonment of the use of force. Since no future peace can be maintained if land, sea or air armaments continue to be employed by nations which threaten, or may threaten aggression outside of their frontiers, they believe, pending the establishment of a wider and permanent system of general security, that the disarmament of such nations is essential. They will likewise aid and encourage all other practicable measures which will lighten for peace-loving peoples the crushing burden of armaments.

FRANKLIN D. ROOSEVELT
WINSTON S. CHURCHILL

Basically, eight was "the number reckoned up to the bloody one," according to believers in divine numerology. Eight is expressive of renewal, revival, regeneration, and resurrection to new life and glory. Above all, it is regarded as the number of the eighth day—Resurrection, the Lord's Day of the Church. It is the first cube, as four is the first square, indicating equal length, breadth, and height (Revelation xxi, 16). Eight stands, therefore, as the number of life. Why it should thus be follows from the theory that if six days, plus the seventh of rest, completed the generation or birth, eight would imply a rebirth, or regeneration. Eight also is the number of the ball behind which Messrs. Roosevelt and Churchill hope to place Adolf Hitler and Benito Mussolini.

Numerology also traces a very definite connection between eight and 1776, since the number of American independence is made up of twice 888, which latter sum consists of three eights. To heighten these allusions, 888 is called the Sibylline number, signifying the name and nature of Christ "in eight units, eight tens and eight hundreds."

The extant Sibylline oracles, approximately four thousand Greek hexameters, written mostly from 200 B.C. to A.D. 300, are Jewish and Christian predictions, partly Messianic, revered in the Middle Ages as pagan witnesses to the divinity of Christ. Book One of these oracles, lines 381 to 388, has been translated:

And then the child of the great God to men
Shall come incarnate, being fashioned like

To mortals on the earth. And He shall bear
Four vowels, and the consonants in Him

Two times are told; and the whole sum I name:
For eight ones, and as many tens to these,
And yet eight hundred will the name reveal
To men who are given up to unbelief.

Jesus is written in Greek as Ἰησοῦς, Iota, eta, sigma, omicron, upsilon, sigma. In the Greek system of arithmetical notation, each letter of the alphabet represented an arbitrary numerical value. In the Saviour's given name, iota, eta, omicron, and upsilon are vowels, while sigma is the twice-told consonant. Their arithmetical values are:

Iota	10
Eta	8
Sigma	200
Omicron	70
Upsilon	400
Sigma	200
Total	888

The possible effect of the lease-lend outpouring on America's national economy is foretold in quatrain 65 of the Second *Centurie*:

Le parc enclin grande calamité,
Par l'Hesperie et Insubre fera,
Le feu en nef, peste et captivité,
Mercure en l'arc, Saturne fenera.

The economy given to great calamity,
It will be brought by the West and north Italy,

Fire in the nave, plague and captivity,
Mercury in the bow, Saturn will speculate.

Nostradamus derived his noun *parc* for "economy" from the Latin adjective *parcus* meaning "sparing, frugal, thrifty, or economical." He shows the war's effect upon Britain's arsenal, North America, and the "Insubrian country"—highly industrialized northern Italy, pressed into service by the German war machine. The third line forebodes troubles in the Church. Mercury symbolizes commerce and Saturn, high finance.

Harold Loeb warned in *Life in a Technocracy*:[11]

War accelerates the evolution of the producing processes. The late war quite proved this. Another war would compel every industry to modernize its technique. When the stress ended, an exhausted world would discover itself able to produce the commodities needed in peace by a mere fraction of its man power. At the same time the greater part of its population would find itself deprived of purchasing power. In other words, a crisis like the present only many times more acute would follow the end of hostilities. And returned soldiers are sometimes impatient breadliners.

Could quatrain 81 of the Tenth *Centurie* refer to the gold hoard buried at Fort Knox?

Mis thresor temple citadins Hesperiques
Dans iceluy retiré en secret lieu:
Le temple ouvrir les liens fameliques
Reprens, ravis, proye horrible au milieu.

---

11. Copyright, 1933, by Harold Loeb; reprinted by permission of The Viking Press, Inc., New York.

The treasure Western citizens put in a temple
Is withdrawn from thence to a secret place:
The starveling bonds open the temple,
Retaken, carried away, a horrible prey in the midst.

Is this what Harry Scherman meant in *Will We Have Inflation?*[12]—the easiest way to wipe out the terrific governmental debt by a drastic devaluation of the gold dollar, bringing on the inflation dreaded so long by American economists?

Such an inflation, "making millions of poor poorer, and magnifying the conflicting interests of all elements in the population—that is the supreme danger that can be identified in our excessive gold, so long as the Government owns all of it and refuses to redeem its paper money on demand." Mr. Scherman calls for the abolition of the Government's monopoly of gold ownership, as a threat to the American way of life, and for a return to the "full convertibility of paper money."

The Federal Government's monopoly of gold ownership, he states, is "at the root of totalitarianism; it is the one power without which it cannot possibly flourish. Thoughtlessly, we have let this foreign weed—it can be traced directly to foreign economic philosophies—establish itself in our own garden."

The author likens the individual citizen's freedom to own gold to "an automatic brake in the governmental machine," and charges that "the present drivers ripped it out" when they abandoned full convertibility of paper money and, at the same time, put what he calls the "Gold Prohibition Law" on our statute books.

"Unless this basic right of protection by economic action is restored to us as a people, and restored soon," Mr. Scherman concludes, "there can be little doubt that one of the main props under

12. Simon and Schuster, copyright, 1941, by Harry Scherman.

the system of individual freedom, built up over thousands of years, will have been effectually destroyed in the world."

It is possible that quatrain 74 of the Eighth *Centurie* presages a repudiation of the British monarchy by North Americans:

En terre neuve bien avant Roy entré
Pendant subges luy viendront faire acueil,
Sa perfidie aura tel rencontré,
Qu'aux citadins lieu de feste et recueil.

In the New World, well before the king enters,
While his subjects will be coming to give him greeting,
His perfidy will have met with so much of that
From the citizens instead of merrymaking and selection.
"Perfidious Albion" again?

Quatrain 48 of the Ninth *Centurie* points an admonitory finger at New York:

La grand'cité d'Occean maritime,
Environnée de marets en cristal:
Dans le solstice hyemal et la prime
Sera tentée de vent espouvental.

The great city of the maritime ocean,
Surrounded with seas of crystal:
In the winter solstice and in the spring
Will be tried by a terrifying gale.

Manhattan is surrounded by water often calm enough to be comparable to "seas of glass." Hurricanes are not unknown in those parts.

New York's destruction has been predicted frequently by

soothsayers. Most prophets agree that "the great city of the maritime ocean" will be the center of an earthquake leveling the skyscrapers and plunging much of the Atlantic littoral beneath the waves. It is even possible that the several light earth shocks felt within the last few years have been premonitory warnings of the greater day of wrath to come. Two Nostradamic stanzas bolster these seismological forecasts:

I-87

Ennosigée feu du centre de terre,
Fera trembler autour de cité neufve:
Deux grands rochers longtemps feront la guerre,
Puis Arethusa rougira nouveau fleuve.

The molten fire of the earth's center
Will cause quaking around the new city:
Two great rocks will wage war a long time
Then Arethusa will redden another river.

Arethusa, in classical mythology, was one of the Nereids of whom Alpheus was enamored, also the name of a fountain near Syracuse, into which she was transformed. Alpheus was said to have mingled his stream with that of Arethusa and it was popularly supposed that anything thrown into the river came up again in Ortygia (Sicily). Arethusa was invoked by Vergil in his tenth eclogue.

X-49

Jardin du monde auprès de cité neuve,
Dans le chemin des montagnes cavées,
Sera saisi et plongé dans la cuve,
Beuvant par force eaux soulphre envenimées.

The garden of the world close to the new city,
In the road of the hollowed mountains,
It will be seized and plunged into the tub,
Drinking by force the poisoned sulphur waters.

The Palisades, picturesque bluffs rising abruptly for thirty miles along the Hudson River to an elevation of from two hundred to five hundred feet, are formed by basaltic traprock which intruded in a molten condition between layers of sandstone and shale and cooled in columnar form. The stanza's first two lines might be taken to describe them.

"Today, seismologists speak of issuing a warning to the eastern seaboard communities of the United States," Albert Carr wrote in *This Week* for March 23, 1941. "This doesn't mean that a great shock is expected in that area this year or next year. What it does mean is that there is a chance—say one in five—that a strong quake will affect some city between New York and Portland, Maine, within the next fifty years."

That Nostradamus foretold a splendid destiny for our United States is among the things not generally known. In several stanzas he refers pointedly to Hesperia (Land of the West) and its brilliant, if tempestuous, future. Most inclusively explicit of these is the fiftieth quatrain of the Fourth *Centurie*:

Libra verra regner les Hespéries,
De Ciel et terre tenir la Monarchie,
D'Asie forces nul ne verra péries,
Que sept ne tiennent par rang la Hiérarchie.

Libra will see the Westerners govern,
To hold the monarchy of Heaven and earth,
No one will see the forces of Asia perish,
With seven not holding the hierarchy by rank.

Interpreted, Libra is the zodiacal sign of the scales, or the Balance, signifying justice and liberty, who will see those dwelling to the west of France—in North America—holding the dominion of Heaven and earth, that is, ruling both spiritual and temporal realms. The cryptic third line appears to indicate that the warring peoples of Asia will be blotted out by a cataclysm in which no witness will be left—possibly a titanic earthquake followed by the reappearance of that Mediasiatic Sea which geologists say once filled most of the vast sandy depression in the interior of the Mongolian Plateau.

The hierarchy of the Roman Catholic Church now is: (1) the Pope, (2) cardinals, (3) patriarchs and primates, (4) archbishops and bishops, (5) regular prelates, (6) abbots and (7) prelates of the Roman court. Perhaps the last line presages acceptance of the teaching of the Council of Trent that the hierarchy is composed of only three elements—bishops, priests, and ministers: "If anyone say that, in the Catholic Church, there is not a hierarchy, instituted by divine authority, which consists of Bishops, Priests, and Ministers, let him be anathema" (Council of Trent, Session XXIII, can. 2).

Speaking of balance, Hermann Rauschning, the ex-Nazi who saw through Hitler, in *The Redemption of Democracy*, which is prophetically subtitled *The Coming Atlantic Empire*, remarks: "Balance belongs to the vocabulary of an altogether different political order, namely the opposing (to the Axis Powers), British-Anglo-Saxon order."

Certain astroanalysts believe that this Anglo-American hegemony embraces the years between 1922, when the Washington Naval Treaty was signed, and 1986.

Attention, too, should be paid to George Berkeley, the prophetic Dean of Derry who later became Bishop of Cloyne. He foresaw North America's future greatness in 1725 with:

Westward the course of empire takes its way;
  The four first Acts already past,

A fifth shall close the Drama with the day;
  Time's noblest offspring is the last.

Bishop Berkeley also proved to his own satisfaction that nothing exists, or, rather, that we cannot know that anything does exist—all that we know is our own sensory feeling. We know the odor of a flower, the feeling of a stone, the color of gold, and the taste of sugar, but there personal knowledge ceases. Whether there actually is any matter which we call flower, stone, gold, or sugar is a topic for investigation.

Doctor Johnson scoffed at this philosophizing, saying: "We know that matter exists and that's the end of it." He kicked his faithful Boswell to prove his contention, which, of course, was no proof at all—he simply proved that kicking Boswell evokes a sensation.

Appendix

Original French of the Letter to King Henry II of France (See Page 46)

A l'Invictissime, Très Puissant et Très Chrestien Henry
Second, Roy de France, Michel Nostradamus, son très humble
et très obéissant serviteur et sujet.
—VICTOIRE ET FÉLICITÉ

Pour icelle souveraine observation que j'ay eu, ô tres-Chrestien et tres-victorieux Roy depuis que ma face estant longtemps obnubilée se présente au devant de la deité de vostre Majesté immesurée, depuis en ça j'ay perpetuellement esblouy, ne desistant d'honorer dignement venerer iceluy jour que premierement devant icelle je me present ay comme à une singuliere Majesté tant humaine. Or cherchant quelque occasion pour laquelle je peusse manifester le bon coeur et bon courage, que moyennant iceluy mon pouvoir eusse fait simple extension de connoissance envers vostre serenissime Majesté. Or voyant par effet le declarer ne m'estoit possible, joint avec mon singulier desir de ma tant longue obtenebration et obscurité est subitement esclarcie et transportée au devant de la face du souverain oeil, et du premier Monarque de l'univers, tellement que j'ay esté en doute longuement à qui je voudrois consacrer ces trois centuries du restant de mes Propheties parachevant la milliade, et après avoir longuement cogité d'une temeraire audace, ay prins mon addresse envers vostre Majesté, n'estant pour cela estonnée, comme raconte le gravissime autheur Plutarque en sa vie de Lycurgue, que voyant les offres et presens qu'on faisoit par sacrifice aux temples des Dieux immortels d'iceluy temps, et à celle fin que l'on ne s'eloignât par trop souvent desdits fraiz et mises, ne s'osoient presenter aux temples. Ce nonobstant voyant vostre splendeur Royale accompagnée d'une incomparable humanité ay prins mon addresse, non comme aux Roys de Perse, qu'il n'estoit nullement permis d'aller à eux ny moins s'en approcher. Mais à un tres-prudend, a un tres-sage Prince, j'ay consacré mes nocturnes et Prophetiques supputations, composées plutost d'un naturel instinct, accompagné d'une fureur poëtique que par regle de poésie, et la pluspart composé et accordé à la calculation Astronomique, correspondant aux ans, mois et sepmaines des regions, contrées, et de la pluspart des villes et citez de toute l'Europe, comprenant de l'Afrique, et une partie de l'Asie par le changement des régions qui s'approchent à la pluspart de tous ces climats et composé d'une naturelle faction respondra que quelqu'un qui auroit bien besoin de soy moucher, la rithme estre autant facile comme l'intelligence du sens est difficile. Et pource ô tres-humanissime Roy la pluspart des quatrains prophétiques sont tellement scabreux qu'on n'y sçaurait donner voye, ny moins aucun interpreter, toutesfois esperant de laisser par écrit les ans, villes, citez, régions, où la pluspart adviendra, mesme de l'année 1585 et de l'année 1606, commençant depuis le temps present, qui est le 14 de mars 1547 et passant outre bien loin jusques à l'advenement, qui sera après au commencement du 7 millenaire profondement supputé tant que mon calcul astronomique et autre assavoir s'est peu estendre, où les adversaires de Jesus-Christ et de son Eglise commenceront plus fort de pulluler: le tout a esté composé et calculé en jours et heurs d'eslection et bien disposées et le plus justement qu'il m'a esté possible. Et le jour Minerva libera & non invita, supputant presque autant des aventures du temps advenir, comme des âges passez comprenant de présent, et de ce que par le cours du temps par toutes regions l'on connoistra advenir, tout ainsi nommément comme il est escrit, n'y meslant rien de superflu, combien que l'on dit: Quod de futuris non est determinata omnino veritas. Il est bien vray Sire que pour mon naturel instinct qui m'a esté donné par mes avites, ne cuidant presager et adjoustant et accordant iceluy naturel instinct avec ma longue supputation uny et vuidant l'ame, l'esprit, et le courage de toute cure solicitude et fascherie par repos et tranquillité de l'esprit. Le tout accordé et presagé l'une partie tripode aeneo. Combien qu'ils soient plusieurs qui m'attribuent ce qui est autant à moy comme de ce que n'en est rien, Dieu seul eternel qui est perscrutateur des humains courages, pie, juste et misericordieux, est le vray juge, auquel je prie qu'il me vueille defendre de la calomnie des méchans qui voudroient aussi calomnieusement s'enquerir pour quelle cause tous vos antiquissimes progeniteurs Roys de France ont guery des escroüelles, et des autres nations ont guery de la morsure des serpens, les autres ont eu certain instinct de l'art divinatrice: et d'autres cas qui seroient longs icy à raconter. Ce nonobstant ceux à qui la malignité de l'esprit malin ne sera comprins par le cours du temps après la terrienne mienne extinction, plus sera mon escrit qu'à mon vivant, cependant si à ma supputation des âges je fallois, on ne pourroit estre selon la volonté d'aucuns. Plaira à vostre plus qu'imperiale Majesté me pardonner, protestant devant Dieu et ses Saincts que je ne pretens de mettre rien quelconque par escrit en la presente Epistre qui soit contre la vraye foy Catholique, conferant les calculations Astronomiques jouxte mon sçavoir: car l'espace du temps de nos premiers qui ont precedez sont tels, me remettant sous la correction du plus saint jugement, que le premier homme Adam fut devant Noë, environ mille deux cent quarante deux ans, ne computant les temps par la supputation des Gentils, comme a mis par escrit Varron: mais tant seulement selon les Sacrées Ecritures, et selon la foiblesse de mon esprit en mes calculations Astronomiques. Après Noë de luy et de l'universel deluge, vint Abraham environ mille huictante ans, lequel à esté souverain Astrologue selon aucun, il inventa premier les lettres Chaldaiques. Après vint Moyse environ cinq cens quinze ou seize ans, et entre le temps de David et Moyse ont esté cinq cens septante ans là environ. Puis apres entre le temps de David, et le temps de N. Sauveur et Redempteur Jesus Christ, né de l'unique Vierge, ont esté (selon aucuns Chronographes) mille trois cents cinquante ans: pourra objecter quelqu'un cette supputation n'estre veritable, parce qu'elle differe à celle d'Eusebe. Et puis le temps de l'humaine Redemption jusqu'à la seduction detestable des Sarrazins, ont esté six cens vingt un ans là environ, depuis en ça l'on peut facilement colliger quels temps ont passez, si la

mienne supputation n'est bonne et valable par toutes nations, pource
que tout a esté calculé par le cours celeste, par association d'emotion
infuse à certaines cures delaissées par l'emotion de mes antiques progeniteurs. Mais l'injure de temps ô serenissime Roy, requiert que tels
evenemens ne soient manifestez que par enigmatique sentence, n'ayant
qu'un seul sens et unique intelligence, sans y avoir rien mis d'ambigue
n'amphibologique calculation: mais plutost sous obnubilée obscurité
par une naturelle infusion, approchant à la sentence d'un des mille et
deux Prophetes qui ont esté depuis la creation du monde, jouste la supputation et Chronique Punique de Joel. Effundam spiritum meum su-
per omnem carnem & prophetabunt filii vestri & filiae vestrae: Mais
telle Prophetie procedoit de la bouche du Saint Esprit qui estoit là Souveraine puissance eternelle, adjoute avec la celeste à d'aucuns de ce
nombre ont predit de grandes et emerveillables adventures. Moy en cet
endroit je ne m'attribuë point tel tiltre ja à Dieu ne plaise: je confesse
bien que le tout vient de Dieu et luy en rends graces, honneur et loüange
immortelle sans y avoir meslé de la divination qui provient à fato, mais
à Deo natura, et la pluspart accompagnée du mouvement du cours celeste, tellement que voyant comme dans un miroir ardent, comme par
vision obnubilée, les grands evenemens tristes prodigieux et calamiteuses adventures qui s'approchent par les principaux culteurs. Premierement des temples de Dieu. Secondement par ceux qui sont
terrestrement soustenus s'approcher telle decadence avec mille autres
calamiteuses adventures, que par le cours du temps on connoistra advenir: Car Dieu regardera la longue sterilité de la grand dam, qui puis
apres conceura deux enfans principaux; mais elle periclitant, celle qui
luy sera adjoustée par la temerité de l'âge de mort periclitant dedans le
dix-huitiesme ne pouvant passer le trentesixiesme qu'en delaissera
trois masles et une femelle, et en aura deux celuy qui n'eut eu jamais
d'un mesme pere, de trois freres seront telles differences, plus unies et
accordées que les trois et quatre parties de l'Europe trembleront par le
moindre d'âge sera la Monarchie Chrestienne soustenuë et augmentée,
sectes eslevées, et subitement abaissées, Arabes reculez, Royaumes
unis, nouvelles loix promulguées, des autres enfans le premier occupera les Lyons furieux, couronnez, tenant les parens dessus les armes
intrepidez, le second se profondera si avant par les Latins accompagné,

qui sera faite la seconde voye tremblante et furibonde au mont Jevis, descendant pour monter aux Pyrénées, ne sera translaté a l'antique Monarchie, sera faite la troisiesme inondation de sang humain, ne se trouvera de longtemps Mars en Caresme. Et sera donnée la fille pour la conservation de l'Eglise Chrestienne tombant son dominateur à la Paganisme secte des nouveaux infidelles, elle aura deux enfans, l'un de fidelité et l'autre d'infidelité par la confirmation de l'Eglise Catholique, et l'autre qui, à sa grande confusion et tarde repentance la voudra ruiner seront trois regions par l'extreme difference des ligues: c'est assavoir la Romaine, la Germanie et l'Espagne qui feront diverses sectes par main militaire, delaissant les 50. et 52. degrez d'hauteur et seront tous hommages des religions lointaines aux regions de l'Europe et de Septentrion de 48. degrez d'auteur qui premier par vaine timidité tremblera puis les plus Occidentaux, Méridionaux et Orientaux trembleront, telle sera leur puissance, que ce que se fera par concorde et union insupportable des conquestes belliques; De nature seront esgaux, mais grandement differents de foy. Apres cecy la Dame sterile de plus grande puissance que la seconde, sera receuës par deux peuples, par le premier obstiné par celuy qui a puissance sur tous, par le deuxiesme, et par le tiers qui estendra ses forces vers le circuit de l'Orient de l'Europe aux pannos l'a profligé et succombé et par voile marine fera les extensions, à la Trinacrie Adriatique par Mirmido et Germaniques du tout succombé et sera la seste Barbarique de tout des Nations grandement affigée et déchassé. Puis le grand Empire de l'Antechrist commencera dans la Arda et Zerfas descendre en nombre grand et innumerable, tellement que la venuë du S. Esprit procedant la 24. degré fera transmigration, dechassant à l'abomination de l'Antechrist faisant guerre contre le Royal, qui sera le grand Vicaire de Jesus Christ et contre son Eglise, et son regne per tempus, & in occasione temporis. Et succedera devant une eclypse solaire le plus obscur et le plus tenebreux qui soit esté depuis la création du monde jusques à la mort et passion de Jesus-Christ, et de là jusques icy, et sera au mois d'Octobre que quelque grande translation sera faite, et telle que l'on cuidera la pesanteur de la terre avoir perdu son naturel mouvement, et estre abysmée en perpetuelle tenebre, seront precedens au temps urnal, et s'en suivant apres d'extremes changemens, et permutations de regne, par grand tremblement de terre avec pullulation de la neusve Babylone, fille miserable, augmentée par l'abomination du premier holocauste et ne tiendra tant seulement septante trois ans, sept mois: puis apres en sortira du tige celle qui avoit demeuré tant long temps sterile, procedant du cinquantiesme degré, qui renouvellera toute l'Eglise Chrestienne. Et sera faite grande paix, union et concorde entre un des enfans des front esgarez et separez: par divers regnes sera faite telle paix que demeurera attaché au plus profond barathre le suscitateur et prometeur de martiale faction par la diversité des Religieux, et sera uny le Royaume de Rabieux, qui contrefera le sage. Et les contrées villes, citez, regnes, et provinces qui auront laissé les premieres voyes pour les delivrer se captivant plus profondement seront secrettement laschez de leur liberté, et parfaite religion perduë, commenceront de frapper dans la partie gauche pour retourner à la dextre, et remettant la sainteté profligée de long temps avec leur pristin escrit, qu'apres le grand chien sortira, le plus gros mastin, qui fera destruction de tout, mesme de ce qu'auparavant sera esté perpetré; seront redressez les temples comme au premier temps, et sera restitué le Clerc à son pristin estat, et commencera à meretriquer et luxurier, faire et commettre mille forfaits. Et estans proche d'une autre desolation, par lors qu'elle sera à sa plus haute et sublime dignité, se dresseront des potentats et maints militaires, et luy seront ostez les deux glaives, et ne luy demeura que ses enseignes, desquelles par moyen de la curuature qui les attire, le peuple le faisant aller droit, et ne voulant se condescendre à eux par le bout opposite de la main aiguë, touchant terre voudront stimuler jusques à ce que naistre d'un rameau de la sterile de long temps, qui delivrera le peuple univers de celle servitude benigne et volontaire, soy remettant à la protection de Mars, spoliant Jupiter de tous ces honneurs de dignitez pour la cité libre, constituée et assise dans une autre exiguë Mezopotamie. Et sera le chef et gouverneur jetté du milieu et mis au lieu de l'air, ignorant la conspiration des conjurateurs avec le second Trasibulus, qui de long temps aura manié tout cecy. Alors les immondicitez des abominations seront par grande honte abjectées et manifestées aux tenebres de la lumière obtenebrée, cessera devers la fin du changement de son regne, et les Chefs de l'Eglise seront en arriere de l'amour de Dieu, et plusieurs d'entr'eux apostasiront de la vraye Foy, et de trois sectes, celle du milieu par les cultures d'icelle, sera un peu mis en decadence. La prime totalement par l'Europe, la plus-part de l'Affrique exterminée de la tierce moyennant les pauvres d'esprit, qui par insensez eslevez par la luxure libidineuse adultèreront. La plebe se levera, soustenant dechassera les adherans des legislateurs, et semblera que les regnes affoiblis par les Orientaux, que Dieu le Createur aye deslié Satan des prisons infernales, pour faire naistre les grand Gog et Magog, lesquels feront si grande fraction abominable aux Eglises, que les rouges ne les blancs sans yeux ne sans mains plus n'en jugeront, et leur sera ostée la luissance. Alors sera faite plue de persecution aux Eglises, que ne fut jamais. Et sur ces entre-faites naistra pestilence si grande, que de trois parts du monde plus que les deux defaudront. Tellement qu'on ne sçaura connoistre ne les appartenants des champs et maisons, et naistra l'herbe par les ruës de citez plus haute que les genoux. Et au Clergé sera faite toute desolation et usurperont les martiaux ce que sera retourné de la cité du Soleil de Melite et des Isles Stecades, et sera ouverte la grande chaîne du port qui prend sa domination boeuf marin. Et sera faite nouvelle incursion par les maritimes plages, voulant le saut Castulum delivrer de la premiere reprinse Mahumetaine. Et ne seront de leur assaillemens vains, et au lieu que jadis fut l'habitation d'Abraham, sera assaillie par personnes qui auront en veneration les Jovialistes. Et icelle cité a'Achem sera environnée et assaillie de toutes parts en tres-grande puissance de gens d'armes. Seront affoiblies leurs forces maritimes par les Occidentaux. Et à ce regne sera faite grande desolation, et les plus grandes citez seront depeuplées et ceux qui entreront dedans seront compris à la vengeance de l'ire de Dieu. Et demeurera le sepulchre de tant grande veneration par l'espace long temps sous le souverain à l'universelle vision des yeux du ciel, du soleil, et de la lune. Et sera converty le lieu sacré en ebergement de troupeau menu et grand et adapté en substances prophanes. O quelle calamiteuse affliction sera pour lors aux femmes enceintes: Et sera par lors du principal chef Oriental la pluspart esmeu par les Septentrionaux et Occidentaux vaincu et mis à mort, profligez et le reste en fuite, et ses enfans de plusieurs femmes emprisonnez, et par lors sera accomplie la Prophetie du Royal Prophète: Ut audiret gemitus compeditorum, ut solveret filios interemptorum. Quelle grande impression qui par lors sera faite sur les Princes et Gouverneurs des Royaumes, mesmes de ceux qui seront maritimes et Orientaux, et leurs langues entremeslées à grande société la langue des latins et les Arabes par la communication Punique, et seront ces Roys chassez profligez, exterminez, non du tout par le moyen de forces des Roys d'Aquilon, et par la proximité de nostre siecle par moyen de trois unis secrettement cherchant la mort et infidies par embûches l'un de l'autre, et durera le renouvellement triumvirat, sept ans que la renommée de telle secte fera son etendue par l'univers, et sera soustenu le sacrifice de la sainte et immaculée Hostie, et seront lors les Seigneurs deux en nombre d'Aquilon, victorieux sur les Orientaux, et sera en iceux fait si grand bruit et tumulte bellique, que tout iceluy Orient tremblera de la frayeur d'iceux freres, non freres Aquilonnaires. Et pource, Sire, que par ce discors je mets presque confusément ces predictions, et quand ce pourra estre, et par l'advenement d'iceux, pour le denombrement du temps qui s'ensuit, qu'il nullement ou bien peu conforme au superieur, lesquels tant par voye Astronomique que par autres, mesme des Sacrées Escritures, qui ne peuvent faillir nullement que si je voulois à chaque quatrain mettre le denombrement du temps se pourroit faire: mais à tous ne seroit agreable ne moins les interpreter jusqu'à ce, Sire, que vôtre Majesté n'aye octroyé simple puisance pour ce faire, pour ne donner cause aux calomniateurs de me mordre; Toutesfois contant les ans depuis la creation du monde jusqu'à la naissance de Noé sont passez mille cinq cens et six ans et depuis la naissance de Noé jusqu'à la parfaicte fabrication de l'arche approchant de l'universelle inondation, passerent six cens ans (si les ans estoient solaires ou lunaires, ou des dix mixtions) je tiens ce que les Sacrées Escritures tiennent qu'ils estoient solaires. Et à la fin d'iceux six ans, Noé entra dans l'arche pour estre sauvé du deluge, et fut iccluy du deluge universel sur terre, et dura un an et deux mois. Et depuis la fin du deluge jusqu'à la nativité d'Abraham, passa le nombre des ans de deux cens nonante cinq. Et depuis la nativité d'Abraham jusqu'à la nativité d'Isaac passerent cent ans. Et depuis Isaac jusqu'à Jacob soixante ans. Dès l'heure qu'il entra en Egypte jusqu'à l'issuë passerent cent trente ans. Et puis l'entrée de Jacob en Egypte jusqu'à l'issuë d'iceluy passerent quatre cens trente ans. Et depuis l'issuë d'Egypte jusqu'à l'edification du temple faite par Salomon au quatriesme an de son regne passeront quatre cens octante ou quatre vingt ans. Et depuis l'edification du temple jusques à Jesus-Christ, selon la supputation des Hierographes, passerent quatre cens nonante ans. Et ainsi par cette supputation que j'ay faite, colligée par les sacrées lettres, font environ quatre mille cent septante trois ans et huit mois peu ou moins. Or de Jesus-Christ en ça par la diversité des sectes je laisse, et ayant supputé et calculé les presentes propheties, le tout selon l'ordre de la chaîne qui contient sa revolution, le tout par doctrine Astronomique, et selon mon naturel instinct, et apres quelque temps, et dans iceluy comprenant depuis le temps que Saturne tournera entrer à sept du mois d'Avril jusques au 15. d'Aoust, Jupiter a 14. de Juin jusques au 7. d'Octobre, Mars depuis le 17. d'Avril jusques au 22. de Juin, Vénus depuis le 9. d'Avril jusques au 22. de May, Mercure depuis le 3. Février jusques au 24. dudit. En apres le 1. de Juin jusques au 24. dudit, et du 25. de Septembre jusques au 16. d'Octobre, Saturne en Capricorne, Jupiter en Aquarius, Mars en Scorpio, Venus en Pisces, Mercure dans un mois en Capricorne, Aquarius et Pisces, la Lune en Aquarius, la teste du Dragon en Libra: la queue à son signe opposite suivant une conjonction de Jupiter à Mercure avec un quadrain aspect de Mars à Mercure, et la teste du Dragon sera avec une conjonction du Soleil à Jupiter, l'année sera pacifique sans éclypse, et non du tout, et sera le commencement comprenant ce que durera et commençant icelle année sera fait plus grande persecution à l'Eglise Chrestienne, qui n'a esté faite en Afrique, et durera cette icy jusques à l'an mil sept cens nonante deux que l'on cuidera estre une renovation de siecle, apres commencera le peuple Romain de se redresser, et de chasser quelques obscures tenebres, recevant quelque peu de leur pristine clarté, non sans grande division et continuel changement. Venise en apres en grande force et puissance se levera ses ailes si haut, ne disant gueres aux forces de l'antique Rome. Et en iceluy temps grandes voiles Bisantines associées aux Ligustiques par l'appuy et puissance Aquilonnaire, donnera quelque empeschement que des deux Cretenses ne leur sera la foy tenuë. Les arcs edifiez par les antiques Martiaux, s'accompagneront aux ondes de Neptune. En l'Andriatique sera faite discorde grande, ce que sera uny sera separé, approchera de maison ce que paravant estoit, et est grande cité, comprenant le Pempétam, la Mesopotamie de l'Europe à quarante cinq et autres de quarante un, de quarante deux et trente sept. Et dans iceluy temps, et en icelles contrées la puissance infernale mettre à l'encontre de l'Eglise de Jesus Christ la puissance des adversaires de sa loy qui sera le second Antechrist lequel persecutera icelle Eglise et son vray Vicaire par moyen de la puissance des Roys temporels qui seront par leur ignorance seduits, par langues qui trancheront plus que nul glaive entre les mains de l'insensé. Le susdit regne de l'Antechrist ne durera que jusques au definiment de ce nay pres de l'aage, et de l'autre à la cité de plancus, accompagné de l'eslu de Modone Fulcy, par Ferrare, maintenu par Liguriens Adriatiques, et de la proximité de la grande Trinacrie: Puis passera le mont Jovis. Le Gallique ogmium accompagné de si grand nombre que de bien loin l'Empire de sa grand loy sera présenté, et par lors quelque temps apres sera espanché profusement le sang des Innocens par les nocens un peu eslevez: alors par grands deluges, la memoire des choses contenuës de tels instrumens recevra innumerable perte, mesmes les lettres qui sera devers les Aquilonaires par la volonté Divine, et entre une fois lié Satan. Et sera faite paix universelle entre les humains, et sera délivré l'Eglise de Jesus-Christ de toute tribulation, combien que par les Azostains voudroit mesler dedans le miel du fiel, et leur pestifere seduction, et cela sera proche du septieme millenaire, que plus le sanctuaire de Jesus-Christ ne sera conculqué par les Infidèles, qui viendront l'Aquilon, le monde approchant de quelque grande conflagration, combien que par mes supputations en mes Propheties le cours du temps aille beaucoup plus loin. Dedans l'Epistre que ces ans passez ay dediées à mon fils Cesar Nostradamus, j'ay assez apertement declaré aucuns poincts sans presage. Mais ici, ô Sire, sont comprins plusieurs grands et merveilleux advenemens, que ceux qui viendront apres, le verront. Et durant icelle supputation Astrologique, conférée aux sacrées lettres la persecution des gens Ecclesiastiques prendra son origine par la puissance des Roys Aquilonaires, unis avec les Orientaux. Et cette persecution durera onze ans, quelque peu moins que par lors défaillira le principal Roy Aquilonnaire, lesquels ans accomplis surviendra son uny Meridional, qui persecutera encore plus fort par l'espace de trois ans les gens d'Eglise par la seduction Apostatique d'un qui tiendra toute puissance absoluë de l'Eglise militaire, et le sainct peuple de Dieu, observateur de sa loy, et tout Ordre de Religion sera grandement persecuté et affligé tellement que le sang des vrais Ecclesiastiques nagera par tout, et un dés horibles Roys temporels par ses adherans luy seront données telles loüanges qu'il aura plus respandu du sang humain des Innocens Ecclesiastiques, que nul ne sçaurait avoir du vin, et iceluy Roy commetra des forfaits envers l'Eglise incroyables, coulera le sang humain par les ruës publiques et temples, comme l'eau par pluye impetueuse, et rougiront de sang plus prochains fleuves, et par autre guerre navale rougira la mer, que le rapport d'un Roy à l'autre luy sera dit: Bellis rubuit navalibus aequor. Puis dans la mesme année et les suivantes s'en ensuivra plus horrible pestilence, et la plus merveilleuse par la famine precedente, et si grandes tribulations que jamais soient advenues telles depuis la fondation de l'Eglise Chrestienne et par toutes les regions Latines, demeurant par les vestiges en aucunes contrées des Espagnes. Pars lors le tiers Roy Aquilonnaire entendant la plainte du peuple de son principal tiltre, dressera si grande armée, et passera par les destroits de ses derniers avites et bysayels, qu'il remettra la plupart en son estat, et le grand Vicaire de la cappe sera remis en son prestin estat: mais desolé, et puis du tout abandonné, et tournera estre Sancta Sanctorum destruite par Paganisme, et le vieux et nouveau Testament seront dechassez et bruslez, en apres l'Antechrist sera le prince infernal, encore par la derniere fois trembleront tous les Royaumes de la Chrestienté, et aussi des infidelles par l'espace de vingt cinq ans, et seront plus griefnes guerres et batailles, et seront villes, citez, chasteaux et tout autres edifices bruslez, desolez, et destruits avec grande effusion de sang vestal, mariées, et vefves violées, enfans de laict contre les murs des villes allidés et brisez, et tant de maux se commettront par le moyen de Satan Prince infernal, que presque tout le monde universel se trouvera defait et desolé, et avant iceux advenemens aucuns oysaux insolites crieront par l'air. Huy huy, et seront apres quelques temps esvanouys. Et aprens que tels coups aura duré longuement, sera presque renouvellé un autre regne de Saturne, et siècle d'or, Dieu le Createur dira entendant l'affliction de son peuple, Satan sera mis et jetté en l'abysme du barathre dans la profonde fosse. Et a donc commencera entre Dieu et les hommes une paix universelle, et demeurera lié environ l'espace de mille ans, et tournera en sa plus grande force, la puissance Ecclesiastique, et puis tout deslié.

Que toutes ces figures sont justement adaptées, par ces divines lettres aux choses celestes visibles, c'est assavoir par Saturne, Jupiter et Mars et les autres conjoints, comme plus à plain par aucuns quatrains l'on pourra voir. J'eusse calculé plus profondement, et adapté les uns avec les autres: Mais voyant, ô serenissime Roy que quelques uns de la censure trouveront difficulté, qui sera cause de retirer ma plume à mon repos nocturne: *Multa etiam, ô Rex omnium potentissime, praeclara & sane brevi ventura, sed omnia in hac tua epistola innectere non possumus, nec volumus: sed ad intelligenda quaedam facta horrida, fata pauca libanda sunt, quamvis tanta sit in omnes tua amplitudo & humanitas homines, Deosque pietas, ut solu amplissimo & Christianissimo Regis nomine, & ad quem summa totius religionis auctoritas deferatur dignus esse videare.* Mais tant seulement je vous requiers, ô Roy tresclement, par icelle vostre singuliere et prudente humanité, d'entendre plutost le desir de mon courage, et le souverain estude que j'ay d'obeyr à vostre serenissime Majesté, depuis que mes yeux furent si proche de vostre splendeur solaire, que la grandeur n'attaint et ne requiers de Salon ce 27 de Juin 1558.

—Faciebat Michaël Nostradamus Salonae Petrae Provinciae

Bibliography

Eugène Bareste, *Nostradamus*, Paris, 1840.

Jacques Romain Boulenger, *Nostradamus*, Paris, 1933.

Dr. Jean de Fontbrune, *Les Prophéties de Maistre Michel Nostradamus*, Sarlat (Dordogne), 1939.

Colin de Larmor, *Les Merveilleux Quatrains de Nostradamus*, Nantes, 1925.

Jean Moura and Paul Louvet, *La Vie de Nostradamus*, Paris, 1930.

Charles Nicoullaud, *Nostradamus: Ses Prophéties*, Paris, 1914.

Anatole le Pelletier, *Les Oracles de Michel de Nostradamus*, Paris, 1867.

Pierre V. Piobb, *Le Secret de Nostradamus*, Paris, 1927.

——, *Le Sort de l'Europe*, Paris, 1939.

Maurice Privat, *La Fin de Notre Siècle*, Paris, 1939.

Émile Ruir, *Le Grand Carnage*, Paris, 1938.

Index

About the Authors

ROLFE BOSWELL was a copyeditor of *The Sun* and one of the foremost translators and interpreters of Nostradamus' prophecies.

NOSTRADAMUS was a sixteenth-century French astronomer and physician. In 1555, he published *Centuries*, a book of prophecies that are still widely read and highly debated to this day.